A Small Sound of the Trumpet

A Small Sound of the Trumpet

Women in Medieval Life

MARGARET WADE LABARGE

Beacon Press   Boston

Beacon Press
25 Beacon Street
Boston, Massachusetts 02108

Beacon Press books are published under the auspices
of the Unitarian Universalist Association
of Congregations in North America.

Published by arrangement with Hamish Hamilton Ltd

93 92 91 90 89 88 87 86   6 5 4 3 2 1

LC 86-47509

ISBN: 0-8070-5626-X

'Implicitly adopting the male life as the norm, they [psychological theorists] have tried to fashion women out of a masculine cloth. It all goes back, of course to Adam and Eve – a story which shows, among other things, that if you make a woman out of a man, you are bound to get into trouble. In the life cycle, as in the Garden of Eden, the woman has been the deviant.'

C. Gilligan, *In a Different Voice* (1982)

'It should not be necessary to write a separate history of half the human beings in any social class. We must, however, do so, whether or not we believe that all women through history have constituted a class oppressed by all men or whether we believe that women's class position was more important than their sex.'

R. H. Hilton, *The English Peasantry in the Later Middle Ages* (1972)

Contents

Foreword

This sketch of the wide-ranging activities of medieval women in northern Europe owes a great debt to the practical encouragement of many scholars. Without their suggestions of fruitful sources or unexplored material it would have been less comprehensive and less lively. I owe special thanks to S. Ady, Prof. D. Angers, Rev. L. E. Boyle OP, Dr. A. de Windt, Dr. J. G. Greatrex, Dr. M. K. McIntosh, Prof. J. Rosenthal, Prof. J. Shatzmiller and Prof. M. M. Sheehan CSB for their generosity in discussing possible avenues and sharing some of their unpublished specialised studies. Like many Canadian medieval scholars I have found friendly criticism and help at the Pontifical Institute of Medieval Studies, Toronto and benefited from the use of its library. In Ottawa, the National Library, the library of the National Gallery of Canada and the libraries of the universities of Carleton, Ottawa and St. Paul have all been hospitable while Frances Montgomery of the Carleton University library provided untiring help in solving bibliographical tangles and tracking down rare titles. In England, I have been equally fortunate in the privilege of using the rich resources of the British Library, the Bodleian Library, and the library of the Institute of Historical Research.

Parts of Chapters 5 and 6 appeared in an earlier, somewhat different form in a paper on 'Medieval Widows: A Second Career' read at the Toronto Medieval Conference of November 1983. The present text has benefited from the criticisms and comments of Prof. J. G. Bellamy on Chapters 1 to 4 and 9; of Dean N. E. S. Griffiths on Chapters 1 and 2; and Sr. K. McCaffrey RSCJ on Chapters 5 and 6. Miss P. Blackstock read the whole text, improving its style and intelligibility. Their work has saved me from many errors and weaknesses while those that unfortunately remain are my sole responsibility.

Other debts remain. My editor, Caroline Tonson Rye, has been generous in her enthusiasm for the original idea, and encouraging during the time it has taken to come to fruition. Friends and family have shared in the arguments and the pleasures of identifying suitable characters for study and the places where they lived. However, it seems appropriate to dedicate this study of a miscellany of medieval women to the wide mix of modern women who have enriched my life – my mother, my daughters and grand-daughters, and my good friends. It is only a small sign of my gratitude and appreciation for their continuing affection and intelligent support.

MARGARET WADE LABARGE

Introduction

To talk about women in medieval life is to deal with their activities at a period when, as one historian has phrased it, 'women were confronted with the closed ranks of a masculine society governed by a thoroughly masculine theology and by a morality made for men by men'[1]. Such a sweeping statement needs some qualification. There is no question that medieval society was predominantly masculine, and the theory which informed it overwhelmingly so, but there were also the realities of everyday life. All men had mothers; some had daughters for whom they cared; and many had wives who either shared in their work, or even took over their responsibilities when they were absent. Thus medieval society displayed a constant, if subordinate, presence of the feminine. Too literal an acceptance of the masculine bias of most medieval thinkers is unfair, since there were also confused efforts to grapple with the opposing poles of Christian belief about woman. Christ himself had preached that the souls of men and women were equal, while a more ambivalent St. Paul occasionally repeated the emphasis of Christ on the equal value of women's souls but more often laid stress on their inferiority. The rest of the intellectual inheritance of medieval thinkers came from sources where women's inherent inferiority was taken for granted – the Old Testament and Greek and Roman philosophy and law. Few of these theorists paid much attention to what was actually happening in their society or what women were doing.

By the twelfth century medieval society had settled into the main lines along which it was to develop through the fifteenth century. The period saw many intellectual and social changes, and inevitably the position of women reflected the wider currents of society. The focus and mental framework of the great twelfth century abbess, Hildegard of Bingen, was naturally far removed from that of the fifteenth century widow of Paris, Christine de Pizan. In the interests of clarity and coherence this study concentrates on the activities of women who can be observed in the strongly feudal society of France, England, the Low Countries and southern Germany from 1100 to 1500. These women shared common ideas, attitudes, and social developments which differed to a considerable degree from those of their sisters of a more urbanised Italy and part-Moorish Spain.

We cannot make sense of the way women lived and (so far as we can discover) felt about themselves without some knowledge of the prevailing ideas about women. By the twelfth century most of Europe was an overwhelmingly Christian society, with generally shared Christian beliefs which were reflected in its laws and patterns of behaviour. By this time the Christian church in the West was becoming increasingly clericalised, structured and hierarchical. Thus most medieval statements about women, whether expressed by theologians and lawyers of both church and state or given concrete application by the preachers and authors of didactic treatises, embodied what celibate clerics thought about women. This was particularly true in the twelfth and thirteenth centuries when these men were the most educated class of society and produced the greatest volume of the literature. Generally perceiving women as threats to their chastity, they were led to a panicky view of the strength of feminine sexuality and harboured a grudging attitude to marriage. They fell back on the convenient stereotype of Eve's responsibility for the existence of sin in the world since this, they felt, provided an adequate explanation to justify woman's inferior position and reinforced man's God-given right to rule over her. Even Bartholomew the Englishman, author of a most widely known medieval encyclopedia, who enthusiastically expressed the wealth of having a good wife (as well as the unparalleled woe of an evil one), still underlined the dominant position of the husband. As head of the family, the wife as well as the children owed him unquestioning obedience.[2] Canon lawyers, while recognising the husband's authority over his wife, also insisted on the need for free consent by both partners to make a valid marriage – a major advance for women. The romances and courtly poetry of the time had a far more secular outlook and often regarded love and marriage as practically incompatible. Nevertheless, when we observe medieval married couples in their everyday surroundings, there seem to be a suspiciously large number of dominant wives as well as examples of real affection between husband and wife. Eileen Power, who portrayed medieval women accurately and sympathetically, once remarked that it was poetic justice that a medieval man 'whose ideal wife was a Patient Griselda, should find himself not infrequently married to the Wife of Bath'.[3]

Given this constant intellectual and legal bias towards a woman's inferiority and her husband's right to domination over her, it is natural that most of the laywoman's activities, bound necessarily to the everyday requirements of life, were either taken for granted or subsumed into the husband's achievements. Yet wives were individually active and documentary traces of what they were doing can be found. Widows often exercised real personal power and influence as independent individuals. Religious women did not have clerical status and they were held at arm's length in the hardening hierarchical structure of the medieval church, but female mystics could benefit from the Christian ambivalence over the reality and use of power and the contradictory gospel value of powerlessness. This latter current encouraged a widespread respect and influence for prophetic and mystical women. Social rank and stage of life also had determining effects on women's position, freedom, and sense of their own worth. For all these reasons medieval women should be seen, as their male relatives are, in relation to their place in society.

It is true that many medieval thinkers never bothered to consider woman's place at all, since her necessary subjection to men was considered too natural to question and obviously part of the divine order of things. The twelfth century saw a general acceptance of the idea of a society organised in a tri-level hierarchical structure, generally described as those who fought and protected society and so were its rulers, those who prayed and provided the necessary link with the divine, and those who by their labour supported their superiors. Surprisingly, one of these twelfth-century thinkers, the rather obscure Gilbert Bishop of Limerick, created a model that did include women as part of each of these groups, though only at the parish level. He explained: 'I do not say that the function of women is to pray or toil, let alone to fight, but they are married to those who pray [in a period when clerical marriage was still common], toil, and fight, and they serve them'.[4] Gilbert expresses the general perception that women shared the social status of their husbands but, because they were subject to them, ranked a half-step below the men, though still superior to the males of any lower order. It has therefore seemed reasonable to adopt this threefold division of society and to illustrate the work of women in all three categories. By the twelfth century women who prayed had gained a separate role for their sex in various forms of religious life. Women in secular society, whatever their status, primarily functioned as wives collaborating with their husbands, or as widows who had a more independent existence. Some women contributed personally to medieval culture while other female unfortunates found themselves exiled to the fringes of society.

It is important to try and discover where theory and fact part company, while bearing in mind the stunting effect these theories of woman's innate inferiority, and often depravity, probably had on many women's development. Brainwashing was not a medieval term, but the effect of all those treatises, denunciations, and sermons must have been to leave many women with a wounding distrust of their own feminity and a tendency to feel that only perpetual chastity was considered an approved calling. Nevertheless, not all women had exclusively religious interests or fitted the submissive stereotype.

It is, of course, true that a woman, in the Middle Ages as through history, could increase her status or influence because of her exceptional beauty or elegance. She might also be recognised and admired for her personal qualities of intelligence, energy or ambition which distinguished her from her contemporaries. This is probably the reason why most studies of medieval women have tended to concentrate on the most spectacular characters – Héloïse, Eleanor of Aquitaine, Joan of Arc, to take only the most obvious examples – because material is more easily available and their vivid personalities appeal to modern minds. Just because they were so extraordinary, such individuals are not a very good guide to the activities and abilities of their less colourful sisters. Fortunately the new historical emphasis on social realities and the everyday activities of all classes of men and women has helped to redress the balance of such concentration and to enlighten us about the lives of a much wider range of individuals, despite the more fragmentary evidence. This book attempts to bring to light the not inconsiderable achievements of a number of women from all levels of medieval society in western Europe between the twelfth and the fifteenth centuries. An account of their own deeds, and occasionally their own words, may only produce 'a small sound of the trumpet',[5] as Hildegard of Bingen too modestly described what she as a woman could do, but its sound comes from the women themselves and should ring true.

CHAPTER ONE

The Precursors

The period of upheaval, devastation, and change which followed the onrush of the invading barbarian tribes and the break-up of the Roman Empire was a time of violence and chaos. For long periods government was rudimentary and decentralised, the adoption of Christianity still tenuous, and intellectual life restricted. Afflicted by a constant fear of revolt or invasion, it is not surprising that early intellectual effort concentrated above all on saving the most important ancient texts from the general destruction; only gradually could early scholars and thinkers develop their own interests and strengths. By the eleventh and twelfth centuries a new, specifically medieval synthesis was to emerge, created from the interaction of the remnants of Roman institutions, the cultural patterns of the vigorous barbarians, and the growing influence of an ever more pervasive church. Although the position of women in the twelfth to fifteenth centuries differed in many ways from that of their precursors it is useful to take a quick look at the situation of women in the early medieval centuries and to point out a few of the outstanding female personalities.

In some ways women were more highly prized in the earlier Middle Ages. Their ability to inherit was more generous so that their legal status was more favourable than it later became. The generally disorganised nature of society allowed more scope for the personal influence of outstanding women, and since women were apparently a minority of the population, they had scarcity value. In a society where life was short and population growth essential for settlement and colonisation, women's ability to bear children was highly prized. Barbarian laws, for example, levied heavy penalties against those responsible for the deaths of women, especially those of childbearing age. The resultant fines were two, sometimes even three, times heavier than those for the killing of men of equivalent status. The fact that it was expensive for a man to marry, as he had to give a heavy dowry to obtain a wife, also suggests a scarcity of females. Female mortality appears to have been high in proportion to that of men. One Carolingian document listing the peasants of St. Victor of Marseilles suggests that the initial preponderance of female children had already disappeared by the age of fifteen and was never regained. Several reasons may account for this. Continual childbearing in itself took a heavy physical toll of all married women, while lower-class women also shared equally with their men in the heavy physical labour of the fields and were often worn-out at an early age. As well, women of all classes were easy prey to the endemic physical violence.

Tacitus at the end of the first century A.D. wrote enthusiastically of the Germans and lauded their attitude towards their women. He reported that a woman at marriage is expected 'to share a man's toils and dangers, that she is to be his partner in all his sufferings and adventures, whether in peace or war'. He emphasised the chastity of the woman and the fact that both sexes waited to maturity to marry, and thus had healthy children, and he recorded the German belief that women embodied an element of holiness and prophecy so that their advice and counsel should not be spurned.[1] It seems evident that the barbarians expected their women to be active and capable. Those familiar with frontier society in more recent centuries find the place of women in the early medieval pattern a vivid reminder of pioneer days. In both cases, society was more fluid and human resources so scarce that they had to be

1 The importance of feasts and spectacles at court continued
throughout the Middle Ages

used according to talents and not restricted to one sex. In such a society women could be active partners in a difficult enterprise.

This was most obvious at the highest levels of society where power concentrated in the person of the king. Thus a dominant wife and mother, who might later serve as regent for a young son, could exercise very real power. In addition, early queens were given actual administrative functions in royal households and the wages of royal supporters and servants were paid through their hands. A queen's central position in the giving and receiving of gifts helped her to make friends and to create ties of obligation. Many of these queens became deeply involved in ecclesiastical affairs, for the ability to make an amenable protégé into a bishop could extend and consolidate her own influence. One of the important functions of an early queen was to organise the spectacle of the royal court and to decorate it herself. The king's wealth and power must impress if he was to overawe his unruly nobles, so that the wealth and status a queen could bring through her own riches and important kinfolk was a natural part of royal ostentation.

In such a personal age, the queen as the mother of the ruling family was not only the central figure in its future, but also played a crucial role in the remembrance and hallowing of the royal tradition through intercession for the royal dead and the creation of a legend around them. Both these functions were often contributing factors in the founding of royal nunneries which harboured dowager queens and unmarried royal daughters as well as repudiated wives, either as privileged residents or actual religious. Queens often founded their own nunneries on their dowerlands, hoping to ensure a safe and peaceful refuge for their old age. The nuns of such royal foundations occasionally wrote lives of their founders or patrons and especially glorified those queens who had become religious. Not surprisingly they put enormous emphasis on the favoured ecclesiastical virtues of such a queen and stressed her religious role. Since this was often only a very brief and relatively unimportant part of her career, it makes the historical usefulness of such lives somewhat limited. What kings and queens did, great nobles and their ladies copied to the extent of their resources, so that similar religious houses with noble patrons and founders also developed in the great fiefs, and for much the same reasons.

A few examples can suggest the calibre of these women and the variety of their activities. Aethelflaed, daughter of King Alfred, who married Aethelred, ealdorman of the West Mercians, was an outstanding tenth century woman. After her father's death she and her husband strove loyally to support her brother King Edward in his effort to create a kingdom of the English. The Lady of the Mercians, as Aethelflaed was called, rebuilt the fortifications at Chester even before her husband died in 911. For seven years after his death she used the military strength of the Mercians to assist her brother, building a number of new fortified towns, of which Warwick and Stafford were the most important. She fought in Wales, led her own troops in the capture of Derby and received the peaceful submission of Leicester. Before her death at Tamworth in June 918 even the people of York had promised to accept her governance. Her work for her brother and for the unification of England had prospered, for all the Mercians under her rule, both Danish and English, accepted King Edward on her death. Aethelflaed has been characterised as 'among the few English women who in any period have permanently influenced the course of history'.[2]

Other ruling women were less successful in their efforts. Agnes, duchess of Aquitaine, was the third wife of Duke William V who ruled that great south-western territory from 994–1030. He already had two sons when he married Agnes, and then had another two sons and a daughter by her. Soon after William's death Agnes, who was still a young woman, married Geoffrey Martel, the heir of the count of Anjou, who was as ambitious and unscrupulous as herself. She encouraged him to make various invasions into Aquitaine for the benefit of her own sons which resulted in the death of their older half-brothers, but she then retained the control of Aquitaine in her hands. Her second marriage was childless and Geoffrey repudiated her by 1050, so she returned to Poitiers. Although her eldest son was of full age and the rightful duke, Agnes continued to govern the duchy herself, allowing her sons only a minor place in its rule. Eight years later another struggle erupted, Geoffrey married again and assigned Agnes's dower lands to his new wife. The infuriated duchess encouraged her elder son to attack Geoffrey on her behalf, an attempt in which he lost his life. His younger brother then succeeded in wresting power in Aquitaine from his mother who retired to the convent of Notre Dame at Saintes, where she lived until her death in 1068. At least in her retirement the headstrong duchess, who also had a reputation for piety, would have leisure for the collection of homilies she acquired at considerable expense. She had earlier given a Benedictine abbey the generous gift of 200 lambs, a large quantity of wheat, rye, and millet, as well as some marten furs in order to get the manuscript for herself.

During her years of power, Agnes had succeeded in negotiating a glittering marriage for her only daughter, another Agnes. The girl married the Holy Roman Emperor, Henry III, in 1043 and when he died in 1056 she became regent for her young son. Agnes was rather colourless and considerably less ruthless than her mother so that after six years of regency two of the most powerful of the German bishops, who were also territorial princes, seized control of her son and ousted her. During the remaining fifteen years before her death in 1077 Agnes was a leading member of the small group of devoted adherents of the reforming popes, especially Gregory VII, and often served as a not very successful ambassador between the pope and her son, Emperor Henry IV.[3]

The life of the Empress Agnes points up one particularly important difference between the lives of men and women, especially noticeable in the early Middle Ages. The men of these centuries were rooted in their own land, which was the source of their wealth and power. Whether it was a kingdom, a lordship, or merely a free peasant's patch of ground, a man clung doggedly to his own, attempted to extend it, and never expected to be uprooted from it. On the other hand, women of royal and noble birth knew from earliest childhood that they were pawns in their family's search for profitable alliances. During these early centuries when the ecclesiastical prohibitions on marriage within the forbidden degrees of relationship were at their strictest (any common ancestor within the last seven generations), the search for legitimate wives of suitable status necessarily ranged far and wide. The foreign wife brought influences from far away to her new home, since a queen or great lady would be accompanied by her own retinue of officials and clerks, as well as her own particular religious interests and favourite charities. In those years of violence and unsettled lines of succession, a foreign queen faced the daunting possibility of serving as regent in a strange country where she would often have to try and defend the rights of her son against serious internal opposition which could easily recruit an endemic anti-foreign sentiment. The Empress Agnes, for example, had already been denounced at the time of her marriage by German clerics as opening the doors to 'the shameful habits of French folly'.[4] A century earlier a Byzantine princess, Theophanu, served as regent for the Emperor Otto III, while in France in the eleventh century the Russian widow of Henry I was also regent for a young heir. Almost unwittingly such women laid the foundations for a rudimentary knowledge of, and connections with, widely separated territories, a development which provided a tenuous network for the exchange of ideas, culture, and patterns of government.

Not only married women had influence and helped in the transmission of culture; some of the great abbesses were outstanding and forceful individuals. Among the most famous were Radegund at Poitiers, Hilda at Whitby, and Lioba, the English nun who followed Boniface to Germany and aided in its Christianisation by setting up convents. The representative abbesses of these early centuries were all women of impressive social standing but they could also be great

2 *This picture from Radegund's* Life *emphasises the value of study for nuns*

administrators and devout religious. The sixth century Radegund, for example, was born a princess of Thuringia. She had been captured as a child by Chlotar, the youngest son of Clovis, the first Christian king of the Franks. Radegund was brought up at a French convent to serve as her captor's queen, and became a well-educated woman able to read Latin with ease. Chlotar was still very much of a barbarian – he seems to have had at least five wives and was brutally cruel. It is not surprising that his marriage to the cultivated Radegund was not a success, particularly as she remained childless, and her husband may have found her uncomfortably active in her devotions and good works. The final break came when Chlotar murdered her brother and Radegund fled from the king and the court, managing to persuade the saintly Bishop Medard to give her the nun's veil which would protect her from Chlotar's pursuit. After some years of seeking a suitable refuge she went to Poitiers where she founded the monastery of Ste-Croix, although she refused to be its abbess. Ste-Croix became a very popular house with a community of some 200 nuns. It was also a centre of letters for Radegund followed the advice given by Cesarius of Arles in his rule for nuns. He felt that all nuns should not only learn to read and write but should also have access to a wide range of books and spend at least two hours a day in such studies.

Radegund's convent was unusual in having a resident poet, Venantius Fortunatus, one of the last verse-writers of elegant trifles in the light-hearted Roman tradition. Fortunatus was born in Ravenna, but his wanderings had finally brought him to Poitiers where he settled happily, warmed by Radegund's patronage and his admiration and friendship for her. He generally wrote charming verses of gratitude for the gifts of food and wine his patroness provided, accompanying them with flowers from his garden. Just once, genuinely moved by the arrival of a relic of the Cross sent to Radegund by the Byzantine emperor, his talent flamed to majesty. The occasion inspired him to write the great processional hymn, *Vexilla Regis prodeunt*, later adopted as a battle hymn by the crusaders. Helen Waddell's translation which begins:

> The standards of the King go forth
> Shines out the blazoned mystery,
> The Cross whereon the Lord of men
> As man was hung,

is perhaps the most felicitous version of a still popular hymn.[5] Fortunatus wrote a life of his friend Radegund as part of the material put forward for her canonisation, as did Baudonivia, one of the nuns of her foundation. The difference in point of view is striking, for, unlike

Fortunatus, Baudonivia's emphasis is not primarily on Radegund's expected virtues of piety and self-denial but, more realistically, on her feminine attributes of maternal solicitude for her nuns, her attempts to serve as peacemaker among her husband's kin, and her effort to develop her monastery into a centre of intercession for the Frankish kings. Radegund died peacefully in her convent in 587, when she was about seventy, and the church of Ste-Radegonde still stands in Poitiers, where she founded it in 552 for her nuns, as a silent reminder of a strong and influential woman.[6]

A century later than Radegund, Hilda of Whitby repeated the combination of royal birth, religious zeal, and able administration, though under less threatening conditions. Hilda was the great-niece of King Edwin of Northumbria and was baptised as a child when he became a Christian. She did not consider religious life until she was in her thirties when she planned to enter the abbey of Chelles near Paris where her mother had retired. Aidan, the saintly bishop of Lindisfarne, called her back home as he wanted her help in his efforts to bring Christianity to the Northumbrians. Hilda founded several convents but is most famous as abbess of Whitby, one of the best-known of all the double monasteries, those unusual communities which had separate sections of monks and nuns who were united under the rule of an abbess. Whitby was noted for its learning and zeal with at least five of its monks being recruited as bishops. When the crucial synod resolving the debate between the Roman and the Celtic church over the proper method of computing Easter was held in Whitby in 664, Hilda and her nuns took an active part. Although the abbess had espoused the Irish cause, she loyally carried out the synod's decision in favour of Rome, which aligned the youthful English church with the Christianity of the continent rather than the Celtic fringe. Hilda's ability was recognised by England's first great historian, the Venerable Bede, who wrote within fifty years of her death, praising her foundations, her fame and her holy influence.

Bede has also preserved the delightful story of Caedmon, the community's cowherd, who was so afraid of being asked to sing at table – a usual form of Anglo-Saxon entertainment – that he would always slip away to the stables when he saw the harp coming his way. One night when this had happened the embarrassed cowherd saw in a dream a man commanding him to sing about the creation, and an original verse in English sprang to his lips. Caedmon's poem was still firmly fixed in his memory when he awoke so he felt he should report to the reeve in charge of the farm. The no doubt bewildered official felt that this certainly was a question for the abbess to decide. Hilda listened to the tale and was convinced that it was a clear sign that Caedmon should become a monk.

When he agreed to this, she arranged for some of the more educated brothers to instruct the illiterate in sacred history and discover if he could render other holy themes into vernacular verse. Caedmon happily spent the rest of a devout life at Whitby making, as Bede records, 'such melodious verse that his delightful renderings turned his instructors into auditors'.[7] Abbess Hilda thus added to her other contributions to Anglo-Saxon culture the patronage of the earliest identifiable English poet.

The Anglo-Saxon church continued to produce able and learned women. The eighth century Lioba, friend of Boniface and sharer in his missionary efforts in Germany, is not as well-known as Hilda but was also remarkable. Lioba came from a noble Wessex family and was related to Boniface on her mother's side. As a girl she was educated at the nunnery at Thanet, and later went to the abbey of Wimborne where she became a nun. Initiating a correspondence with Boniface after he had been sent to Saxony and Thuringia, she reminded him that they were bound by a dual tie – her mother was his relative and her father his friend – and she would like to look on him as a brother. The young nun sent him a small gift and, perhaps to distract his mind from his missionary hardships, asked him to correct her letter and also give her guidance in the rules of verse. This unusual opening seems to have led to a lifelong friendship. In 748 Boniface asked the abbess of Wimborne to send him Lioba and some companions so that he could set up monasteries for women in the newly converted sections of Germany. Lioba soon became abbess of Bischofsheim, a community highly esteemed as a centre of prayer, wise counsel for the great, and help for its poor neighbours. The tie between Lioba and Boniface was so strong that before he left on his final journey he asked that her body should be buried near his. Lioba had served as abbess for twenty-eight years before retiring and her prestige remained high, for Charlemagne's queen, Hildegard, even invited her to court. When she died in 782 she was buried at Fulda near Boniface. Her life was written from the testimony of her companions and draws an attractive sketch of an intelligent, kind, and beautiful woman who ruled her community according to the Benedictine rule. She punctuated public prayer with the study of Latin and service in the abbey's scriptorium, as well as the usual manual work of kitchen, brewery, bakery, and garden.[8]

These three abbesses suggest a lively picture of convent life in the early centuries when study was still an essential element, and the personal influence of well-connected and remarkably able women could be brought to bear on the great men of both church and kingdom. They illustrate the high level of literacy among the noble women in the convents, which was encouraged by such men as Cesarius of Arles in the sixth century and Aldhelm in the seventh century. Aldhelm, who was monk, bishop and poet, suggested to the abbess of Barking that her nuns should work like bees, culling honey not only from sacred scripture but also from their knowledge of ancient law, history and allegory. He put forward an ambitious course of study, ranging from the rules of grammar, orthography, punctuation and metre to how to arrange events chronologically. The description of the education given to two eighth-century nuns, who were sent to Valenciennes to study at the monastery there, suggests that Aldhelm's programme was not merely an ideal. The young women at Valenciennes were not only taught religious studies, arts and letters through books and lectures, but were also well grounded in all the varied forms of the ecclesiastical ceremonies and monastic hours with their appropriate readings and chants. They were instructed in the purely feminine arts of spinning and weaving, making designs and interlacing in gold and embroidering flowers in silk, but they also learned how to copy and illustrate manuscripts.[9] It seems abundantly clear that nuns in the early medieval centuries were not allowed to sink into laziness through lack of work for either hand or brain.

Charlemagne's insistence on having his daughters as well as his sons educated in the liberal arts is attested by Einhard, the great emperor's biographer, and may have provided a good example to encourage the education of both sexes. The emperor expected his daughters to be adept in the accepted feminine occupations – the working of wool and the use of the distaff and the spindle – but felt that this was not enough to occupy their time and that they should also learn to read and write. There were certainly some other young girls in the palace school under the authority of Alcuin as well as Charlemagne's sister and one of his

3 The distaff, the spindle, and later the spinning wheel were the common symbols in many pictures of medieval women

wives. They seem to have studied the first elements of grammar, a little rhetoric and logic, and acquired a few vague notions of arithmetic, geometry and astronomy. Such a syllabus covered, at least sketchily, much of what was then known. A religious house like Chelles, much favoured by Charlemagne and used as a retirement home for his sister Gisela and his daughter Rotrod, had an extensive library of which Rotrod and Gisela took advantage. They corresponded with Alcuin over serious literary matters and their opinions were considered. He asked for their criticism on his unfinished commentary on the gospel of St. John, and sent them the works of Bede. In return they urged him to finish the commentary but also to explain some difficult passages of St. Augustine. These early nuns not only read, some were definitely encouraged to act as professional scribes, and several nunneries had their own scriptoria.

During the ninth century it became evident that this emphasis on schooling and books had gone beyond the court and the monasteries to influence also the higher nobility. Some of these upper-class laymen and women not only owned books but even disposed of considerable libraries in their wills. Count Ekkehard, a Burgundian nobleman, bequeathed both religious and secular works. The religious manuscripts comprised several theological texts, canon law, some saints' lives, and a German gospel, while of more secular interest were *The History of the Franks* by Gregory of Tours, a history of the Lombards, copies of several law codes, a book on agriculture, one on the military art, two on prognostics, one on medicine as well as one of the works of the great early encyclopedist, Isidore of Seville. Like many lovers of books Ekkehard also borrowed from his friends, and he anxiously warned his executors to be sure and return to the Benedictines at Fleury some books he had borrowed from their monastery which could be found safely put away in a hutch in his closet. Although most of these books were given to ecclesiastical institutions or to clerical friends, one of the law codes was given to a namesake, the other, along with the text on the military art, to a lay friend, and the medical book to an important noble lady. Another contemporary, Count Eckhard of Autun and Macon, left a couple of religious books to an abbess, a psalter and book of prayers to his sister Adana, and a book on gynaecology to his sister-in-law.[10] It was particularly suitable that the gynaecology text should be left to a woman, since childbirth and its resultant problems were dealt with by female practitioners and such a work might well be kept for reference by the nearest great lady. The fact that the medical book also went to a woman suggests the early recognition that the lady of a household had considerable supervisory responsibility for the treatment of the wounds and ailments of her own household and those directly dependent on it. Much of early medicine was based on common sense, experience, and a knowledge of the healing properties of herbs. Monasteries in the early centuries, whether of men or women, with their large infirmaries and their own herb gardens were likely to have the most skilled practitioners, and outsiders were often brought to them for care. Nevertheless, the first treatment was generally that of the lady of the manor or castle. The possession of such reference books would be valuable to her personally and allow her to pass on the relevant information to lower class practitioners who would probably have been illiterate.

The educated women of these two centuries included two really remarkable authors: Dhuoda and Hrotsvitha. Dhuoda is an extraordinary and rather pathetic figure. She was born into a family of the higher nobility at the beginning of the ninth century, and in 824 was married to Bernard, duke of Septimania and a cousin of Charlemagne, whom Louis the Pious had assigned to the overseeing of the Spanish Marches. Dhuoda and Bernard's son, William, named after a renowned and holy grandfather, was born in November 826. Soon after that – just when and why are not known – Bernard dispatched his wife to Uzès, just west of the Pont du Gard, where she appears to have spent most of her life apart from her husband. Several rumours circulated explaining his abandonment of Dhuoda, including the suggestion that Bernard had become the lover of Louis's second wife, Judith, but none of these insinuations was ever proved. In 840 Bernard returned briefly to his wife, and their second son was born the following year. Before the baby had even been christened his father had taken him away from his mother, leaving Dhuoda alone. Meanwhile the older son had been sent as a pledge of Bernard's loyalty to the court of Charles the Bald, the successor of Louis the Pious, whom Bernard had originally opposed. During this period of sorrow and concern Dhuoda decided to try and do something useful for her elder son and wrote a *Manual* designed for his instruction.[11] The treatise explains both her religious and secular ideals for him and is also a remarkable picture of a dignified and well-educated lady, buffeted but not overcome by life's trials.

The *Manual* displays very clearly the dual system of values which Dhuoda wished to put before her son: service to God, of course, but also the proper upholding of the ideal of noble existence in this life. She insists that he must act nobly – respecting rank and giving largess, but also showing gentleness to all, not only his equals. She is convinced that such proper behaviour, when combined with Christian devotion, will bring him both worldly felicity and eternal salvation. Her book paints a remarkable portrait of Dhuoda herself in all her human longing for a normal life with her children, yet with a genuine religious devotion and the dignity and self-control that were expected from one of her station. In one of the most touching passages she reminds her son that she had gone heavily into debt in order to help her husband in his struggles, and to try and ensure that he would not abandon them both. She had borrowed from both Christians and Jews and had tried to repay them all as well as she could but, if any of her debts remain after her death, she begs her son to endeavour to find out to whom the money was owed and to make sure they were all repaid.

Her work is clear evidence of her reliance on faith and prayer, and her realistic knowledge that the high ideals she puts before her son would be difficult to maintain among the splendours and intrigues of the court. The most recent commentator on her *Manual* has described her Latin as 'unorthodox and at times incorrect', but lays great emphasis on the fact that she was indeed striving to express something new, something which was very much her own and which allows her to emerge as an unforgettable personality.[12] There is a tragic footnote to all this, for her treatise was to have little use for the son for whom she had so carefully composed it. Dhuoda's husband was executed for treason in 844 by Charles the Bald. The elder son then joined the Aquitanian rebels, was captured and executed in his turn in 849. We know nothing of Dhuoda except what her *Manual* tells us, but it transmits the distinctive voice of a woman, speaking in an imperfect classical Latin but with her own sensibility and sense of values. Her affectionate treatise of instruction for her son was not to be paralleled for several centuries.

Hrotsvitha, the extraordinary resident of Gandersheim, was the outstanding female author of the early Middle Ages. Her output included eight metrical legends, histories in verse glorifying Emperor Otto I and the early foundation of Gandersheim, and – most surprising of all – six dramas modelled on the comedies of Terence, an unlikely exemplar in a tenth-century convent. Gandersheim itself was an unusual nunnery, since from its foundation it maintained close links with the ruling Ottonian dynasty and its abbesses were members of the reigning family. In 947 Otto I went so far as to invest the abbess of Gandersheim with supreme authority, so that the abbey became an independent princedom with its own courts, its own army, the right to mint coinage, to be represented at the imperial assembly, and to answer directly to the pope without episcopal interference. Gandersheim was therefore one of the most striking examples of the common royal tendency in the early Middle Ages to encourage the foundation of convents where women of royal blood might have a place where they could exercise power and where there was an intellectual milieu. All the inhabitants of Gandersheim, except the servants, were of noble birth.

There were two classes of residents: those who had taken vows as full religious, and the canonesses who preserved the right to retain their own property, have their own servants, and buy their own food. Such canonesses could come and go, entertain guests, and might even leave to be married without incurring any condemnation.

Hrotsvitha is now believed to have been one of these canonesses, not a nun. She was certainly of noble birth, and the most recent commentator on her work believes that she spent quite some time at court, probably at an early age.[13] This hypothesis may be reinforced by the nature of her *Gesta Ottonis*, which was a commission for her to celebrate Otto I in a long epic poem. The *Gesta* is not one of the best of Hrotsvitha's works for she did not have the written models or the first-hand reports she would need to write convincing epic, much less serious history. As well, such a work designed to glorify the emperor as the ideal Christian ruler was not best suited to her mischievous sense of humour. On the other hand, her pseudo-Terentian comedies, written in the manner of Terence but based on current legends of the saints, are both amusing and a remarkable literary achievement. Critical argument rages over the intention behind these plays. Were they written as purely literary exercises and only for the amusement of her fellow religious at Gandersheim, or were they perhaps used to entertain a wider audience as theatrical readings with a certain elementary use of impersonation or even of mime? The question is necessarily an open one.

Probably the most comic of her plays is *Dulcitius*, which deals with the heroic refusal of three beautiful young Christian girls to sacrifice to the Roman gods, preferring torture and death to abjuring their faith. In an almost farcical scene Dulcitius, the Roman governor who wished to seduce the girls for his own pleasure, has them locked up in a storeroom next to the kitchen. When he comes secretly at night to carry out his evil scheme he is so seized by delusion that he embraces the pots and pans and the kitchen utensils, thinking they are the lovely girls he seeks. Meanwhile his prisoners peek through the door and laugh at his ridiculous situation. In perhaps the earliest example of kitchen-sink drama, Hrotsvitha has the unfortunate governor, blackened with soot, terrifying his own soldiers who did not want to allow their unrecognisable superior to enter his own palace. Her version of the happy ending has all three girls showing up their judges as foolish and incompetent but succeeding in gaining the martyrdom they desire.[14]

Hrotsvitha's works suggest a most attractive personality, somewhat handicapped by her inability to work without stiffness in the classical metres she copied from Terence. The canoness from Gandersheim was trying to adapt new ideas and sensibilities to the older, more formal expression but her effort was not totally successful, nor did she gain much fame for herself. She seems to have had little influence during the Middle Ages, although a few of her plays were copied with no attribution. Only in this century have four more manuscripts of her work been added to the one comprehensive collection copied soon after her death and discovered at the end of the fifteenth century by a German humanist. This unique manuscript was preserved at the convent of St. Emmeram at Regensburg, where Hrotsvitha's abbess and friend had been educated. It has been suggested that it had some influence on the rather coquettish poems the young nuns of Regensburg wrote a century later, poems which share Hrotsvitha's fluctuations between self-assurance and the deference considered suitable for women.[15]

In talking of the women of the early Middle Ages and the parts they played it is inevitable to concentrate on those of the upper classes because they were the most visible and their activities more fully recorded. At that time towns had not begun to grow and develop and commerce was very limited, so society did not yet encompass a bourgeoisie. Apart from the court and the monasteries there were country estates all over Europe which fed these upper classes. On them, peasant husbands and wives worked together to carry out the necessary agricultural tasks. Some light is thrown on the lives of the peasants, the overwhelming numerical majority of the population, by such documents as the detailed estate book of the abbey of St-Germain-des-Prés. The polyptych, as it was called described each estate held by the abbey, named all the inhabitants, their wives and the number of their children, and specified the exact services and rents for which they had to answer to the abbey's estate officials. Eileen Power was one of the first to use these documents as a means of throwing light on the life of a peasant woman. From them, and the regulations issued by the Emperor Charlemagne she acquaints us with the peasant Bodo, his wife Ermentrude and their three children. Ermentrude, apart from the usual household duties, worked with her husband on the land and, in addition, had special responsibility for the eggs and chickens, the making of cloth and of thread, the washing of the clothes, and the shearing of the sheep. Female household serfs were put to work in segregated workrooms on the estate to spin, dye cloth, and make up garments. It is pleasant to know that Charlemagne had specifically ordered his stewards to make sure that the houses where the women worked had stoves and cellars, as well as being protected by surrounding hedges and a strong door.[16]

The women we can identify as precursors in these early medieval centuries, despite the harsh and violent conditions of their lives, had a

*4 A peasant woman
shearing her sheep*

certain freedom and influence that their successors were to lack. The
greater organisation and departmentalisation which developed in royal
and noble courts gradually moved the queen and the great noble lady
from their position of supreme influence at the centre, making them
more figures of ceremony than of power. Abbeys of nuns gradually lost
their reputation as intellectual and cultural centres as cathedral schools
and universities became the new centres of scholarship.

Their decline was gradual and did not become very evident until
the fourteenth century. However, the rural life of Ermentrude and
the generations of her counterparts on the farms and manors of
northern Europe, although made somewhat easier by improvements in

agricultural practice, legal position, and food supplies, did not basically alter. The peasant family retained its partnership with the land through the centuries.

CHAPTER TWO

The Mould for Medieval Women

A: Physical Conditions and Social Patterns

The once popular notion that Europeans, in a manner reminiscent of millenarian sects, suspended all activity as they awaited the end of the world in the year 1000 has long been discredited. In reality very few men of the time would have been able to agree on the date when the year began, or to compute it; most simply would not have cared, for in an agricultural world artificial calendars are generally irrelevant. Nevertheless, the eleventh century did mark an upsurge of energy as Western Europe finally emerged from the dark centuries of invasions and general breakdown in which the glory of the Carolingian empire had shone with fleeting splendour. New energies were harnessed to the elaboration of the structures of church and state. The revival of Roman law, the movement for reform in the church, the rediscovery – often through translations from Moslem authors – of many of the great philosophical and scientific works of the past; all these contributed to a new vitality and great intellectual advance for men. How did these changes affect women and their place in the developing medieval society?

The usual modern approach to such a question would be to begin with basic statistics – the percentage of women in the population, their life expectancy, and the average number of births per mother – but such information is extremely difficult to uncover in the Middle Ages. Looking for accuracy in the medieval use of numbers is rather like chasing the proverbial needle in the haystack. The remaining records are fragmentary, so that comparisons are difficult and often inappropriate, while the contemporary scribes were usually uninterested in what they considered unimportant facts. Much of the information we can find is incidental, culled from the lives of queens, saints, or abbesses who cannot be considered representative of the general female population. Laws setting the age of marriage can suggest when girls were expected to attain puberty, and legal case records and tax rolls occasionally provide useful hints about women's ages or time of death. At best these are only able to suggest the range of possibilities, not provide a general average.

There is a more specialised difficulty. Any discussion of women in medieval society quickly brings to light another problem related to the extraordinarily masculine nature of that society, especially in its upper ranges. What accounts for the general invisibility of noble women except in very small numbers? The queen and her ladies were always part of the scenery of the royal court, but they were relatively few and heavily outnumbered by male officials, clerics, and men-at-arms, as well as the vast crowd of male hangers-on that swarmed around the court. In the fifteenth century Christine de Pizan emphasised that it was the normal duty of a noble wife to stay at home and run the estate while her husband sought honour by attendance at court, the bearing of arms or travel, but there is the same extraordinary preponderance of men in the great noble households. The ratio might be as high as four to one in a household actually headed by a woman, where one would expect more female companions, and soared to thirty-seven to one at a feast which boasted of its large number of women.[1] Clerics did not have wives and some of the spouses of royal or noble officials were undoubtedly at home on their husbands' lands managing the family estates, but where were the rest? It cannot be presumed that they all went to nunneries, for even there the disproportion between men and women was considerable. In England during this whole period the number of nuns ranged from 21% to 30% of the male religious, a figure which does not even include the large number of secular clerics, by this time officially celibate.[2] The ratio of religious women was higher on the Continent, especially in Germany and the Low Countries, but was still unbalanced. According to the documents available, women were more visible in the urban centres, and in the manors and villages where peasants tilled the land, extant records suggest that there may even have been a slight predominance of women, especially widows. As medieval society had no niche for the unmarried woman who was of too high a rank to be active in trade or on the land, what happened to the daughters who did not succeed in marrying or entering a convent? Were superfluous infant daughters neglected to encourage early death as a solution to the parents' concern over establishing their children, or did they somehow find occupations not yet recognised? Are we perhaps accepting too easily the natural biases of the often clerical chronicles, and not seeing the women who were there but who were not mentioned because they were considered unimportant? It is a complex topic which would repay detailed research.

However many women there were, medieval thinkers had very specific ideas about their role. The Middle Ages had inherited from the ancients the belief in a doctrine of humours which conditioned people's temperaments and had far-reaching effects on their appearance, behaviour, and susceptibility to illness. Almost all medieval writing about

*5 Men illustrating
the four humours:
melancholic, choleric,
sanguine, and
phlegmatic*

physiology worked within this accepted framework and it became the
standard pattern used by both clerical and secular authors, and was
familiar even to the slightly educated. The body was believed to be
composed of the four contraries – hot, cold, moist, and dry – which
combined to form the humours. These were sanguine, a mixture of hot
and moist; choleric, hot and dry; phlegmatic, cold and moist; and
melancholic, cold and dry. A modern scholar talking of the humours
considers them a realistic classification, which also paid some attention
to the effect of bodily secretions on moods. He relates them to Pavlov's
rediscovery of the fact that people respond to stress either actively, that
is aggressively, or by ignoring it, that is inhibitedly; and that they do so
in two degrees, either with control or uncontrolledly. To put medieval
concepts into modern terms, the sanguine type was aggressive but
controlled; the phlegmatic, inhibited but controlled; while the choleric
type was uncontrolledly aggressive. Such a modern definition would
perceive the melancholic as one naturally predisposed to depression, or
reduced to such a state by stress. Hildegard is the only medieval woman
who defines the humours and applies the characteristics of each specifically to her own sex, with special emphasis on their effect on female

sexual behaviour. Women were usually considered to be naturally melancholic and Hildegard certainly placed herself in that category.[3] Such melancholic humours were generally believed to encourage women in what might now be termed neurotic behaviour. Certainly, since medieval women were so constantly lectured on their natural inferiority and their inheritance of Eve's guilt, as well as hedged by so many prohibitions about their behaviour, their level of stress must often have been unbearably high. Because they were felt to be primarily influenced by cold and dry humours which pushed them towards death, the coldest and driest state of all, it was taken for granted that they died sooner than men who generally were of the more healthy sanguine type.

This theory of women's length of life was backed by the authority of a statement by Aristotle, though with no physical evidence adduced, and many medieval writers were happy to parrot a dictum from such a respected source. Some tried to look at the facts. Albert the Great, the famous German Dominican of the thirteenth century and the teacher of Aquinas, was far more interested in actual physical phenomena than his more famous pupil. Albert looked at what he could actually observe in the world at the time and added a note of realism to the discussion. He bowed to Aristotle's authority by agreeing that the philosopher was right in saying that men lived longer than women 'by nature', but then went on to explain that 'by accident', that is by actual conditions rather than basic principles, women in fact lived longer. Albert gave three reasons for this: sexual intercourse was less exhausting for women than for men, the flow of menstrual blood cleaned impurities from women's bodies, and women worked less hard and therefore were less worn out than men.[4]

This was the theory. Is there any way of discovering how long women were actually living as the twelfth century began? Unfortunately, the question cannot be easily or accurately answered. Women's life expectancy was improving and generally continued to do so, despite the great increase in plague and plague-related deaths during the mid-fourteenth century. Physical conditions had begun to improve for the whole population in the eleventh century as the increasing area under the plough meant more generous crops which benefited the peasants as well as the lords. It has been argued that the beans and legumes were the most valuable segment of these crops since they not only provided new and necessary protein, but also a more generous source of iron. This latter was especially valuable for women, whose need for iron during the years of menstruation and child-birth is two to three times that of men. Such additions to the diet, and even the extra traces of iron which came from food now generally being cooked in iron pots, served to lower the rate of female anaemia with its predisposition to early death, especially in childbirth.[5]

As governments became more organised and the danger of random violence was reduced, the physical weakness of women was less exploited while men continued to die, often long before their time, in crusades, tournaments, wars, and even in hunting accidents. The development of towns and the growth in the number of religious houses provided new ways for some women to live out their lives in less exhausting conditions than those of unrelieved hard physical labour. Even by the twelfth century a change in the proportion of women in the population is suggested by the fact that it was now the girl's family who usually had to provide the dowry, and that its amount continued to rise. By the end of the fifteenth century it appears that cities, especially those north of the Alps, had a definite preponderance of women. Calculations suggest that women outnumbered men by ratios of from 109 to 120 females to 100 males, and that the imbalance was even higher among the elderly. Some of this may well have been due to the greater attraction of the town over the country for single or widowed women, but it also suggests that women, though little talked about, were indeed present in greater numbers. Efforts to arrive at some reasonably based statistical approximation of the life expectancy of women in the Middle Ages have so far tended to be more approximate than statistical. Perhaps it is wisest to echo the most reliable guide in these matters and content ourselves with the observation that it certainly seemed to the men of the later Middle Ages that women were in reality living longer than men.[6]

Other factors concerning women's health, such as the ages of menarche and menopause, the average numbers of childbirths per marriage, and the frequency of deaths of either infant or mother in childbirth are equally difficult to quantify in the absence of continuing statistics. Canon law, and most customary law, set the age of marriage for a girl at twelve and for a boy at fourteen, these being the original classical standards, but there seems to be enough evidence to show that people knew that menarche was often closer to fifteen. Hildegard of Bingen, who wrote very specifically on these subjects, describes a girl as feeling the first awakening of passion at twelve, but added that she should be well guarded then since she was infertile and might easily fall into lasciviousness, losing her sense of honour and shame. Hildegard felt that if a girl was of a vigorous and humid nature she would be mature and fertile by fifteen, otherwise by sixteen. Such ages might be true of the upper classes and the nuns, who led easier lives and often had better, or at least more regular, food. Even now menarche can be much delayed by poor nutrition and hard physical labour, conditions which constantly affected lower class women in the Middle Ages. It is interesting to note that it was also Hildegard, the twelfth century abbess, who wrote most clearly and fully of menstruation and all the complaints which have traditionally accompanied it. It seems possible that Albert the Great even borrowed from her the idea that menstruation cleansed a woman's blood and humours, thus improving her health. She placed the menopause around the age of fifty, though she thought passion might continue to seventy if the woman was strong. In her realism and concern for women's problems Hildegard displayed still another facet of a truly remarkable mind.[7]

If girls survived infancy and childhood the next great hazard was childbirth. Many women died in childbirth or from its after-effects, though it is, as always, difficult to provide statistics. Families, especially in the upper classes, might be very large and it is often easiest to track the number of children born to a single wife in royal families, since court chroniclers might mention daughters as well as sons, and even refer to stillbirths. For example, Blanche of Castile, one of the most remarkable women of the thirteenth century and mother of King Louis IX of France, had ten other pregnancies at intervals of approximately

6 Childbirth in rather luxurious conditions

two years. She was seventeen at the birth of her first child and her husband died when they were both thirty-eight. Blanche must have had a very strong physique for she went on to live a most active life as regent for her young son until his majority and again, twenty years later, when he was away on crusade. She was deeply involved in the political affairs of the kingdom until her death at the age of sixty-four. On the other hand, Mary de Bohun, who married Henry of Derby (later King Henry IV of England) when she was about ten, also had her first child at seventeen, but in the ensuing seven years produced three more sons and two daughters. The physical strain was too great and she died at the birth of her last daughter, aged only twenty-four.

Survival for any woman during the hazardous years of childbirth depended on natural strength, uncomplicated births, and some time for recuperation. The upper-class habit of providing wet-nurses for their babies often shortened the interval between children. In addition, princesses and the daughters of great nobles tended to be married very young, since they served as useful pawns in the cementing of alliances or the building up of land holdings. They also seem to have had children very young, and in their immaturity were more subject to complications, because it was considered essential that a wife should fulfil her duty of providing not only one male heir but several, to provide insurance against the all too frequent infant deaths. From what we can learn about peasant marriages and those of the less affluent townspeople, their families appear to have been kept small in order to allow the members to survive. At these social levels the age of marriage was often considerably older because of the need to have sufficient land or resources to make marriage and an independent household possible. Because of this the couple's period of fertility was somewhat shorter while the mother often nursed her baby which helped to delay a subsequent pregnancy.

How frequently births were consciously limited and by what means is almost impossible to ascertain. Certainly medieval medical treatises described contraceptive and abortive substances, and theologians included both practices in their denunciations. Occasionally they mentioned that contraception was normally to avoid impoverishment or shame. There was a medieval Latin proverb on living cautiously, if not chastely, which was quoted by Peter Abelard in his poem of advice to his son, and which seems to have been the ancestor of that once well-known phrase, 'if you can't be good, be careful'.[8] I have seen only one case recorded among people of high rank of an expressed desire to limit the family. The wife took the initiative and her reasoning in the matter is most interesting. According to the chronicler, Herman of Tournai, Clemence of Burgundy, who was the wife of Count Robert II of Flanders, had three sons in three years. She then practised 'womanly arts' lest another should arrive, *because* (added emphasis) she feared that if more sons were born 'they would fight among themselves for Flanders'. Certainly fourteenth-century priests involved in penitential work, such as William of Pagula and John Bromyard, talked of contraceptive practices, and both William and the influential St. Catherine of Siena testify that married people tended not to consider contraception a sin. Catherine certainly thought it very prevalent in her milieu.[9]

There was, however, another large group of women whose very choice of life exempted them from the hazards of childbirth – those who adopted the religious life in any of its forms. Although the evidence about their life span is mainly anecdotal, many of them seem to have lived into their sixties and more. Unfortunately, any knowledge of the avenues open to unmarried women who did not adopt a religious life is very sparse. It seems that they were most generally to be found among the minor servants on manors and in town households, and appeared as the poorly paid fringe of hucksters and unskilled workers in the towns, and as prostitutes. In any of these occupations life-spans were probably even shorter than the average, but information is lacking. The known existence of so many widows in both town and country suggests that once the perils of childbearing had been surmounted, women frequently enjoyed a number of active years, particularly in the upper classes. Such noble women benefited from better nourishment throughout life, warmer clothing, better housing, what medical care there was and freedom from exhausting physical labour. As well, they were usually protected from much of the violence to which the lower classes were so often exposed. It is easier to know something of their lives because of the greater number of records in which they appear but is also true that any woman in the family of a great feudal lord, a minor noble, or even, in the later period, a rich townsman had inherent physical advantages.

Nevertheless, social status was even more important for a medieval woman than her physical inheritance, for it defined how she would be regarded by others, whom she could marry or what form of religious life she might undertake. Status was determined by birth, for medieval thinkers firmly believed that royal and noble blood was indeed different from the substance which pulsed in the veins of the bourgeois and the peasants, and that it should not be intermingled with that of a lower rank. It was this solid conviction which accounted for the fury of widows and wards whose lords sold their marriages and thus their fiefs to men below their own station and explains their willingness to pay large sums to avoid such disparagement. Women shared the status of their family and their husband all the way up and down the social scale, though a married woman was always a step below her husband for he was her lord and master. Nevertheless, such subordination was restricted only to her husband; all other men, if of lower rank, must display respect for her higher status, for actual behaviour was based primarily on the subservience exacted by rank. One flowery rhetorical example of this is to be found in the exaggerated humility of Archbishop Lanfranc's letter to Queen Margaret of Scotland:

> In the brief span of a letter I cannot hope to unfold the joy with which you flooded my heart when I studied the letter that you sent me, O Queen beloved by God. With what holy cheer the words flow on which are uttered by the inspiration of the Holy Spirit! . . . It is as a result of Christ's teaching here that you, who are born of a royal line, brought up as befits a queen and nobly wedded to a noble king, are choosing me as your father – a foreigner of neither birth nor worth, who is ensnared in sin.[10]

The consciousness of their privileged position protected the women of the upper classes, but worked to the disadvantage of those lower down the scale. Courtesy was a noble virtue; it was not considered necessary towards poor townswomen or, even more noticeably, towards peasant women, because their low rank excluded them from consideration. Most men felt that violence, even rape, practised on such base creatures quite literally did not count and should be overlooked. Such an attitude was encouraged by the fact that high tempers and violence were general in the Middle Ages in both sexes. In addition, the law recognised the right of men of all classes to beat their wives, so long as they did not kill them or do excessive damage. It appears to have been a frequently exercised right, for many of the cautionary tales warn women of the wisdom of being humble and not arousing their husband's wrath, lest a beating and permanent disfigurement or worse should follow. The women themselves seem to have been quick with words and occasionally with blows.

There is another factor which must be considered in coming to grips with the actual position of medieval women. The various stages of her life defined her quite differently and required varying abilities as she passed through them.[11] Men could see their lifespan as a clear progression through infancy and youth, when they had little or no power and served a training period to fit them for the future; to full age and maturity, when they married and exercised all the rights and privileges of their state in life; to old age, when physical, and perhaps mental, decay, might finally compel the regretful passing of power to the rising heir. It was all very straightforward and required no particular

7 *Wedding ceremonies usually took place at the church door before witnesses*

shift in self-image along the way, though it was recognised that the normal progression might be interrupted at any time by violent death.

The pattern was far more complex for women, as society demanded different virtues and skills at the different stages of her life. The young girl or infant was in the same state of legal powerlessness as her brother, but her upbringing was mainly devoted to inculcating the feminine ideal of passivity and submissiveness to her parents and a future husband, whoever he might be. Her marriage, often at a very young age, meant total domination by her husband and, for all practical purposes, the extinguishing of her legal rights during the term of the marriage. Despite this, she was also supposed to be competent and resourceful in running the household once she was married, since its material comfort and maintenance was primarily her responsibility. Finally, widowhood, if she had any resources, opened to a woman the possibility of the exercise of personal power. She regained her legal personality, was entitled to a certain share of her husband's holdings and, for the first time in her life, could make independent decisions. Widowhood could be perilous, with the danger of violence and intimidation being used to overturn legal rights, but its possibilities for action seem to have exhilarated many medieval women, and the challenges brought forth quick responses. Because men tended to marry somewhat later and usually preferred younger partners, even when they themselves had reached middle age, the widow, especially of a third or fourth marriage, might well be quite a young woman. Such a young woman might have to deal for some years with the guardianship of minor children and be responsible for maintaining the family assets for their benefit against considerable outside pressure. It is a tribute to the flexibility of medieval women that such a number managed to reconcile successfully the contradictory attributes they were admonished to display at different periods of their lives.

Occasionally women recognised their need of assistance in their complex duties and even found female helpers. A ninth-century saint, Liutberga, provides an unexpected new model of holiness, that of the executive housekeeper. Gisla, daughter of a Saxon count, was a widow with a young son and had to travel a great deal to supervise his estates and her own. She must have had some previous knowledge of Liutberga's potential for she removed the young woman from a convent and trained her to be her assistant. During the day Liutberga oversaw her patroness's household and estates, while at night she retired to pray. When she grew old she was finally allowed to retire to the convent of Wendhausen. Even there she received many aristocratic visitors from the surrounding area as they wanted her advice and brought their daughters to learn some of her specialised domestic skills. Her career was in fact that of 'a professional housekeeper and teacher of domestic science'. The use of such quasi-religious continued, for the young wife of the fourteenth-century Ménagier de Paris had Dame Agnes the Beguine to teach her wise and mature behaviour and to help her fifteen-year-old mistress in supervising the servants and their labours, as well as apportioning the work.[12]

The pattern for the married women did not apply in the same way to the religious or the spinster. Till quite late in the Middle Ages spinsterhood was relatively rare and developed most easily in the growing towns where single women had less difficulty finding work and could act independently throughout their lives. The religious, in a sense, sidestepped the whole problem, since her vows removed her from a personal place in the social structure and kept her from individual legal concerns. Her life might well follow the same familiar round from her childhood to her death. The decision to enter a convent was not usually left to her, for in most cases parents placed their daughter in a convent at a very early age. This was rarely because the child had shown some aptitude for religious life but rather a parental response to the need to dispose suitably of an extra daughter for whom it was too expensive, or even impossible, to arrange a marriage. Often placed with the nuns as early as five or six, the little girls grew up familiar with the atmosphere, and received at least a minimal education. Apart from religious satisfactions, if a girl had intellectual interests or other abilities, the nunnery might provide an outlet for her talents or grant her authority as a convent official. Even in a small house the responsibility placed on the lower officials could be extensive, while an abbess, as head of the house and representative of its corporate existence, was always an important woman in her neighbourhood. She was not only busy with immediate administration and the need to keep on good terms with the officials of both king and bishop, but was often involved in legal struggles supporting the convent's claims to its lands, rents and rights. It could be a very satisfactory niche for an able woman.

B: Theories, Laws and Teaching

When we turn from physical realities and women's place in the social structure and at the various stages of life, we come to the influence of a literature where male theories about women and their proper role reigned almost unchallenged. Medieval thinkers' understanding of women was based on their easy acceptance of woman's essential inferiority, which they explained as the natural result of Eve's sin. A few struggled to work out the implications of the New Testament concept that the souls of men and women were equal so that, throughout the Middle Ages, canonists and theologians endeavoured, not very successfully, to harmonise these two principles. The extreme denunciations of women by such authoritative church fathers as Jerome strongly influenced later monastic writers. They were happy to adopt his emphasis on the glory of virginity as woman's best choice and his vivid description of the disadvantages of the married state – bloated pregnancy, howling babies, the troubles of managing a household, and the tortures of jealousy. Their tone became still more shrill as the Gregorian reforms of the eleventh and twelfth centuries struggled to impose general clerical celibacy, a situation which encouraged the depiction of women as merely seducers and temptresses. At the same time, and in line with the increasing devotion to Christ's humanity, new stress was laid on the unique value of the Virgin Mary and her compassion and maternal concern for all who sought her help, however unworthily. The contrast between most women as fallen daughters of Eve, and the glory of the

Virgin Mary, which was shared to a degree by all virgins, contributed to the profound dichotomy in the medieval outlook on women. A thirteenth-century monk's pious tale puts this dualistic approach in human terms. A novice troubled by demons saved herself by calling on the Virgin, whom the demons denounced as 'that woman'. The shocked novice retorted that 'woman' was a name of natural corruption only, while 'virgin', 'Mary', or 'Mother of God' were names of glory.[13]

Both theologians and canonists regarded consecrated virgins as almost a separate division of humankind and felt they were exempted from women's general subordination because their destiny was determined by their consecration to Christ rather than to any living man. As an extension of this extreme praise of virginity almost all theologians denigrated marriage as a poor second choice, existing only as a cure for sin and the procreation of children. It was not to be enjoyed, but only to be used for those purposes. This theological attitude and the preaching that resulted from it, helped to widen the rift between the ideal preached to a lay congregation and the nature of everyday married life as they experienced it.

A woman was most interesting to the law, especially canon law, as it tried to regulate marriage, for it was primarily concerned with her function as wife and mother. Medieval Europe lived under a variety of laws – royal, canon, customary, and manorial – and these were enforced by different courts. Thus the church had its own courts where canon law ruled and which claimed jurisdiction over marriage cases and often over wills. In at least one respect, canon lawyers were considerably more generous to women than their secular counterparts. It was through the consistent efforts of the canonists, that regulations insisting on the necessity of free consent to create a valid marriage were enforced by the church courts. In the twelfth century this insistence still ran counter to the earlier secular practice, which regarded marriage as primarily an alliance with social or economic advantages rather than a religious rite controlled by church legislation. Parents had been convinced that they had not only the right but the duty to arrange their children's marriages and, if necessary, to force them into the desired contract against their wills and under extreme pressure. Freedom of consent was an illusion when the couple were betrothed in infancy, and when there were so many subtle – and not so subtle – forms of pressure open to determined parents. As well, the secular authorities had a legitimate concern that marriages of rich heiresses should ensure loyal and adequate service by their husbands of the obligations with which their lands were burdened, and which were of interest to the whole community. Nevertheless, despite social resentment, church courts heard cases concerning forced marriages, though the need to balance free consent with suitable respect for parental authority could lead to questionable hairsplitting. For example, in a Canterbury court a girl fiercely beaten with staves prior to her marriage was allowed an annulment, but in a similar case where the family piously said that they had only brought staves to the signing of the marriage contract to help them get over ditches on the way, the marriage was upheld.[14]

There was another more unfortunate aspect to the canonists' insistence on untrammelled free choice, and that was the church's recognition of the validity of secret marriages. By the beginning of the thirteenth century a respected theologian, Thomas of Chobham, could write that valid marriage did not require either witnesses or the presence of a priest. This led to many abuses, including false pretences, rash promises and occasionally deliberate fraud, since church courts almost always upheld the first secret marriage against a later publicly attested one and required a return to the first spouse. The case of Edmund de Nastok and Elizabeth de Ludehale in 1290 is a particularly vivid example of carefully planned fraud. In 1277 Edmund and Elizabeth had wished to marry but found their resources insufficient so they concocted a plot. They married secretly but then, with mutual agreement, Edmund negotiated with Richard de Brok to marry his daughter Agnes. He obtained a valuable dowry of more than £60, made up of goods, animals, clothes and 100s in money. It was given him prior to the marriage and he took it, with suitable publicity, to his home in Essex some forty miles away. He disposed of the items even before the marriage legitimated his claim to them. Sometime after the wedding,

8 This initial of the relevant chapter of a canon law handbook depicts a woman's right to accept one spouse and refuse another

Edmund encouraged Elizabeth to initiate a suit in the ecclesiastical
court claiming the prior marriage. When Edmund admitted the previous contract, the court divorced him from Agnes. The aggrieved wife
then sought the return of her dowry and finally sued in the king's court
where Edmund tried, by several specious arguments, to maintain his
rights to it. The court found fraud and malice in the whole affair, and
not only rewarded Agnes with the return of £66 but added a further £16
in damages.[15] Later church statutes did not totally condemn secret
marriages, but tried to arrive at a system encouraging, if not requiring,
public notice of marriage within the local community.

Although canonists insisted on the authority of the husband during
marriage they believed in one area of equality. Both spouses had equal
rights over each other's body, so that neither could take a vow of
chastity, retire to religious life, or even go on crusade without the
willing agreement of the other. In the crusading era this last case caused
considerable soul-searching as the canonists struggled with the need to
encourage more crusaders, but foresaw both moral and practical problems if too many wives decided that their husbands could not go on
crusade without taking them along. Innocent III, anxious for crusaders, allowed men to leave without their wives' consent, but later in
the thirteenth century Aquinas felt that this practice, made legal by
papal fiat, was morally reprehensible.[16] Churchmen also claimed the
right of the married woman to make a will, and even without her
husband's consent, – a position opposed to that of the secular law – on
the grounds that attention to almsgiving and the settling of debts was
necessary for her spiritual health at the time of death. One final freedom
the married woman was allowed – she did not have to share her
husband's tomb, but could choose her own burial place.

Canonists obeying the Christian tradition that a special care should
be taken for the welfare of widows, were particularly concerned with the
woman's situation when her husband predeceased her. When they
translated this idea into practical measures in England, church legislation tried to protect a widow's rights over the property she had
brought to the marriage, her dower from her husband, and her rightful
share of his chattels, that is, what would now be called personal
property. They sought proper maintenance for her until her dower was
assigned from her husband's estate, and insisted that she had the right
to live in widowhood or to remarry at her own choice. Although
ecclesiastical courts were open to widows in England, they could only
deal with chattels, which more and more became sequestered in the
husband's hands and distributed entirely at his volition. They had no
jurisdiction over lands or rents. By the beginning of the thirteenth
century, and especially after the clause in Magna Carta protecting

widows' rights, most upper-class widows in England turned to the secular courts to seek redress and claim their rights.

As well as dealing with legislation regarding marriage, canonists also wrestled with the place of women in ecclesiastical matters. It was generally felt that women were necessarily excluded from the sacrament of orders, although a few canonists admitted that they might have the theoretical capacity. Aquinas resolved the question somewhat differently. He considered women incapable of receiving orders, but able to receive the greater gift of prophecy.[17] His solution provided an approved niche for the female mystics who were such an influential force in the medieval religious consciousness. In principle the church did not recognise any female right to ecclesiastical jurisdiction except in the 'maternal' government of nuns. Nevertheless, some women named clerics to benefices, chaplaincies, and canonries, because the right to do so was tied up with their secular position and property rights. Very powerful ladies, though less commonly than in the earlier Middle Ages, assisted at church councils and even convoked synods. They were frequently addressed by clerics of a lower grade than themselves in the most slavish terms.

Abbesses were a constant source of distress to canonists and popes because of their use of their authority. These men were upset by the fact that – obviously against the natural order of things – abbesses directed monasteries of men and women. Double monasteries were gradually eliminated, although the Brigittine order revived the practice at the end of the fourteenth century. However, abbesses of certain specially favoured nunneries, which rejoiced in vigorous and consistent royal backing and drew their nuns from the highest ranks of society, saw no need to kowtow to ecclesiastics. Such abbeys as Las Huelgas in Spain, Quedlinburg in Germany, and Fontevrault in France exercised almost episcopal powers and were buttressed by extensive royal privileges. The Cistercian abbots regarded the activities of the abbess of Las Huelgas with special horror. They reported to Innocent III in 1210 that she not only held councils of abbessess and made visitations of her affiliated convents, but also blessed the nuns, read the gospel, preached publicly and – worst of all – heard confessions. The monks had overlooked these excesses because Las Huelgas was so far away and the Castilian king, its protector, so powerful. Pope Innocent found this state of affairs both incongruous and absurd and ordered the nearest Spanish bishops to forbid it. He explained that although the Virgin Mary was worthier and more excellent than all the apostles, it was still to them, and not to her, that Christ had committed the keys of the kingdom.[18]

The provisions of canon law were generally uniform throughout

western Europe, but the secular law affecting women varies so greatly
from jurisdiction to jurisdiction that it is almost impossible to be both
brief and accurate in describing its general framework. It reflected local
customs, the greater or lesser influence of the old Roman law, as well as
the specialised laws for various groups. Peasant tenures and customs,
borough regulations, and the pattern of inheritance for noble fiefs
frequently differed from place to place. Despite this necessary dis-
claimer, there were some basic likenesses because all medieval lawyers
easily accepted the natural and proper inferiority of women. On the
whole, public law perceived women as having no rights, but also no
duties, in the public field. A woman was required to pay taxes if she had
sufficient property or goods, and she was responsible for the services in
the lands she held, even though they might have to be performed by
deputy, as in the case of military service. A woman could not serve as an
official – royal borough, or manorial (although there were rare exceptions) – nor as a juror in court, nor even as a witness unless the case
touched her personally. Despite these public barriers, the unmarried
woman of legal age or the widow was almost the equal of a man in
private law. By this time she could inherit even the greatest fiefs, though
her brothers would be the preferred heirs. By the fourteenth century,
only France among the European kingdoms did not allow the woman to
inherit the crown or to transmit a claim to it. A woman had the freedom
to hold land, make contracts, to sue and be sued in her own person. A
queen could serve as a regent for the kingdom and the average widow
was often named guardian for her minor children. Everywhere the
married woman was in a position of legal inferiority, though on the
Continent a budding concept of community of goods restricted to some
degree the husband's absolute power over his wife's property.

In England the common law was particularly restrictive of women's
rights. One legal historian has remarked forcefully that women were the
great victims of the Norman conquest and the law code it elaborated, for
the 'common law crushed women more than any other western law has
ever done'.[19] Under its provisions a woman once married, or a widow
remarried, saw all her legal rights suppressed for the period of the
marriage. Some minimal protection was given to wives since the
marriage portion or dowry which she brought to marriage, and the
dower with which she was endowed by her husband (usually one-third
of his lands), were not supposed to be alienated without her free
consent. A married woman's chattels, including her clothes and
jewelry, were also in her husband's possession and he could dispose of
them as he pleased. Since a married woman's subordination in England
was so complete, she was considered legally incapable of making a will
without her husband's authorisation or consent, since in legal terms she

owned nothing. In this case, reality did not always reflect the theory for more and more married women made wills on their own initiative and husbands usually acquiesced. However, as it becomes possible to study the greater number of wills which have survived from the fourteenth and fifteenth centuries the difference between the wills of wives and those of widows is very great. A student of a large number of English wills of this period has discovered that wives' bequests of money averaged about £5 while the average for widows was £30. As well, wives had fewer and less valuable chattels.[20]

Some practical exceptions had to be made to this theory of the total incapacity of married women in order to reflect the realities of a society in which long drawn-out legal struggles seem to have been one of the amusements of the age, and husbands were often absent for years at a stretch. In such cases a wife could legally act for her husband, and he sometimes appointed her his attorney. As the commercial system expanded and women began to play an active part in trade, the law accommodated itself to the changed circumstances by agreeing to recognise a married woman trading on her own as a *fame sole*, i.e. as if she was unmarried. This not only gave her more freedom, but also protected her husband, since in such a case his assets could not be attached to pay her business debts.

These abstract and often chilly provisions of the law need to be seen against the more human face of reality. Even in the period of arranged marriages, wives could be highly prized by their husbands. A twelfth-century epitaph for Avice, wife of Walter of Auffay, described her as 'fair of face, well-spoken, and full of wisdom', and as having lived with Walter 'in felicity' for fifteen years during which she 'gave him in gladness twelve goodly children'. The most touching eulogy of wife and daughters, however, comes from that persecuted section of medieval society, the Jews. Eliezer son of Judah penned a passionate lament for his wife and two daughters, killed by intruders who broke into his school in Mainz in 1197. Echoing the Old Testament description of the wise woman, Eliezer praised not only his wife's industry and attention to prayer but affirmed that 'the heart of her husband had safely trust in her'. The loss of his two daughters, especially the six-year-old, who, in a beloved child's timeless fashion, amused her father and sang for him, left him lamenting piteously.[21] A mother might occasionally have a lasting influence, especially if her sons were clerics. There is the well-known eulogy of his mother by Peter the Venerable, abbot of Cluny, which not only mentions her piety but adds how generously she and his father had always welcomed guests, and how much she was loved even when she retired to the convent in Marcigny. John de Shillingford, canon of Exeter, paid a more intimate tribute. He stated in

his will that he wanted to be buried in the Dartmoor church of
Wedecombe-in-the-Moor beside his mother, 'so that where I received
my first greeting, I may take my last farewell'.[22]

Reality can also present a less than rosy picture of medieval marriage.
Given the burdensome legal, and often practical, disadvantages for a
woman who had little choice as to whether, or to whom, she was
married, it hardly seems surprising that many medieval women welcomed widowhood as a release. Mrs. Noah in the Towneley Plays may
speak for many of the active city women who formed such a large part of
the audience for these miracle plays. She answers Noah's complaints
about her lack of meekness with the quick response that she would be
easy of heart if she were a widow. She would willingly pay the
mass-penny for his soul and so, she is sure, would many other wives,
who wish their husbands were dead because of the lives they lead.[23] The
poor widow without lands, rentals, trade, or dutiful family was still a
synonym for great need, but the activities of many medieval widows
suggest that their new state of legal and personal freedom inspired fresh
energy and competence. They may also have gained valuable support
through their female friends. A statistical survey of women's wills
shows that they laid particular emphasis on bequests to female friends,
since these occurred in some 75% of the cases. Although bequests were
also made by women to men outside the family these often seem to have
been conceived as a practical strategy to make sure the will was carried
out, while the ones to women appear to be genuine marks of
friendship.[24]

If the laws and beliefs of both ecclesiastical and lay society combined
to insist on the inferior place of women, how was the male ideal of her
suitable behaviour presented? The clerics found it easiest to get their
ideas across to all classes because of the ubiquity of sermons, especially
after the foundation of the Franciscans and Dominicans, whose main
work in life was preaching. In the thirteenth century, well-known
preachers like Jacques de Vitry and Etienne de Bourbon compiled
whole collections of *exempla*, or moral stories, generally based on
heightened versions of everyday life or popular legends. Preachers
interspersed their more serious matter with such *exempla* to add
necessary liveliness to their lengthy sermons. They also tailored their
remarks to their audience, so, when talking to women, preachers
naturally spent much of their time denouncing feminine vanity and
interest in personal adornment. When sermons were preached at
marriages, they emphasised the dignity of the sacrament and the need
for true love and unity in terms strongly reminiscent of the preamble to
the contemporary marriage service of both the Anglicans and the Roman
Catholics. Naturally, medieval preachers also liked to add warning

9 Despite all the sermons women never lost their interest in personal adornment

stories on the unhappy fate of contrary wives and the dangers of marital discord.

Sometimes the more misogynist clerics got so carried away by their theme of the perfidy of all women that their offended auditors finally interrupted them. There was a Dominican who was particularly enthusiastic in his denunciations of women, and was allowed by a noble lady to preach in her chapel on this subject. The friar embarked on a tide of impassioned rhetoric until he reached his climax, in which he attributed to Pilate's wife, attempting to rescue Christ from the Jews, the insidious goal of hindering the redemption of the human race. That was more than the lady of the castle could bear. Rising in the middle of his sermon, she cried brusquely to him to stop slandering her sex. Such independence of judgment, and lack of embarrassment in expressing it, seems to have been obvious even among the lower classes. There was the case of the vain cleric who, in a Palm Sunday sermon, praised Christ's great humility in entering Jerusalem on an ass. He himself was riding a superb palfrey and was not at all pleased to be asked by an old woman if that was the Lord's ass which he had praised so highly.[25] Medieval women, to the discomfiture of many men, had quick, sharp tongues which they delighted in using to deflate male pomposity.

Another Dominican, Robert Holcot, once a judge in the king's court, expressed the typical male's dissatisfaction with women's liberal use of their tongues.

> This is the whole end and apparatus of womenhood, that it should be garrulous and wandering, impatient of quiet, not wishing to stay at home. The Gloss says that it is a matter of astonishment that women who have fewer teeth than men (and teeth are needed for talk) should yet have, not less to say than men, but a good deal more.

In a remarkable biological deduction Holcot suggested that this was because women had more superfluous moisture than men, and so their tongues found it easier to move than in men's drier mouths.[26]

In an age which craved treatises of instruction in all areas of life, both clerical and secular writers provided works setting out their ideals for women. These were generally written in the vernacular, since by the thirteenth century only some nuns and a few extremely well-educated noble ladies could be expected to have more than the bare minimum of Latin required for their devotions. The learned abbesses and ladies of the sixth to the twelfth centuries had no real successors, and true literacy in Latin continued to decline among women as the vernaculars developed and became accepted literary languages of their own. All these treatises were quite naturally addressed to women of the upper classes and to religious, for only they were likely to be able to read, or to be read to, or to have the riches and opportunity to accumulate such manuscripts.

Such texts abounded during these centuries, and although many are dull, repetitive, or excessively patronising, a few sparkle with vitality and charm. The thirteenth century was particularly prolific in providing treatises written with secular women in mind. Two general texts on proper behaviour were composed for upper class women by Robert of Blois and Philip of Novara, both comfortably at home in noble society. Robert laid down specific rules for courteous behaviour, while Philip was rather more general and emphasised especially that a woman's only necessary virtues were chastity and obedience. He thought reading unnecessary except for nuns, and considered writing downright dangerous, as it might lead to the perilous exchange of love letters. Vincent of Beauvais, the learned Dominican who was a favourite of the French court, wrote a high-minded treatise in Latin for Queen Marguerite of Provence, the wife of Louis IX, on the education of noble children. He gave much less space to the girls than the boys, contenting himself, like Philip of Novara, with laying enormous emphasis on the importance of female chastity. He condemned as leading to temptation not only elegant coiffures and exquisite clothes, but even soft beds, warm baths, and too much food. He grudgingly accepted girls reading, thinking it was a less dangerous pastime than others. It is characteristic of the impractical attitude of these male advice-givers that they took for granted that such a sheltered, strongly repressed, and inadequately educated young girl would, once married, suddenly find herself competent to run a household, live peacefully with a husband, discipline her children and servants, and deal prudently with the domestic economy.[27]

Unlike Vincent's austere treatise for the queen, Louis IX's *Enseigne-mens*, which the king wrote with his own hand for his oldest daughter, the queen of Navarre, show both common sense and piety. Louis displays a genuine paternal affection and the quick recognition that his daughter would accept advice more easily from a beloved father than from others. Conscious of the duties of her estate, the king urges her to show practical pity for the poor and the sick, warns her to protect her own reputation by surrounding herself with irreproachable women, and tells her that she should obey her husband, and her father and mother, out of love for them and love for God. He suggests that she should not have too many robes or jewels, though she should have what was suitable for her estate, but he adds that it would please him better if she gave alms of the surplus. She should pray for his soul if he predeceased her, and he ends his brief text with the hope that she will be as good, or even better, than he can desire.[28]

About a hundred years later the Knight of La Tour Landry, a minor noble of Anjou, wrote a full-length book of instruction for his three daughters. He compiled his work by having his chaplains and clerks read him the bible, lives of past worthies, and assorted chronicles so that he could cull praiseworthy or cautionary examples. His purpose was to teach his daughters 'that they might understand how they should govern them, and know good from evil'.[29] The knight obviously expected all his daughters to marry and he gives them a number of practical warnings about how to get and keep a good husband. He has tales of evil, stupid, or headstrong women, but also many stories which sing the praises of good women from his own time as well as the past – a collection of secular *exempla*. The knight strongly favoured sending children to school, though he hoped they would read edifying literature rather than romance. In fact he specifically states that every woman who can read and know the law of God and learn virtue and science is closer to salvation for it. His own praises of particularly good contemporary women reflect his pragmatic approach and the favoured charities of the time, for he emphasises practical good works. Feeding the poor, providing medicine for the sick, visiting those in childbirth, and having a special care for poor gentlewomen so that they could be suitably married and their funerals decently celebrated: these, he felt, were much more important than prayers and ascetic practices. He lets his wife insist that love should not conquer all, arguing that a woman should respect estate and degree even in love, for if she weds one lower than herself she loses the respect and friendship of her family and her acquaintances. Of course it is even worse if a married woman falls in love with such a one. The book breathes a practical piety and warmth that proclaim the truth of the knight's statement that he had made the book for the love of his daughters, hoping to turn them to love and serve their creator and to be loved by their neighbours and the world.[30]

Equally sensible and affectionate in his tone, and even more concerned with practical affairs, was the Ménagier de Paris, whose treatise for the edification and instruction of his young wife has been made known to a wide public by Eileen Power. The Ménagier wrote near the end of the fourteenth century and represented the rising class of the rich bourgeoisie of the larger towns. He provided with almost photographic clarity a picture of the way life was run in such an urban household. Certain elements remain the same – the Ménagier wanted to be sure that his wife took proper care of her husband and made his comfort her first concern. He expected her to be meek and submissive but within limits. Although he repeats at considerable length the story of Patient Griselda, he concludes roundly that he does not expect her to be that obedient, for he is neither worthy of it, nor that foolish, nor yet that cruel.[31] He obviously loved his young wife – she was only fifteen – but he wanted to be quite sure that she knew how to conduct both herself and her household, for what would seem to us an unusual reason – so that she would do him credit if she married again after his death.

A fifteenth-century work in English verse, *How the Good Wijf taughte Hir Doughtir*, provides no real evidence that its author was a woman, despite having the wife as the narrator. It was designed for a group considerably further down the social scale than the Ménagier and his wife, and suggests the household of a reasonably well-to-do peasant or townsman, where there are servants to be supervised but the wife sells her cloth to help the family fortunes and is warned against spending too much time or money in taverns or going to wrestling matches, definitely lower class amusements. At that level too the husband insisted on obedience and the wife was faced with the duty of running the household and making sure that the work was properly and thriftily done.[32] Perhaps the most interesting question the verse provokes is how those meant to benefit from it got the message. Could they read by this time, or was it recited to them – and if so, by whom?

The last book of instruction for women is certainly the most unusual because it was actually written by a woman, and thus stands out among the plethora of treatises written by men to impress on women masculine ideals for their behaviour. For the first time since Dhuoda, the voice of admonition and practical advice is that of a woman herself, Christine de Pizan, daughter of the Italian-born doctor and astrologer at the court of King Charles V of France. Christine was brought up on the fringes of the court, and also benefited from her Italian father's more serious view about the importance of education for his daughter. When she was left a widow at twenty-five with three young children and a widowed mother to support, she turned to her pen as the only way of making a living. Aided by influential friends and the useful connections with the ruling Valois princes she had through the court, she made a triumphant success of it. Christine accepted the traditional religious, moral and social structure of her time, but she felt strongly that women were unjustly treated and much undervalued by their male contemporaries – and was both willing and able to argue the point. Her two most important books on women were written one after the other in 1404–5. *The City of Ladies*, inspired by Boccaccio's *Concerning Famous Women*, merely sung the praises of important women. However, Christine extended the range from which she drew her examples, including her own contemporaries and expressing a strongly moral point of view. *The Treasure of the City of Ladies* or *Book of the Three*

10 The Menagier's interest in his garden would encourage his wife to supervise her servant in the necessary digging.

Virtues as it is variously called, was intended to be a more practical work.[33] In it Christine aimed to provide rules of conduct for women at all levels of the social structure and all stages of life. Since it was dedicated to Margaret of Burgundy, recently married at the age of ten to the seven-year-old dauphin, Louis of Guyenne, it devotes more than half of its pages to the duties and difficulties of princesses and great ladies. Several sections are devoted to the proper conduct of such women when they become widows, perhaps a premonition of the unfortunate fact that Margaret herself would be widowed before she was twenty.

In the subsequent chapters Christine went on to deal fairly fully with women who lived at the court or were responsible for country estates, and then continued down the ranks of officials' wives, rich towns-women, and the lower classes in town and country. So as to neglect no one, she ended with reflections for the old and the young, the widow and the unmarried girl, the religious and even the prostitute. What emerges from a careful reading of her treatise is the strong practical emphasis in Christine's work. She agrees that chastity is important for a woman and must be safeguarded so as to protect her reputation, but she is far more concerned about the practical virtue of prudence, devoting eight chapters to the different ways it should be exercised.[34] Profiting from her own difficult experience after her husband's death, she was convinced that women at any level of society must be involved and knowledgeable in the safeguarding of the family goods. Even a princess should watch over the finances of her court and supervise the master of her household, for only in this way could she make a sensible division of her revenues so as to be able to meet all her obligations, especially wages, and still give adequate largess. Christine realised that not all wives were trusted by their husbands with knowledge of the family resources, but she also knew that it was the wives who suffered when male extravagance allowed expenditures to exceed income. She would certainly have applauded Mr. Micawber's dictum on how to balance annual income and annual outgo so as to achieve happiness.

It is typical that one of the most vivid and attractive of Christine's very human illustrative vignettes is that of the lady in charge of a country estate while her husband is away. The indefatigable lady is pictured as well informed on all the legal rights concerning the prop-erty, knowledgeable about crops and their marketing, and with a constant eye on the accounts. As well, she was not too proud to be up to her knees in the farmyard mud while she bustled everywhere to be sure that all her servants were working hard and not sneaking a nap under a convenient hedge.[35] The stereotype of the canny French wife carefully supervising the family assets seems to have a long and distinguished tradition. Christine's book of advice was well-known in France during the fifteenth and early sixteenth centuries, but was then forgotten. Nevertheless, as we look at the reality of medieval women's lives, as opposed to the ideals that were proposed for them, we must often recall Christine's strictures and suggestions. She described the accommodations women of her time had to make to live in their predominantly masculine world, and she did so through a woman's eyes and in a woman's voice. In so doing she sheds light on the ways in which woman's work was done and where feminine influence could best be applied.

CHAPTER THREE

Women who Ruled: Queens

Queens in the twelfth to fifteenth centuries did not normally exercise the independent power that had often characterised the powerful royal consorts of the earlier Middle Ages. As royal courts became more complex and required more organisation the queen tended to lose her central position, since power began to flow to newly influential officials. Nevertheless, in the hierarchical social structure of the time the queen still represented the highest rank and position open to a woman and her special character was generally recognised. It is typical of the mental attitude of that feudal period that a favourite title of the Virgin Mary was 'Queen of Heaven' and many of her most popular legends emphasise her queenly prerogative of mercy, even overriding justice.

By the twelfth century the queen's primary role was to ensure the passage of the royal blood to a male heir whose existence was considered essential for the peaceful transmission of power from one generation to the next. This was unlike the situation in the early Middle Ages when the barbarians newly settled in European lands had generally followed the Germanic tradition of choosing a king from among the most suitable members of the whole royal family. Gradually this kin-right had become narrowed into a direct hereditary right and was further refined to recognise the prerogative of the first-born son to succeed to an undivided kingdom, an idea firmly implanted in both France and England by the late twelfth century. The civil war in England in the mid-twelfth century, when the Empress Matilda, daughter and only surviving child of Henry I, battled for the throne with Stephen, Henry's nephew and nearest male heir, was felt to be a notorious example of the evils that might befall when the queen had not produced a surviving male heir.

As primogeniture became the norm, and the oldest son the expected heir, queens did not have to struggle for the rights of their sons against the ambitions of royal uncles, and were no longer the almost invariable choice as regent when the heir was a minor. The contrasting decisions in England and France at the beginning of the thirteenth century when the nine-year-old Henry III ascended to the throne of England in 1216 and the twelve-year-old Louis IX to the throne of France in 1226, indicate how the choice of regent appears to have been affected by the suitability of the individual queen. In France, Blanche of Castile had been specifically named by her husband in his will to serve as regent while the heir was under age. The French barons were not pleased, but she was strong enough to enforce her position. On the other hand in England, where the country was menaced by a French invasion, Isabella of Angoulême, Henry's mother, was passed over by the English barons, with the advice of the papal legate, in favour of the highly respected and formidable William Marshal, earl of Pembroke. It was a wise move for England. Isabella returned to Angoulême less than two years after her husband's death and by 1220 had decided to replace her own ten-year-old daughter as the wife of Hugh Le Brun, count of La Marche. Four of their sons and a daughter battened on the generosity of their royal half-brother, ultimately acquiring valuable lordships and marriages in England.

Besides the chroniclers' descriptions of actual queens, we occasionally find an abstract statement of the contemporary ideal. Before 1325 James de Cessolis, a Lombard Dominican, summed up his very popular preaching before noble audiences in a treatise entitled *The Solace of the Game of Chess*. He used the rules which governed the play of the various pieces in this approved noble amusement as an allegorical structure to describe the duties of the various states of life. His work was soon translated into French, became very popular, and was one of the first books that Caxton printed in English. The queen is the only woman mentioned and her responsibility was seen as twofold. Because of the importance of unquestioned hereditary succession the queen must be chaste, and the friar lays great emphasis on this, but he felt she must also be wise. She should be discreet, able to keep confidential matters secret, and careful in the education of her children. Her chastity should also serve to remind others 'for as she is above all other in estate and reverence so should she be ensaumple unto all other in her lvyng honestyle'.[1] When Cessolis deals with the play of the various pieces his explanation of the pattern of the queen's moves suggests what were then felt to be the queen's special privileges and duties. She had the right to pass in front of the judges (whom the friar substituted for the bishops), and also of the rooks, who represent the knights and officials commissioned by the king, because she had in herself the grace and authority that the rooks had only by commission, and she should have perfect wisdom as should the judges. She should not go into battle and usurp the place of knights – if she does, it should only be as a solace to the king – but remain safely within the fortresses. When Cessolis assigned the various pawns and labelled them as representing various occupations (e.g. the pawn to the right of the knight was the smith because the knight had the most need of his skill), he described the pawn assigned to the queen as representing physicians, spicers and apothecaries, symbolising her particular concern with the maintenance of health and wellbeing. The queen was not only the apex of the social structure but added to her own family responsibilities the exercise of mercy and compassion to the larger family of the realm.

How was the choice of a queen arrived at? There was a strong feeling throughout medieval society that the status of a wife and her family should match that of her prospective husband. Despite the popularity of the story of Patient Griselda as an example of the ideal wife, most practical people agreed that much of her trouble arose from the disparity of her condition, for she had no natural group of supporters who could protect her against the calculated debasement by her husband. Since the choice of a queen should be profitable to the kingdom, a prospective queen should have treasure, land and supporters she could bring with her to help solidify the royal position, which meant that she should come from royalty or the very high nobility. Profitability was defined in different ways at different times. Thus Henry I of England,

11 Eleanor of Aquitaine's effigy at Fontevrault

who had seized the throne after the murder of William Rufus, almost immediately made overtures for a marriage to Edith (whom the Normans always referred to as Matilda), daughter of Margaret, queen of Scotland, who was descended from the old Anglo-Saxon ruling family. Such a link could help lend legitimacy to his position. On the other hand, both Louis VII of France and Henry II of England coveted the hand of Eleanor of Aquitaine because she was heiress to an extensive block of southwest France and would bring the rich duchy of Aquitaine to her husband. During these centuries the kings of France and England searched for queens who would provide useful alliances to bolster their power, extend their territories, or disarm their enemies. Marriages between the members of the French and English royal families became common during the fourteenth and fifteenth centuries since it was believed such unions might be the means of ending the continuing hostilities between the two kingdoms. The marriages had enthusiastic papal encouragement but little success in affecting the political bitterness of that struggle and often envenomed it.

As the twelfth century wore on, royal marriage ceremonies became more solemn and queens too had coronations, though marriage and coronation might not coincide. The influence of the queen depended on two things – her position as king's consort and her own personal power. As long as the court was small the queen's opportunities for individual influence could be very great. Adelaide of Maurienne, queen of Louis VI of France (1108–37), marked the high tide of a queen sharing in royal power as a matter of right. The royal acts included the queen's regnal year as well as the king's, and her name appears in some forty-five charters as participating in the decision. The queen's share in government was recognised in Adelaide's time in both theory and practice, not only in the accepted matters of benefactions, ecclesiastical appointments and settlements of cases brought before the king's court, but also in such unexpected fields as charters of special privileges and royal protection, the issuing of safe-conducts in her own name, and a joint oath of allegiance to Innocent II by both king and queen in their own names. The French pattern changed sharply with the accession of Louis VII and the rise to power of his advisor, Abbot Suger. The monarchy was becoming more stable and needed to digest its recent expansions; more officials were required and the court became less intimate, so that the queen, although she retained her social status, began to lose her official powers. From the late twelfth and early thirteenth centuries, as separate households for king and queen began to be the accepted order, the royal pair led far more individual lives and the possibilities of intrigue between ambitious members of the two households multiplied. A dowager queen retained her title but normally retired to the lands given her as dower and exercised only the powers which belonged to the lands she actually controlled. The English situation was similar, although no English queen exercised the powers of Adelaide of Maurienne. By the thirteenth century in both countries it was the personal influence of the particular queen which tended to define her actual power.

The eleventh century Queen Margaret, wife of Malcolm Canmore, king of Scotland, was still powerful in her own right and also mother of a queen of England. Educated on the continent within the orbit of the pious Empress Agnes, the widow of Emperor Henry III, Margaret had absorbed the continental ideas of church and monastic reform and brought them with her to Scotland. Her position as one of the few remaining members of the Anglo-Saxon royal house lent her prestige; her rather domineering devotion to the church and her introduction of Benedictine monasticism was carried on by her sons' efforts; while her canonisation enshrined her prestigiously in the select company of sainted queens. Margaret died in 1093, a few days after her husband, but her daughter Edith/Matilda had been previously sent for education and protection to her aunt Cristina, abbess first of Romsey and then of Wilton.

When Henry I seized the throne of England and began to contemplate the advantages of a marriage to Matilda, controversy arose over whether his proposed bride had ever been veiled or not. This was an important matter, for if she had been veiled any subsequent marriage would not be legitimate. It may well have been that her aunt was anxious to see her as a nun, but this career did not appeal to the girl who had no doubts of her continued secular status. She insisted that her aunt Cristina had put a black hood on her head for fear of the raiding Normans, but that she had thrown it off and trampled on it, even though her conduct had brought her a beating and a harsh scolding from the abbess. Matilda also stated that her father had once seen her thus veiled and he too had snatched off her head-covering and torn it to pieces, declaring that he would have married her to his worst enemy rather than consigning her to a house of nuns.[2] The problem was put before Anselm, the archbishop of Canterbury. As general feeling favoured Matilda as the king's bride Anselm diplomatically agreed and their marriage was celebrated in November 1100. During the eighteen years of her married life Matilda demonstrated many of her mother's qualities for, like her, she was a formidable woman, uncomfortable to cross but active in good works. With filial devotion she not only commissioned a life of Margaret and had it read to her, but apparently inspected the pages herself. William of Malmesbury, the finest monastic historian of the century, was rather lukewarm in the queen's praises. He acknowledged her blameless reputation and charity to the poor but was very dubious about her marriage after her stay in the nunnery and remarked rather censoriously that after two children, one of either sex, she was content to desist from childbearing, leave the royal court and live in great splendour at Westminster.[3]

The queen believed in practical works of mercy – her interests were wide and her benefactions both generous and useful. She founded the leper-hospital of St. Giles in Holborn just outside the city walls, as well as a priory of Augustinian canons, Holy Trinity at Aldgate, which was to be the only major religious house within the city walls until the coming of the friars. The canons were generally more concerned with practical social needs than contemplation and liturgy, and were helpful neighbours. As well, Matilda built at Queenshythe, the great riverside wharf which bore her name, one of the first public lavatories in the city which seems to have also accommodated public baths. Her correspondents included some of the important men of the day, above all Anselm of Canterbury. Even when he was in exile she poured out fulsome praise on the excellence of his letters, insisting that they combined the best points of Cicero, Quintilian, Paul, Jerome, Gregory, and Augustine, a fervid devotion which the archbishop regarded with considerable reserve.[4] The queen also patronised writers and musicians. She asked the author of the *Voyage of St. Brendan*, originally written in Latin, to provide an Anglo-Norman version for her ladies and the members of her household who did not know Latin. He did so, making a few changes for the benefit of such a noble lay audience. The story was so good, and so popular that, when Matilda died, the author, with a quick eye to the advantages of court patronage, re-dedicated it to Henry's second queen. William of Malmesbury admitted that Matilda was particularly fond of music and generous to good church musicians. Her liberality attracted foreign singers whom she rewarded so well that they spread her fame far and wide, though the monk added grudgingly, these gifts were often at the expense of her own dependents.[5]

During the fifteen years between the birth of her last child and her own death in 1118 Matilda was also involved in the affairs of the kingdom. She was left as regent on several occasions when Henry was in Normandy and appears to have enjoyed the administrative routine, though many of her judgments in specific cases were made in concert with Roger of Salisbury, the king's justiciar who exercised the real power. The queen died in her late thirties, and within two years of her death the seventeen-year-old Prince William was lost in the wreck of the *White Ship*, depriving the kingdom of its male heir. Although the monastic chroniclers always had some doubts about Matilda – that question of the veil may well have continued to rankle – the queen was admired and remembered by the common people for many years after her death. Her good example in encouraging and patronising important works of mercy inspired nobles and ecclesiastics to follow a similar path, for the private foundation of hospitals and leper-houses in England expanded rapidly in the twelfth and early thirteenth centuries.

The best-known of all medieval queens is unquestionably Eleanor of Aquitaine, the headstrong heiress to the rich, powerful, and extensive duchy of Aquitaine, who was successively queen of France and of England. Her vivid personality has been a constant source of inspiration to lovers of literature who have praised her patronage of the troubadours and overstressed her connection with the courts of love, while incidents in her life have provided historical novelists with more startling material than they might have dared to imagine. Undoubtedly her passionate and strong-minded moulding of events to suit her own purpose, and her struggles with her wildly dissimilar husbands have always provided good theatre. More sober historians have had considerable difficulty in coming to terms with her personality and her actions, and arguments over her actual importance and influence continue to rage. She seems to have had what is now described as 'star quality', that indefinable attribute which fascinated such onlookers as the unknown German student who scribbled his homage in a brief verse preserved in the *Carmina Burana*:

> Were the world all mine
> From the sea to the Rhine,
> I'd give it all
> If so be the Queen of England
> Lay in my arms.[6]

Undoubtedly both intelligent and well-educated, Eleanor could read Latin as well as the vernacular, and had broad literary interests. As queen of England she patronised the clerks who provided popular history for the court and they paid tribute to her learning, beauty, and virtue.

Eleanor was married to Louis VII of France immediately after her father's death, and, as heiress to Aquitaine, was an enormously valuable bride. All through her life, Eleanor was passionate, wilful, and deeply attached to the interests of Aquitaine, where she tried to keep the reins of government in her own hands. She found Louis a rather dull husband and, to his dismay and that of his advisers, she succeeded in producing only two daughters in the fifteen years their marriage lasted. The breaking point came on the crusade that Louis VII insisted on leading personally in 1147 and on which Eleanor accompanied him. Her obvious delight in the elegant society of the crusader kingdom and her growing intimacy with Raymond of Antioch, her uncle although only eight years her senior, provoked the usually mild Louis to firmness. His exercise of husbandly authority suggested to the irate Eleanor the possibility of using to her own advantage the church's strict laws on the invalidity of marriages between relations as a way to break a tie she found irksome. After the royal pair's return to France she began to lay her plans to seek an annulment of her marriage. The French bishops were quite willing to pursue the matter, since the ties of relationship were undoubtedly within the forbidden degrees, and she had neither provided an heir to the throne nor seemed likely to do so. There seems little doubt that Eleanor had carefully planned the scenario of the divorce and also knew what she proposed to do next.

As soon as the marriage was dissolved in March 1152 Eleanor travelled at once to Poitiers, leaving her daughters with her divorced husband, and notified Henry Plantagenet, son of the Empress Matilda and her second husband the count of Anjou, that she wanted to marry him. By this time Eleanor was thirty and Henry a young man of nineteen, but she was the richest heiress in Europe with power and resources to aid his ambitions. In addition, there seems to be little question that a passionate attraction had sprung up between them during a meeting at the French court in 1151. They married in May; before the end of 1152 Henry had succeeded his father as count of Anjou and in 1154 was crowned king of England, succeeding Stephen. Eleanor had four sons and a daughter in the first five years of their marriage, and two more daughters and another son, John, were born in the 1160s – John, when his mother was forty-five. However, frequent childbearing did not interfere with the queen's political activity. During the early years of the reign, Eleanor was often involved in affairs of state, frequently served as regent when Henry was in his continental lands, and probably encouraged the campaign against Toulouse in 1159. However, by 1163 Henry, now in his prime, controlled all political decisions, although Eleanor was later encouraged to resume the active management of her duchy of Aquitaine. Relations between Henry and Eleanor cooled and her energies were increasingly devoted to forwarding her childrens' interest, even against their father. Her important share in her oldest son's rebellion was more than King Henry could stomach, and from 1174 until Henry's death in 1189 she was kept under close watch, either in France or England.

It is a striking commentary on Eleanor's physical and mental powers that the accession to the English throne of Richard, her favourite son, could spur her at the age of sixty-seven to a vigorous display of supportive activity. During the period that Richard was in captivity, having been seized while returning home from the crusade, his mother practically ruled England, keeping the ambitious young John under control. Not until 1194, after Richard and John had been reconciled through her mediation, did Eleanor finally retire to the abbey of Fontevrault to which she had close ties of affection and patronage. She was then seventy-two, but emerged again from her retreat five years later to aid John's accession to the English throne. She not only ensured the loyalty of her duchy of Aquitaine to him but also foiled the intrigues of Arthur of Brittany, her grandson but her son's rival. By 1200 eight of Eleanor's ten children had predeceased her but the old queen was still sufficiently alert, active, and politically astute to journey personally over the Pyrenees in winter to visit her daughter at the court of Castile and arrange yet another marriage. She hoped that the wedding of one of her Castilian grand-daughters, who at the time were John's closest heirs, to the heir to the French throne might help bring peace between her son and the French king. Her choice of the younger daughter, Blanche, to fill this role was her last public act and that extraordinary young girl was to set the tenor of French history for the first half of the thirteenth century. Queen Eleanor died at Fontevrault in 1204 and was buried there in a nun's habit. Her effigy in the Fontevrault church may have little relation to her actual appearance but is an impressive reminder of a powerful and wilful woman who played an extraordinarily large part in the political intrigues of more than half a century. Through her manoeuvrings as mother and grandmother she left an indelible impression on the royal power in both England and France.

Her grand-daughter, Blanche of Castile, has her own niche in French history. The devout and ascetic mother of France's only canonised king was also an active and able administrator of the realm, not only during Louis IX's minority, but also when the king went on crusade in 1248 and left the regency in her hands. While Louis was under-age, she overcame vigorous baronial opposition to hold the royal power for her son, faithfully carrying out the aggressive and expansionist policy of her father-in-law, Philip Augustus. Brought to France as a pawn in a peace treaty between England and France, her early married life gave no suggestion of the politically active role she was to play. Her first child was stillborn in 1205, when she was seventeen and her husband a year older. In the next twenty-one years she had eight living children, as well as three others who died at birth or soon after, so that much of her time was given to the supervision of their education and moral training. The three short years of Louis VIII's reign (1223–26) coincided with his full maturity and were crammed with ambitious projects against the county of Toulouse and the Albigensian heretics. Louis died at Montpensier in the Auvergne on 8 November 1226 while returning from the siege of Avignon. Although the tragic news devastated the queen, she assumed her responsibility as regent and was capable of moving rapidly to ensure the immediate coronation of her twelve-year-old son; thus legitimising his position, before the rebellious barons could move against him. The ceremony took place in Reims exactly three weeks after his father's death – a triumph of speed and organisation given contemporary conditions, though many of the most important barons failed to attend. Disaffection was rife. The barons muttered that it was quite unsuitable that Queen Blanche should 'govern so great a thing as the kingdom of France'.[7] After all, she was a stranger, a Spaniard and a woman – a triple indictment.

Nevertheless, she continued to rule the kingdom of France most successfully for the next eight years. By the time Louis IX came of age Blanche had managed through judicious campaigns to conclude satisfactory treaties with all the disaffected nobles, except in Poitou where the English king was strong and had local supporters. Even in the queen's forays with her army, she combined practicality with a clear grasp of the issues at stake. She moved her army unexpectedly against Brittany in January 1229, an unheard of time for campaigning, but she wished to prevent the rebellious count from acquiring English help. The French settled to a siege of the strong fortress of Bellême but the queen was so concerned about the effect of the cold on the soldiers and

12 Blanche of Castile teaching the young Louis IX

the horses that she gave orders for fires to be lit and had her men cut down trees and even destroy wooden houses in the nearby villages to stoke the fires.[8]

Although a competent strategist and a careful administrator, Blanche was a domineering woman who occasionally failed when she tried to push royal power too far. Two cases are noteworthy. The first was in 1229 when she engaged in a long drawn-out struggle with the university of Paris, always fiercely protective of its independent privileges. On the occasion of a riot erupting between students and townspeople the queen intervened by sending royal soldiers to settle a matter in which they did not have jurisdiction. In the fracas they killed some of the scholars and the university reacted vigorously. The masters shut down their lectures and declared a boycott of Paris and the whole diocese by all members of the university until they had received satisfaction. It took two years, and some prodding from the pope, before the court and the university finally arrived at a settlement, which generally upheld the university's claims.[9] The second case arose when Louis was absent on crusade and Blanche battled with the chapter of Notre Dame. Her struggle with the Paris canons concerned their rights to tallage their serfs of the manor of Orly and the queen's attempt to bring the case to the royal court. Offended by this encroachment on their rights, the chapter threw the serfs, along with their wives and children, into the chapter's prison where some died. The queen's anger led her into another questionable step. She entered the canons' cloister, accompanied by her officials and men-at-arms who broke down the prison door, rescuing the serfs. The matter went to arbitration but dragged on so long that sentence was not finally given till after the queen's death when the judgment asserted that her interference had overstepped her rights.[10]

Queen Blanche was sixty years old when Louis departed on crusade, and was an active regent, but her task was less difficult than in the early years, since many of the more aggressive barons had joined her son's expedition. The news of Louis' capture at Mansourah, as well as the death of his rash younger brother, Robert of Artois, and so many other French knights, came as a thunderbolt. Blanche worked frantically to raise the sums needed for the king's ransom, soliciting contributions from the pope, the French clergy, the barons and the towns. She originally welcomed the unruly *Pastoureaux* in Paris because she hoped they might really save the Holy Land – the mission they claimed – and thus avenge her sons. Unfortunately the *Pastoureaux* were merely one more of the wild, undisciplined movements of medieval ne'er-do-wells with charismatic leaders that were sparked by the emotional fervour of the crusades. Such groups were almost always violently anti-clerical and disruptive of the social structure and had no resources to maintain them. The queen finally became disillusioned by their brutalities and ordered their capture, but they succeeded in devastating much of France before their spellbinding leader was slain and the movement fell apart. Matthew Paris, the conservative English chronicler, reported rather grandiloquently that they were the greatest trouble to the church since Mohammed.[11] Blanche died in November 1252 at the Cistercian abbey of Maubuisson, before Louis returned from the Holy Land. Her deathbed, as described by her youngest son, seems remarkably characteristic of the woman. As death approached she had herself laid on a pallet on the floor, but the priests and clerks around her hesitated to initiate the prayers. Suddenly the queen herself began to intone the prayer for the dying and 'gave up her soul little by little, muttering between her teeth the rest of the prayer'.[12] Even in death the old queen insisted on taking charge.

Blanche was in many ways an unattractive character. She was harsh with herself, harsh with her son, and particularly harsh with her daughter-in-law, who nevertheless wept at the news of her death because of the sorrow it was for Louis. Joinville, the king's great friend, disapproved of the old queen's efforts to keep her son away from his wife except at night. He tells how the young couple enjoyed the royal palace at Pontoise best of all because there was a connecting staircase between their rooms which allowed them to meet in the middle and yet be warned by their servants if the queen was about to arrive.[13] There seems little doubt that Queen Blanche was fiercely jealous of any challenge to her primacy with Louis whom she had moulded according to her demanding and religious ideal of kingship. Seen in human terms, she was a difficult and dominating personality, characteristics accentuated by her successful struggle against great odds to protect both her son's inheritance and the kingdom of France. She achieved her aims with a Castilian rigidity and an emphasis on strict, almost monastic, behaviour for both herself and her son. Many of their subjects found the pious atmosphere of the court oppressive and unsuitable in its minimising of royal display for, as one of Louis' more modern biographers once phrased it, the French 'always preferred amiable vices to inconvenient virtues'.[14] Nevertheless, Blanche was a most successful and powerful queen and well deserved the tribute of the chronicler, Guillaume de Nangis: 'she was the wisest of all women of her time, and all good things came to the realm of France while she was alive'.[15]

Blanche was a remarkable example of a queen whose political activity was essential and generally constructive. The two queens who sat on the thrones of France and England for over fifty years during the later years of the thirteenth century display very different models of the ways in which queens could attempt to wield political power. Marguerite and

Eleanor of Provence were sisters, the elder daughters of Count Raymond Berengar of Provence and his wife, Beatrice of Savoy. The counties of Provence and Savoy assumed new importance in the thirteenth century because of their strategic position, and alliance with them was eagerly sought. Raymond Berengar and his able officials were excellent strategists and used his four beautiful daughters to forge highly advantageous marriages with both the French and the English royal houses. Queen Blanche had picked the eldest, Marguerite, as a bride for Louis in 1234, hoping that such a marriage would further extend French influence into Provence, a territory which the French kings were now beginning to regard with an acquisitive eye. Henry III of England married Eleanor, the second daughter, two years later. Sanchia, the third daughter, became the second wife of Henry's brother, Earl Richard of Cornwall. The French influence became predominant when Louis' youngest brother, Charles of Anjou, married the youngest daughter, Beatrice, after her father's death and when his will had named her as the heiress of the county. The result of this intermingling of the royal families of France and England was to provide both affection and rancour in a familiar pattern, which in this case had wider political repercussions.

The more amiable side of this inter-relationship can be perceived in the chroniclers' description of the great family reunion in Paris in December 1254. Louis had just returned from his six years in the Holy Land and Henry, who had been in his duchy of Gascony, proposed to return to England by the land route, stopping at Fontevrault to transfer his mother's body to a more dignified spot within the abbey church. The English king also wanted to make a pilgrimage to Pontigny and was most eager to see the wonders of Paris, that metropolis of the north. Louis was delighted to grant his permission and rode as far as Chartres with a resplendent retinue to welcome his brother-in-law. Henry's intelligent passion for building must have made even a brief visit to the almost completed cathedral a special pleasure, while in Paris he was so entranced by the beauties of the Sainte-Chapelle that a contemporary song suggested that he would have liked to roll it off in a cart. The atmosphere in Paris was extremely festive. The widowed Countess Beatrice had come to join all her daughters and the citizens of Paris put themselves out to greet their distinguished visitors with songs, dances, and lighted torches as the procession passed through streets adorned with festive hangings. There were banquets and the exchange of valuable gifts, although Henry must have been astounded when Louis gave him for his zoo in the Tower of London the elephant the sultan of Egypt had presented to the French king. However, the family meeting had undercurrents of jealousy as well as pleasure, Marguerite and

Eleanor, meeting again after twenty years, were truly delighted to see each other but were joined in dissatisfaction that their youngest sister had inherited all of the county of Provence while their original marriage portions had not yet been completely paid. The two younger sisters were envious of their elders' rank as queens when they were only countesses, although before they died both Sanchia and Beatrice had also reached that pre-eminence with Richard's election as king of the Romans and Charles of Anjou's as king of Naples and Sicily.[16]

Countess Beatrice seems to have enjoyed this festive reunion with her daughters. It was on another such occasion, perhaps two years later, that she brought along a useful compendium of health information for women, compiled for her by her physician, Aldobrandino of Siena. The Italian doctor wrote the first such treatise in French, full of practical advice, including how to keep healthy while travelling – very useful for women of such peripatetic households. The doctor also provided suggestions for the pregnant woman at all stages of her pregnancy – what she should do and what she should avoid, the way to deal with

13 Countess Beatrice's physician, Aldobrandino of Siena, lecturing to other, less distinguished pupils

newborn babies, and the characteristics a mother should look for when acquiring a wet nurse for the baby. Aldobrandino also dealt with beauty care, providing recipes for dying hair blond, red or black, as well as for removing superflous hair, although the suggested ointment containing arsenic or alum sounds rather drastic.[17] The countess's desire to take this text with her when she visited her daughters suggests that medieval mothers felt that informing their daughters on health care was one of their responsibilities.

Marguerite of Provence was a courageous and passionate woman. She bore Louis eleven children, three of them during his crusade and under difficult conditions. Joinville describes the distraught queen in the last stages of pregnancy at Damietta after the king had been taken prisoner at Mansourah. She suffered from such nightmares of Saracen attackers that she had an old knight of eighty sleep by her bed and hold her hand when she cried out. Before her labour started she privately begged the knight on her knees that if the Saracens should capture the town he would kill her rather than allow her to be captured – a move with which he agreed and on which he had already decided. The day her son was born, the queen learned that the western merchants proposed to abandon Damietta, the major bargaining counter the crusaders had to ensure the deliverance of Louis and the other captives. The indomitable Marguerite called the merchants into her chamber and begged them to desist from such an action which could destroy the king and the army, as well as her newborn son. At least they could delay their departure until she could rise from her bed and take charge. The reluctant traders claimed that they were dying from hunger, so the queen bought up all the town's provisions at great expense and engaged the merchants at the king's charge, thus persuading them to stay. Damietta served its purpose, being surrendered to the Saracens as part of the king's ransom, while the queen, still weak from childbirth, took ship for Acre to await Louis' arrival.[18] Marguerite was at her best when she could take decisive action. One night on shipboard returning to France, a careless serving woman left her scarf where it was set afire by a guttering candle and the queen wakened to find her cabin full of flames. Marguerite speedily threw the scarf into the sea and beat out the fire with her sheets without pausing to cry for help.[19]

Louis was a strong king who allowed political influence only to his mother, not his wife – a situation which Marguerite obviously resented and often tried to circumvent. Her early political activities in the years after Blanche's death were concerned with rallying support for her sister Eleanor when the English barons rose against King Henry or, more personally, with her own claims in Provence. She never ceased to intrigue against Charles of Anjou, whom she felt had unfairly taken

Provence from her. Her ambitions and resentment led her to extract a secret oath from her eldest son Philip that he would hold the kingdom of France under her wardship until he was thirty, not appoint anyone to his council without her agreement, nor sign any treaty or alliance with Charles of Anjou. Louis got wind of this secret agreement and moved quickly to obtain a papal dispensation for his son from such an injudicious oath.[20] Even after Philip became king Marguerite kept up her struggle against Charles, leading the faction at court which was anti-Anjou and pro-English as opposed to the party of Marie of Brabant, Philip's second queen, who encouraged Charles' Italian ambitions. Undoubtedly Marguerite had a very real fondness for her sister Eleanor and her children, especially Edward. The French queen mellowed somewhat in her widowhood and spent her final years in pious foundations and good works, even showing friendly kindness to the exiled countess of Leicester, the widow of Simon de Montfort whose revolt against King Henry had so infuriated her ten years before. When the countess died at Montargis in 1275 Marguerite obeyed her dying request and wrote to her nephew King Edward urging him to carry out the countess's will and to restore her son Amaury de Montfort to royal favour, something the king continued to refuse. When the dowager queen herself died at a ripe old age in December 1295, Edward's continuing fondness for his aunt was signalled by his request for public prayers for her in England, even though he was currently at war with France.[21]

Eleanor of Provence exercised a great deal more personal political power than her older sister. She was as vigorous and partisan as Marguerite, but Henry was a far more malleable husband than Louis. Within two years of their marriage Richard of Cornwall was already reproaching his brother for giving gifts to all the relations and hangers-on of his wife, reminding him that his brother-in-law refused to do this.[22] Eleanor fulfilled her first duty as queen by bearing nine children in the first twenty years of her marriage, although four died in infancy. The queen's major involvement in English politics came between 1259 and 1265 when she threw herself heart and soul into supporting her husband against the demands of the barons. A peace treaty between England and France had finally been achieved by December 1259 and when Henry and Eleanor arrived in Paris for its formal publication they lingered until April. They found the atmosphere of the French court congenial and the support of their sympathetic relatives more attractive than returning to face the irate barons and the restrictions of the Provisions of Oxford.

The queen became active in opposition after an incident in London in the spring of 1263. She and Henry had been staying in the Tower, centre of royal power, but the citizens of London were active baronial supporters who disliked all aliens, particularly the foreign queen with her expensive entourage. When they discovered that Queen Eleanor was trying to escape in a skiff upriver to Windsor Castle, still held by Prince Edward, they gathered at London Bridge and attacked her with mud and stones as well as curses and reproaches. The queen was rescued by the mayor of London and lodged in the house of the bishop of London since the king timidly refused to re-admit her to the Tower. Neither Henry nor Eleanor ever forgot or forgave this insult while in France such behaviour towards a crowned queen offended King Louis' sense of propriety and fuelled Marguerite's partisan passion.

Henry and Eleanor travelled to Boulogne in September, where Louis made a final attempt to achieve some settlement between king and barons. When Henry returned to England Eleanor remained in France, encouraged by her sister's sympathy and a large number of royal supporters who had sought the friendly French court. In this adversity Queen Eleanor proved herself Henry's most vigorous auxiliary. She set herself to raising both money and arms for the royal cause, borrowing heavily from Louis against the terms of compensation set down in the 1259 treaty. When the baronial victory at Lewes in May 1264 left Henry and Edward captives in Simon de Montfort's hands Eleanor, with the assistance of her Savoy relatives, redoubled her efforts. She raised more money, hired mercenaries and tried to launch an invasion of England from a Flemish port. She and Marguerite both wrote vigorously to Louis' younger brother, Count Alphonse of Poitiers, endeavouring to enlist his help in seizing English ships in the ports of Poitou and turning them over to Eleanor for use in her invasion force, and also in arresting English supporters. Both Alphonse and King Louis were too prudent to appear so openly partisan. Nevertheless, the fear of Eleanor's invasion force caused much apprehension in England during the summer of 1264. As Eleanor's finances became exhausted, the mercenaries gradually melted away and it finally became obvious that the force would not sail.[23] Eleanor had to await her son Edward's success at Evesham in August 1265 when the barons were routed, King Henry freed, and her enemy Simon de Montfort killed.

The queen came back to England in triumph in October, eager to second the king in his malicious revenge against the baronial supporters, but her period of political importance was over. Henry died in 1272 and for nearly twenty years the dowager queen moved among her dower estates, such as Marlborough, Ludgershall and Guildford. These had been familiar to her throughout her married life, and the records are full of Henry's many architectural improvements, often for the queen's benefit. Guildford, for example, had not only been given many glass windows but also a fireplace and adjoining privy chamber in each room, while the king had also ordered the construction of a small building specifically to warm the queen's food. As the kitchen was usually outside the building to avoid fire, and the food inevitably cold, this warming pantry must have been a considerable luxury. At Ludgershall Eleanor had the gift of twenty-four oaks in 1285 to rebuild a chapel and chamber, which suggests that she proposed to spend more time there.[24] Its location was convenient, only fifteen miles west of Amesbury, the favourite royal nunnery in which she had persuaded Edward to place his seven-year-old daughter Mary as a nun. The queen herself took the veil at Amesbury in 1286, a year after her granddaughter, but retained her influence. In April 1290 King Edward, his brother Edmund, his uncle William of Valence and a number of bishops all converged on Amesbury for a meeting. It was in the nature of a family council, for Edward was again thinking of going on crusade. His daughter Joan was soon to be married to the powerful earl of Gloucester and the peaceful succession of the kingdom had to be assured. In such matters it could be useful to have the advice of the old and experienced queen mother. A year later Eleanor was dead.

The two sisters were vivid examples of the virtues and deficiencies of the feudal women of their time. They could be both gracious and compassionate, but they held strongly to their own rights, as well as to their rights and duties as queens. Well educated, both knew and were interested in the literature of the time. Eleanor had her own book of romances and Matthew Paris dedicated to her his life of Edward the Confessor. Probably in 1274, one of Eleanor's clerks recast his Latin poem *Philomena* into Anglo-Norman for the old queen, describing her in his envoi as 'the pious pure mother to King Edward the wise'. He hoped that it might please her and be repeated to her.[25] Eleanor was the first English queen whose correspondence has survived, including several personal letters like the amusing example of her note to Edward explaining that she had left Gillingham for Marlborough because the air was polluted by too much smoke in the evenings – a singularly modern concern.[26] Her sister Marguerite was also an active letter-writer with an equally strong feeling for the maintenance of family relationships. She once wrote to King Henry asking him to send her Henry of Almaine (son of Richard of Cornwall and thus her nephew), as she had heard that he was ailing, 'because he will be better with us than in foreign and unknown places where he might have to stay alone'.[27] The sisters were warm-hearted as well as passionate,. brave women who took their queenly position seriously. Their ability to exercise power and influence depended on their husbands' differing characters, but they left their individual marks.

The French and English queens of the late thirteenth, fourteenth and fifteenth centuries provide examples of both extremes of queenly behaviour. On the one hand, there are such gracious figures as Eleanor of Castile, Edward I's much loved first wife, and Philippa of Hainault, who married Edward III. Both these queens were extremely fertile. Eleanor of Castile is estimated to have had fifteen or sixteen children between 1255 and 1285, although only one son and five daughters were still alive when she died in 1290 at the age of forty-nine. Philippa had better fortune. She had twelve children, of whom only three died in infancy, and when she died she left her husband with five vigorous and

14 Eleanor of Castile's effigy in Westminster Abbey

combative sons. Queens like Eleanor and Philippa presided with elegance at court functions, obeyed the recognised obligation to be generous to the poor, and could lead an active life within their own households. A recent study of the household of Eleanor of Castile in 1290 suggests how varied such a queen's interest might be – her concern for her servants, her letters to family members, including her redoubtable mother-in-law, her fondness for elegant imported objects, a Spanish passion for tapestries and hangings, and a very real concern for books. She even asked John Pecham, the archbishop of Canterbury, for a treatise in French which compared the court of heaven to the royal court of England and wrote to an Oxford master about one of her books.[28] Eleanor seems to have been a good, even rapacious businesswoman and she was certainly informed on public affairs as she corresponded with the archbishop of Canterbury and several other bishops, various earls and important knights.

Queen Philippa is probably best known for Froissart's dramatic story about her successful efforts after the surrender of Calais to move her angry husband to mercy for the town's dignitaries brought out in chains to their conquerors, the scene so touchingly portrayed by Rodin.[29] The queen was constantly in debt, whether through extravagance or because she did not have sufficient dower. Her debts of £5,851 8s were paid off after the merger of her household with that of the king. It is a clue to her personality that her creditors were chiefly tailors, furriers, embroiderers, jewellers and goldsmiths, for she seems to have had unquenchable desires for their elegant goods. As well, the queen took a special interest in the royal gardens with occasional major construction. She ordered the building of a large enclosed garden in the park of the royal castle at Odiham, which was to be surrounded with 2,000 feet of new hedging. Within, medicinal herbs as well as flowers were planted in beds among the green turf, perhaps including the rosemary that Philippa's mother had sent her after her marriage. The garden was designed for privacy and comfort for it had a board fence with five doors, the seats were protected by turfed roofs, and there was even a garderobe screened by a hedge.[30]

Many of the French queens were equally gracious but remote figures whose personalities do not emerge. However, Jeanne of Bourbon, the well-loved wife of Charles V of France, had an enthusiastic publicist in Christine de Pizan, who included a rhapsodic eulogy of Jeanne in her life of Charles V. More representative of the contemporary political understanding of the queen's role is the rite for the consecration and coronation of the queen, with its accompanying cycle of miniatures, in the *Coronation Book of Charles V of France*.[31] Both the treatise itself and its illuminations were designed to emphasise essential parts of the royal

*15 Idealised statue of
Jeanne of Bourbon
emphasising her
queenly attributes*

symbolism included in a coronation. In the fourteenth century the office of the French queen had become more ceremonial and symbolic, although her most important function was to ensure the necessary heirs to the throne. A natural emphasis on the fertility of the queen in the *Coronation Book* prayers had particular poignancy in 1364 when Charles and Jeanne were crowned. Already married for fourteen years, the queen, now in her mid-twenties, had not yet provided a living heir. Since the Capetian dynasty had finally expired for the lack of male heirs and the Valois occupation of the throne was somewhat shaky, sons were desperately needed. Much of the symbolism touching the queen emphasised her subordinate political position and lack of sovereignty, with the intention of reinforcing the political decision of 1328 that the royal succession could not even pass through the female line.

The coronation ceremonies nevertheless emphasised the queen's responsibility to uphold the church, practise generosity to the poor and disadvantaged, and 'take favorable counsel for the people'. The attributes a queen was expected to exhibit in her role as royal consort were authority, judgment, and an abundance of such secular virtues as prudence, wisdom, and understanding. The esteem and affection in which Jeanne was held by Charles helps to explain the place given to the queen, not only in the coronation liturgy, but also in a number of public testimonies of his confidence in her. In 1374 Jeanne was appointed guardian of the royal children (four had been born after their coronation) in the event of the king's death. She also played a remarkably prominent part in the greatest propaganda event of Charles V's reign – the solemn visit of the Holy Roman Emperor Charles IV to Paris in 1377/78. Jeanne died of childbed fever in 1378 when only forty and her husband mourned her until his own death two years later.

Christine de Pizan not only eulogised Queen Jeanne in her life of Charles V, she also drew a detailed portrait of the ideal queen in her *Treasure of the City of Ladies*. Much of the first section of the book was devoted to a detailed portrait of how the ideal queen should behave, emphasising her necessary virtues of prudence, compassion and wise counsel.[32] Christine may have been merely drawing on the virtues she had observed in Queen Jeanne, or during her father's years in close attendance on Charles V and her own later knowledge of the royal library she could have seen or heard of the *Coronation Book* and borrowed from it the virtues which it sought for a French queen.

The pattern of such an ideal marriage did not recur. Unfortunately, the fourteenth and fifteenth centuries provide several examples in both

England and France of queens who indeed exercised personal power, though not in a way which benefited the king or the kingdom, but instead encouraged civil war. The problem of monarchy based on the hereditary principle is that genetic chance can inevitably throw up a totally unsuitable heir. Hereditary weaknesses within the royal lines tended to be reinforced by the constant marriage of cousins, since papal dispensations for marriage within the closest degrees of kindred were easily granted for political reasons. One particularly unfortunate example appears among the descendants of Charles V and Jeanne de Bourbon. Charles' father, John the Good, was somewhat unstable while the Bourbon connection had a history of mental weakness and Jeanne herself had suffered a nervous breakdown in her thirties. Their son Charles VI had his first attack of madness in 1392 and from then until his death in 1422 his periods of lucidity declined. Their grandson Charles VII was a hesitant, shy youth who came to maturity and self-confidence only very late in his reign. His sister, Catherine, who married Henry V of England, bore only one son before her husband's early death, the feeble-minded Henry VI. Where kings were weak and incompetent it is not surprising that queens moved to fill the vacuum, but their own weaknesses often led to even more dire results.

Isabella of France, queen of Edward II; Isabeau of Bavaria, queen of Charles VI; and Margaret of Anjou, queen of Henry VI, were the most notorious queens of the later Middle Ages and in two cases added overtly scandalous behaviour to the already bubbling political cauldron. Their reputations were not aided by the fact that the nationalistic chroniclers of both England and France found it safer and more emotionally satisfying to blame all the trouble on the foreign women rather than to take sides among the internal factions which often manipulated the queens as their puppets. Later descriptions were even less forgiving. Isabella, though poorly thought of by her contemporaries, was first described as the 'She-wolf of France' by an eighteenth-century English poet, while Louis XI is reputed to have referred to his grandmother Isabeau as 'La gran putana' (the great whore). Margaret of Anjou was accused of responsibility for the factional warfare that flared throughout England in the fifteenth century because of her domineering control of Henry VI and her obstinate, though unsuccessful, attempts to maintain him on the throne. Shakespeare, never a very accurate historian of English kings but a superb propagandist, had the duke of York describe her as the 'She-Wolf of France but worse than wolves of France, whose tongue more poisons than the adder's tooth'.[33]

The personal activities of these three queens were so tied up with the general history of their husbands' reigns and involved such tortuous manoeuvres that any summary runs the risk of being either unbalanced or impossibly detailed, but the basic outlines can suggest the problems. In 1308 the twelve-year-old Isabella of France, daughter of King Philip the Fair, was married to the 24-year-old Edward II. The marriage was meant to assure peace between England and France but instead multiplied the difficulties and infuriated the chauvinistic English. The young girl was faced with a very difficult situation. Edward II's great weakness was his excessive and probably homosexual dependence on favourites, of whom the most intimate and the most hated by the English nobles were Gaveston and the Despensers. Piers Gaveston was the son of a royal household knight from Gascony and had been part of Edward's household when he was Prince of Wales. Even before his father's death the Prince had already showed Gaveston such excessive generosity that Edward I sent Gaveston from the country, an exile that was immediately revoked when Edward II became king. After Gaveston's death at the hands of the infuriated nobles the Despensers took his place as the king's intimates. Hugh Despenser the elder was an experienced royal official who took on many burdens for the king but it was above all his son, Hugh Despenser the younger, who as a contemporary of the king and an early member of his household was the ambitious and greedy dominant partner.

The young queen bore Edward four children – Edward III was born when she was only sixteen – and tried to wean her husband from his favourites. However, the Despensers so demeaned her as to rouse her hatred, encouraging her to seek their overthrow by making common cause with their many enemies in the kingdom. Isabella became not just a figurehead but the moving spirit behind the invasion of England in 1326, the capture and execution of the Despensers, and the capture and deposition of her husband in favour of her fourteen-year-old son. These moves were made in concert with Roger Mortimer, one of the marcher barons aggrieved by the Despensers, who had become the queen's lover. Mortimer used the enamoured queen as his tool to achieve personal power and riches, but, like the Despensers, became the over-mighty subject and a danger to the realm. In 1330 young Edward escaped the tutelage in which he was held, captured Mortimer and had him executed despite the queen's pleas for her lover. As king, Edward III treated his mother with consideration. Although she was sent into retirement and her newest acquisitions taken from her, her situation was not uncomfortable. No public statement was made of her liaison with Mortimer, she was given an allowance which was gradually increased until she had regained all her dower estates, among which she was allowed to move as she pleased. Her brief period as instigator of a revolution gave way to twenty-eight years in comfortable and uneventful retirement. Isabella amused herself with hawking, entertaining, reading – or having read aloud – her considerable library of romances. It has been suggested that she may have acquired this taste by her association with Richard de Bury, the great bibliophile of the fourteenth century. At the end, like many medieval ladies and perhaps with more reason than most, she turned to pious works and on her death in 1358 was buried in the Grey Friars church in London.

Isabeau of Bavaria was the daughter of the duke of Bavaria and Taddea Visconti, whose extraordinarily wealthy father Barnabo was the ruler of Milan. Isabeau was their only daughter and she seems to have inherited a full measure of the sensuality and passion for luxury which were characteristic of both her parents, as well as the rapacity and unbridled egotism of her Visconti forebears. She married the seventeen-year-old Charles VI in 1385 when she was fifteen. The young queen bore twelve children, though several died in infancy and the three eldest boys all died before they reached twenty. The young king and queen loved feasting, celebrations and all sorts of entertainments, so Isabeau's solemn entry into Paris for her coronation in 1389 was one

16 This portrayal of Isabeau's solemn entry into Paris reflects the richness and pageantry of the scene

of those fantastic pageants so beloved in the later Middle Ages. Every curious and costly device was employed to add glamour to the occasion, encouraging the urban population to forget their underfed and over-taxed situation.

From 1392 when Charles suffered the first of his spells of madness, which continued and grew more frequent until his death thirty years later, Isabeau's conduct began to deteriorate. While the king's uncles wrangled over the control of the kingdom, the queen sought to augment her own income, endeavoured to gain French support for her family's policy in France, encouraged her household in the riotous pursuit of pleasure. Her dissolute behaviour did not become public knowledge until the middle of 1403 when the queen and Louis of Orleans, her brother-in-law and almost certainly her lover, attempted to kidnap the dauphin in an effort to counteract the power of the duke of Burgundy. Even Christine de Pizan, who had praised the queen as her patron, felt impelled to write her a letter imploring her to use her position and influence to lead France away from civil war.[34] The situation continued to worsen. When Louis of Orleans was assassinated in 1407 on the orders of the duke of Burgundy, while returning from a visit to the queen, the civil war became even more envenomed.

Charles VI was a sad puppet whom both sides coveted, since control of his person gave legitimacy to their rule, while Isabeau, now a gross figure of a woman suffering from dropsy but still bent on pleasure and passion, had no policy except opposition to the faction that tried to control her. The harsh reality of the English victories, especially Agincourt, and the steady Burgundian pressure for an alliance with England were the catalysts for the Treaty of Troyes with Henry V in 1420. Isabeau, as one of the treaty's chief negotiators, not only accepted the marriage of her daughter Catherine to King Henry but recognised, for her husband and herself, Henry's adoption as their son and heir to the kingdom of France, and declared the Dauphin Charles incapable of ruling. The death of Henry and Charles VI within a few months of each other in 1422 left the infant Henry VI as the heir to both kingdoms. Isabeau died alone and disregarded in 1435 at the palace of St-Pol, her husband's favourite residence. It is one of history's grim jokes that the queen should have died in the year the Congress of Arras celebrated the Burgundian withdrawal from its alliance with England and looked to the reunification of France under Charles VII, the son whom she had been so willing to deprive of his inheritance.

Margaret of Anjou came to England in 1445 as the sixteen-year-old bride of Henry VI. Well-educated, arrogant, and steeped in the artificial chivalric ceremony of the court of her father King René, she was unprepared for the problems she would face. Margaret never really understood the English people, the many cross-currents of English policy, or the bitter factions at court. During the final phase of the Hundred Years War, English partisans of peace manoeuvred against those who favoured ever more vigorous attacks on the French, while England itself slid towards civil war. Henry VI was weak and incompetent, easily manipulated by his ruthless wife, and by 1453 had lapsed into insanity. Margaret became more fierce with the birth of her son, trying desperately to maintain his right to the throne. She distrusted the duke of York who was given the position of Protector when the king fell ill and Yorkists and Lancastrians waged open combat with the foolish king as their pawn. Despite a victory at St. Albans Margaret was unable to prevail against the Yorkists, whose leader was proclaimed as Edward IV. During the next ten years Margaret, though forced to flight and exile with her son, struggled with gallant bravery but little political realism to gather forces which might turn the tide in her son's favour. The end of all her dreams came in 1471 when the Lancastrian army with the queen and Prince Edward was defeated at Tewkesbury by Edward IV. Her son was killed and she was taken to the Tower of London for a last glimpse of her unfortunate husband. Kept in captivity for five years until Louis XI agreed to ransom her for 50,000 crowns, Margaret was reduced to poverty after the death of her improvident father and died almost penniless in 1482. The avaricious King Louis had already seized whatever of her assets he could to recover his ransom payment so that by the time of her death all that was left were her dogs – and he insisted on having them too.[35]

Medieval queens were a collection of vivid personalities who could often exercise considerable power. It was usually unfortunate for the kingdom when weak kings were married to ambitious and dominant women, for despite the growing depersonalisation of the royal court, the queen still had a strong influence and often set its tone. A queen was a woman and thus theoretically submissive, but the king had to be able and willing to exercise his authority over her lest she create her own party and supporters who could split the realm. Some were unable or unwilling to grasp the issues or were manipulated by favourites who flattered their way to rewards and power. A queen who served as regent for a young king might be able, like Blanche of Castile, to rule the kingdom wisely and well. In other cases, such as that of the young Henry III and the infant Henry VI the queen was – quite reasonably – not trusted by the royal council to fill such a position. During these centuries of growing nationalism queens were often handicapped by their very foreignness, which was held against them by their subjects. Even this brief survey makes abundantly clear that there was no simple, stereotyped queen. The women whose lives we have scanned dealt with their position, its difficulties and opportunities, according to their own abilities and circumstances. Frequently they were vivid, strong personalities in their own right.

CHAPTER FOUR

Women who Ruled: Noble Ladies

Queens were certainly the most visible women of the Middle Ages and those whom we are most likely to be able to observe as individuals, but noble ladies could also make an impression on their time and leave traces to be discovered. The range among the noble ladies was very great, as the category included royal princesses married to the greatest nobles, duchesses and countesses whose state might easily rival that of queens, and the many ladies, noble by birth, who occupied descending rungs on the hierarchical ladder. Ultimately even rich city heiresses were included. A lady might improve her status through an advantageous marriage, or succession of marriages, which would add to her wealth and give her access to new networks of local importance. These women understood power and were not shy of exercising it. A rather plaintive letter from Archbishop Pecham to Isabella, daughter of Roger Mortimer, in which he tried to dissuade her from prosecuting the bishop of St. Asaph in the king's court, suggests that the Archbishop was not optimistic the lady would give in, despite his similar letter to her father urging him to put pressure on her also, and the threat of excommunication.[1]

Although the noble woman might be the heiress of the title and the lands and riches that accompanied it, her husband normally (always in England) took over during the marriage the title, the wealth and the accompanying duties. During the marriage the wife was usually occupied with considerable supervision of the household and the upbringing of the children. Real power for a woman came with widowhood when she took full control of her dower lands and frequently, if the heir was a minor, the management and supervision of all the lands and revenues until he came of age. Widows might still be forced into subsequent marriages by royal command (though many bought from the king the right to remain single or to choose their own husbands), by abduction, or by various social pressures. A letter of Queen Margaret of Anjou in the fifteenth century suggests the pattern. She wrote to Dame Jane Carew, a widow with a moderate inheritance of seventeen manors, to persuade her to look favourably on a marriage proposal from Margaret's squire, remarking rather ominously that acquiescence would improve

*17 A dignified noble
lady with her daughter*

her standing with the queen. Dame Carew refused, fortified herself
with a licence from the bishop of Exeter and remarried very profitably
the brother of the earl of Oxford.[2] By the late fourteenth and fifteenth
centuries the daughters and widows of the wealthy merchants who
controlled London and Paris began to be considered as suitable marriage partners since merchant riches could be very great and were badly
needed by impecunious nobles.

The remarriage of widows of London merchants might take them a
long way up the social ladder, as the case of Matilda Fraunceys
illustrates. She was the daughter of an important fourteenth-century
London alderman and married three times. Her first husband was John
Aubrey, a rich young merchant; her second, Sir Alan Buxhall, keeper
of the Tower and a Knight of the Garter; and her third the ill-fated John
Montague, earl of Salisbury who was executed for treason in 1400. Her
children continued their mother's social success. Her son married the
co-heiress of the earl of Kent and all the daughters married nobles, one
even attracting the duke of Exeter as a third husband.[3] Since noblemen
were much attracted to rich widows with shares in merchant fortunes
which might support their expensive tastes, Matilda's success was not

too unusual. Widows were common in noble families but spinsters were almost unknown. Girls who could not be married – whether for lack of dowries or some physical or mental handicap – were normally placed in nunneries while quite young. Girls who remained in their family's care were usually those for whom marriage negotiations were actively in progress.

Feudal law had never really anticipated that great fiefs would end up under the control of women, but frequently a lack of sons and the greater mortality of male heirs in various violent activities, or even hunting accidents, put the inheritance into the hands of the daughters. Feudal law, though it favoured the males of the family, did not exclude females in direct descent but usually divided the inheritance equally among them. As well, during the great period of the crusades from the late eleventh to the late thirteenth lords might be away from their lands for five or six years. During these long absences wives had to fill their husbands' shoes and maintain the family interests by law and by force. Such circumstances might produce a situation like that of France in the twelfth and thirteenth centuries when women ruled in Aquitaine, Burgundy, Champagne, and Flanders, often for many years. In England too great noble families could lack male heirs in successive generations, as the earldom of Salisbury illustrates. It had been inherited by Ela, an only child, in 1196 and the title finally passed to her granddaughter because her son died young on crusade and her grandson in a tournament. One of the greatest landowners in thirteenth-century England was Isabella de Fortibus, widow of the count of Aumale and sister and heiress of the earl of Devon. In the fourteenth century the male line of the Clare family, the powerful and prestigious earls of Gloucester, died out and the last earl's three sisters divided the extended nexus of family lands.

Such women could indeed be extraordinarily rich. In France more than in England, their wealth often involved local territorial power and gave them very great political importance. Noble ladies in England, primarily because of the Norman conqueror's careful policy of separating geographically the estates with which he rewarded his followers, did not hold the great blocks of land which allowed political action. Nevertheless, their far-flung estates appear to have encouraged or required them to spend much of their time in the royal law courts enforcing their various rights.

What was expected of such women? The short answer might well be – a very great deal. Apart from the normal burdens of childbearing and responsibility for the children, the wife would usually be concerned with at least partial supervision of what could be a complex household mechanism. In thirteenth-century England models describing the proper organisation of a household had already been drawn up for barons and their wives, adapting to a lesser degree the rules governing the larger households of royalty and the greater nobles. One such ordinance exists for the medium-sized barony of Eresby in Lincolnshire which provides for a common establishment for the lord and his wife. They had a household steward, who was a knight, with two deputies. The chief clerical officer was known as the wardrober, and was responsible with the steward for examining the daily expenditure every evening. He also served as auditor of the steward's account. His deputy was the clerk of the offices. The household staff included a chief buyer, a marshal in charge of the stable, two pantrymen and butlers, two cooks, one man in charge of the sauces and another of the poultry, as well as a laundress, a porter, a baker, a brewer and two farriers for the horses. Most of the men had boy assistants, while the laundress had a girl. The chaplain, who doubled as almoner in charge of the daily alms to the poor, was also required to write any necessary letters or documents, and to serve as controller of expenses when the wardrober was away. He had some friars to help him and a boy clerk. All these individuals had at least one horse, and the greater officials two, besides the horses of the lord and lady and those required for the carts which carried the produce or helped in the household moves.[4] Eresby was a relatively simple household but it presupposed a staff of twenty-five, as well as the knights or esquires in attendance, and suggests how many individuals could be economically tied to the fortunes of a small lordship. These numbers ballooned as one ascended the social ladder where increasing complexity demanded separate households for the lord and lady.

When the wife or widow had to take over control, the existence of such entrenched patterns of organisation meant that she had an established structure through which to operate and such women often proved very competent managers of family resources. Occasionally they even had practical reference material to aid them in their many-sided duties. Robert Grosseteste, the famous thirteenth-century bishop of Lincoln, wrote an Anglo-Norman treatise around 1240 for the widowed countess of Lincoln. His *Reules Seynt Roberd* was exceedingly practical, dealing not only with the production needed on the countess' manors, but also on the management of her resources of foodstuffs and money, and the proper discipline for her household. The range of talents and the amount of prudence and forethought required of the young countess as the final arbiter and overseer of her various officials and servants would require considerable executive skill. More intellectual, and obviously presuming educational interest and competence on the mother's part, is the rhyming vocabulary of French written by

*18 The example of St.
Anne teaching the
young Virgin Mary to
read suggested still
another responsibility
for mothers*

Walter of Bibbesworth for the lady Denise Montchesney at the end of
the thirteenth century. Walter was an Essex knight who had served
Henry III and who felt that his work, with its English interlineations,
would help Denise to teach her children the vocabulary of social life,
management, and husbandry required by their position. By this time
English was obviously their mother tongue but French was still the
language of the gentry and they must learn it well. Even more surprising
as required reading for a noble lady is Christine de Pizan's insistence
that she should know the law of arms and how to stock and guard a
castle.[5]

It is difficult to form a picture of such a lady. The troubadours and
writers of the romances usually provide stereotypes of beautiful young
women whose principal activity was being charming to men. Rarely are
there any suggestions that the ladies had any practical abilities,
although Nicolette, when she discovered that Aucassin had dislocated

his shoulder in a fall from his horse, immediately puts it back in place and then bandages it firmly with the hem of her shift in a remarkable display of competence.[6] Somewhat more realistic are the occasional descriptions by devoted sons, frequently monks, of the special qualities of their mothers. Not surprisingly they extol their extraordinary piety and many virtues, but once in a while a more secular note creeps in. Guibert de Nogent, a twelfth-century monk, was particularly struck by his mother's beauty, as well her more conventional attributes of virtue, ability, and care for his education. He writes almost apologetically of his gratitude for a mother who was beautiful, yet chaste and modest, and he insists, in opposition to those who would condemn natural beauty as merely worldly, that all beauty is a reflection of the eternal beauty of God.[7]

Bernard of Clairvaux was much impressed by his mother's almost monastic piety, and emphasised as most unusual that she would not let her children be nursed by anyone else, but absorbed their mother's goodness with her milk. This practice was not general in the upper classes, but a few mothers felt strongly about its possible effects. The story is told of Countess Ida of Boulogne, who bore her husband three sons and nursed them herself exclusively. According to the romanticised life of Duke Godfrey of Lorraine, who captured Jerusalem in the First Crusade, Godfrey himself and his brother Baldwin, who became king of Jerusalem, were so much more successful than their brother Eustace, merely count of Boulogne, because he once had milk from an outsider. The baby had been howling vehemently while Countess Ida was at mass and her serving woman was at her wit's end, so she suggested to a woman in the place that she suckle the child. The countess returned, found Eustace's chin milky and was so infuriated that she rolled the unfortunate child on to a table and shook him until he had vomited the stranger's milk. The romance insists that, despite this immediate drastic action, his deeds and renown were always less than his brothers.[8]

Although twelfth century noble families were firmly attached to their territorial power base, they looked for any means by which to extend their holdings and, if possible, endow their younger sons. The crusades encouraged such ambitions, as did Duke William of Normandy's conquest of England and the accession to the English throne in 1154 of Henry, count of Anjou and husband of Eleanor of Aquitaine. Naturally, many noble families in the west of France, who supported or encouraged the successful adventurers, were rewarded with lands and titles on both sides of the Channel. For a considerable period of time family relations took feudal ties more seriously than national ones. This process had its effect on the women as well. Adela of Blois, for example,

was the daughter of William the Conqueror and married Count Stephen
of Blois in 1081. She seems to have been a naturally domineering lady
whose pride was deeply offended by what she felt was the cowardice of
her husband. Stephen had joined the First Crusade at her insistent
urging, leaving Europe in 1096 and regularly writing home to his wife.
Stephen had a healthy desire to save his own skin so when the crusader
siege of Antioch in 1098 dragged on with no signs of success or progress
towards Jerusalem, Stephen abandoned the army. Unfortunately for
his reputation, he had miscalculated and Antioch fell almost immediately after his departure. He returned home, blamed by many
crusaders and most of the chroniclers, only to be nagged constantly by
his wife. Adela gave him no peace even in their bedchamber, urging
him not to accept the scorn of such men.[9] In 1101 Stephen finally gave
in to his wife's reproaches and joined another French expedition to
the Holy Land where he died fighting bravely in an unimportant
skirmish.

Stephen's death made little difference at home where Adela had been
ruling the county ever since his departure and where she continued to
be in charge as long as her sons were minors. Two of them, Stephen and
Henry, were to make their careers in England, benefiting from the
generosity of their uncle Henry I. Henry, the youngest, had been an
oblate at Cluny but by 1126 he had been named abbot of Glastonbury
and, in 1129, bishop of Winchester, the richest bishopric in England.
Stephen rose even further for he went to England on his uncle's death
when there seemed to be little popular enthusiasm for the succession of
the Empress Matilda, Henry's daughter and only direct heir. He gained
the support of the Londoners and some of the lords and had himself
crowned, though the civil war continued during much of his reign. The
Countess Adela remained a widow, keeping a court acclaimed for its
literary and cultural interests. She was praised for her prudent government by Hildebert of Lavardin, the scholarly bishop of Le Mans,
flattered by Baudri de Bourgueil in a lengthy and highly ornamented
Latin poem. Baudri was a versifier, an abbot whose ambitions to be a
bishop might, he felt, be aided by the countess's favour. His poem
is distinguished by its romantic vision of the magnificence of her
chamber, its exceedingly obsequious remarks about her distinguished
parents and her father's conquest of England, as well as her own
knowledge of the classics from which its allusions were taken.[10]

Adela had no doubts about her pre-eminent place in feudal society.
In 1119 she happily received at her court Thurstan, archbishop-elect of
York, after her brother Henry I exiled him from England. The countess
had begun to consider religious life and there seems little doubt that her
timely acquaintance with Thurstan, a sensitive encourager of female

vocations, influenced her decision to retire to Marcigny. She took the veil at the aristocratic convent founded by Hugh of Cluny in 1120, to which she was accompanied by Thurstan and other prelates, and died there seventeen years later. Orderic Vitalis attributed her decision to renounce the world after her sons had come to full age to the sins connected with the 'great riches and many luxuries' which she had enjoyed.[11] The disapproving monk was inclined to underestimate the very real piety and desire for retirement of many of these high-born women. They felt the need to attend more closely to their souls when they had fulfilled their secular responsibilities with suitable dignity, effectiveness, and elegance. It was a practice which continued through-out the Middle Ages as many fourteenth and fifteenth century widows demonstrated. The type of pious refuge might change; the motivation remained the same.

Ermengarde, a twelfth-century viscountess of Narbonne, ruled a small territory in south-east France centred on the prosperous trading city founded by the Romans. She inherited her title from her father and personally led her troops in struggles against the count of Toulouse, her feudal overlord, who had attempted to seize her viscounty. Although Ermengarde married twice, neither husband seems to have been allowed any share in the government of Narbonne where the viscount-ess resolutely pursued a policy of closer relations with the French king as a counterbalance to the local power of the count of Toulouse. During her fifty years of rule – she retired in 1192 in favour of a nephew – she kept peace with her immediate neighbours, signed agreements with both Genoa and Pisa which protected Narbonne's commerce and merchants, and was also renowned for presiding over one of the most brilliant courts of Languedoc. As well, she befriended the Cistercians and was particularly generous to their abbey of Fontfroide, hidden in a remote valley some fifteen miles from Narbonne. The historians of Languedoc who chronicle her achievements claim that she 'distin-guished herself not less by masculine virtues than by those proper to her sex, and by the wisdom of her government'[12].

Nicolaa de la Haye also became famous for her military role. Like many noble women in the twelfth century she had inherited lands on both sides of the Channel, in Normandy and Lincolnshire including a claim to the hereditary wardship of Lincoln Castle. Her husband, Gerard de Camville, who exercised her rights, served as sheriff of Lincolnshire on several occasions during the reigns of Richard the Lionhearted and John but died by 1215. When Prince Louis of France invaded England in 1216, hoping to attract those English barons who had revolted against John, Lincoln was one of the places attacked. Lincoln Castle was the key to the town and the surrounding countryside and Nicolaa organised its defence, retaining the castle for King John. Her spirited resistance impressed her fellow citizens, for, sixty years later, their representatives reported to the royal officials how Nicolaa, after her husband's death, had 'held the castle in time of war and in time of peace'. They added that when John came to Lincoln just before his death she went out of the west gate, carrying the keys, and offered them to the king. She claimed that she was now an aged woman, who had borne many labours and anxieties in the castle and could no longer do so, but John gently gave her back the keys and her charge[13].

The thirteenth century seems to have been particularly blessed with vigorous, determined, and competent women who left their mark in many fields. Countess Marguerite of Flanders and Isabella de Fortibus, countess of Aumale and Devon, can serve as lively examples of the outstanding women who exercised power during those years on either side of the Channel. Marguerite was the younger of the two daughters of Count Baldwin of Flanders who joined the Fourth Crusade, shared in the capture and sack of Constantinople in 1204, was named Latin emperor there but died within a year. The elder sister, Jeanne, inherited Flanders on her father's death and was pushed into two marriages designed to increase French influence in her lands, but neither produced children. When Jeanne died in 1245 Marguerite inherited the county which she was to rule for over thirty years. She had two main problems: the constant struggle to maintain some independence for Flanders, and the difficulty over her two marriages. She had married Bouchard d'Avesnes in 1212 and they had two sons. However, this marriage was put aside, either because of Bouchard's genuine concern about his clerical status as a sub-deacon which would have rendered the marriage invalid, or because King Philip Augustus made use of a fraudulent excuse to free Marguerite to make another marriage more favourable to French interests. Her second marriage to William of Dampierre, a younger brother of Archambaud de Bourbon, one of the most loyal of French vassals, probably took place between 1220 and 1223. She had three sons by William, as well as a couple of daughters, but both husbands were dead before she inherited Flanders.

All the ingredients were in place for a bitter family quarrel among the sons, for if the marriage to Bouchard was truly invalid, the Dampierre sons were her only legitimate heirs. The first ten years of Marguerite's rule were spent in fruitless arbitrations ending in civil war between the Dampierre and d'Avesnes factions and their followers. When John d'Avesnes captured his Dampierre brothers at the battle of Walcheren in 1253 and tried to use his hostages to make his mother sue for peace, Matthew Paris, always happy to report a highly coloured story, wrote up the whole struggle luridly. He describes Marguerite as 'another Medea' who was responsible for the death of good knights. He even quotes her as replying to John d'Avesnes' offer with a vigorous blast, 'Sacrifice them, truculent meat-eater, and devour one of them cooked with a pepper sauce, and the other roasted with garlic'.[14] Peace was finally achieved with the help of King Louis after his return from the crusade.

Marguerite could now spend the remaining twenty odd years of her rule in a far more congenial and constructive fashion. She gave great impetus to the effort of making Bruges a major international trading centre, improving the network of canals and giving privileges to the merchants of Poitou, Gascony, and Spain, as well as encouraging the established trade with England and the Rhineland. As a further means of stimulating commerce, Marguerite struck moneys which corresponded easily with English and Rhenish coins. Like so many of the noble ladies of the time, she favoured poetry and literature in her lighter moments and, above all, had close and friendly relations with the church. Her youngest daughter was a Cistercian but the countess's own patronage appears to have been given primarily to the Dominicans. They owed special gratitude to both Marguerite and Jeanne, for the countesses had encouraged their existence and power in Flanders. Jeanne had founded Dominican houses at Ghent and Bruges; Marguerite confirmed a Dominican foundation at Valenciennes, and founded two more at Ypres and Douai. She also made continuous effort to get the houses at Ghent and Bruges transferred from the German province to the French and finally succeeded with the help of a friendly cardinal and a papal bull of incorporation. Her warmest eulogy came from the French Dominican province.

Marguerite also knew individual Dominicans, some quite well. The most intriguing example is a letter from Thomas Aquinas answering her questions about moral problems of government. The elderly countess (she was at least seventy at the time) may have developed scruples about her treatment of the Jews and about the morality of putting the offices of her officials up for sale for she wrote for advice to Aquinas, then teaching at Paris. His letter sounds a little dubious about answering her questions, since he was busy lecturing and thought others might be more experienced. Nevertheless, he admitted that he felt he owed her what help he could since anything else would be a poor requital of her affection. His answers were morally argued according to the accepted standards of the time – usury, in the sense of taking interest, was seriously sinful, and should reward neither the Jews who practised it nor the rulers who seized their ill-gotten goods. He was also realistic when dealing with the vexed matter of buying offices, reminding the

19 A devout noblewoman who founded chapels or religious houses might be rewarded, as Jeanne of Evreux was, with a statue in which she held a representation of her gift

countess that such a practice was not likely to provide her with faithful and useful officers, but with those who are prone to extortion.[15] By 1278 the countess passed the government of Flanders to her son, Guy of Dampierre, and died two years later, aged at least eighty. The two countesses of Flanders had ruled their rich and turbulent territory for three-quarters of a century, struggling against great difficulties to maintain their power and to ensure peace and commercial prosperity for the people and towns under their rule.

Isabella de Fortibus did not have any apparent political power, but she was certainly the richest woman in thirteenth-century England, and among the ten wealthiest barons. She has left copious traces in the records of her time, not only through the administrative paper-work about her estates, but also in the court records, for she was a lady with a passion for litigation and for every iota of her rights. Isabella was born in 1237, the daughter of Baldwin de Redvers, earl of Devon, and his wife Amice, sister of Richard de Clare, the powerful earl of Gloucester. In 1249 she became the second wife of William de Forz, count of Aumale who held important lands in Holderness, Yorkshire. When he died in 1260 he left his widow a considerable patrimony there. For four years Isabella, her children, and her widowed mother lived together at Burstwick, the administrative centre of the estates. When her only brother, now earl of Devon, died without children in 1262, Isabella inherited his title and his lands which included the whole of the Isle of Wight.

Such a widow, still only twenty-five, was obviously a considerable prize, and the lands she controlled could be of great political importance, depending on the side she took during those tense days of the baronial uprising. Once again politics encouraged family friction. Her mother and sister-in-law, Margaret of Savoy, a niece of Queen Eleanor of Provence, were strong royalists, whereas Isabella seems to have been a baronial supporter. She appears as a guest of the countess of Leicester at Odiham during the Easter weekend of 1265 and letters passed between them in May.[16] It is hard to know exactly what happened at that time. Certainly when Isabella launched a court case in 1267 she declared that she took shelter at the priory of Breamore when 'robbers and disturbers of the peace of the kingdom rode ravaging with horses and arms throughout England'. The prior was a friend of Simon de Montfort the younger to whom, Isabella claimed, she had been sold seditiously for 500 marks. In despair the young widow offered on the altar of the priory a charter confirming to it her father's gift of the manor of Lymington. The bribe being successful, she asserted that she was allowed to escape from the priory but that young Simon de Montfort continued to pursue her with horses and arms, trying to abduct her, until she found refuge in Wales.[17] Isabella's account is exciting but questionable, since she was not the royalist she so expediently claimed. She succeeded in winning her case and got both her charter and her manor back.

Meanwhile another legal confrontation was brewing between Isabella and her mother over their respective rights and revenues in Holderness. In 1269 Isabella decided to sue her mother for the issues of all the possessions in the north during the four years they lived together. Typical of so many medieval law cases, this one was constantly called and as constantly adjourned, until mother and daughter were formally reconciled, withdrew their mutual claims, and returned to at least surface friendship, although they never lived together again. Isabella's acquisitive instincts must have been encouraged when she hired her chief official Adam de Stretton, a man described as 'the great Christian usurer'.[18] He first appears as one of the executors of her brother's will and had been a successful royal official before he became Isabella's deputy at the exchequer. Adam improved the machinery of collection of her revenues, but was not above such nefarious practices as confiscating charters or tearing off their authenticating seals. Isabella seems to have been sufficiently astute to have dismissed him from her service before his many misdeeds caught up with him. The huge sum of £12,000 was found in his house in London when it and his goods were confiscated; he was considered a felon, and probably murdered.

The final drama of Isabella's life was played out on her deathbed. The crown was extremely anxious to gain possession of the Isle of Wight, so crucial to the safekeeping of the south coast. When Isabella's only son died in 1269 her daughter, a girl of ten, was quickly married to King Henry's younger son Edmund, thus safeguarding the inheritance. Unfortunately the girl died childless within five years, and discussions on the future of the island had to begin again. Isabella's heir was a cousin, a young man for whom she had no particular feeling and who was such a distant relation that, as she herself remarked, she could have legally married him. In such circumstances Isabella was quite willing to make a bargain with the king and discussions were under way in September 1293. King Edward had not perceived any need for haste, but Isabella suddenly took ill in November while returning from Canterbury. The royal treasurer hurried to her deathbed at Stockwell in a last ditch effort to conclude the matter before it was too late. Her condition was so alarming that the concerned treasurer sat in the garden writing the final charter himself. Its terms provided for a royal payment of £4,000 for possession of the Isle of Wight and four of her manors on the mainland and was read to the sick woman in the presence of her household. Isabella signified her agreement, but was so weak she had to have one of her damsels affix her seal to the document. It was truly a last-minute settlement, for she was barely able to make her will, point out her executors, and receive the last sacraments before dying soon after midnight on 10 November 1293.[19]

There is little evidence with which to sketch Isabella's personality, although her continued insistence on maintaining her rights and using any advantageous loophole is well documented. Her human contacts seem to have been primarily with her own household. It is pleasant to note that Agnes de Monceaux, who sealed the royal charter at her mistress's request and remained at her deathbed, had been in Isabella's service for nearly thirty years, and had been rewarded for her faithful service with lands and rents. Having outlived husband, children and mother, at least Isabella's household provided a familiar background for her last years.

One of the noticeable developments of the fourteenth and fifteenth centuries is the appearance of more personal material, allowing us to penetrate further into the everyday lives of the upper class. Since important men were always much more visible to medieval chroniclers, more interested in their warlike, knightly, or ecclesiastical activities, the growth and survival of such records as private household accounts, a wide range of wills, and the beginnings of truly personal correspondence redress the balance somewhat, for they often trace the occupations and interests of women, who were generally overlooked in the more public records. Countess Mahaut d'Artois and the Lady Elizabeth de Burgh are examples at the highest social level of how the existence of household accounts and wills can suggest a more rounded picture of women's lives and interests.

Countess Mahaut of Artois could be seen in the fourteenth century as the greatest lady of France. As great-niece of St. Louis IX, cousin to one king, mother-in-law to another, and godmother to yet another, her position was impressive. The date of her birth is not known but she was married in 1285 to Count Othon of Burgundy, a man of about forty-five who was considered generous and a valiant fighter but light-minded and incapable. Her father was killed at Courtrai in 1302, her husband the following year during the French struggles in Flanders. Since Mahaut was her father's only surviving child she was left with the titles of countess of Artois, as well as countess of Burgundy and lady of Salins, with the responsibility for the administration of these territories as well as the care of her two daughters and a son of about five. The daughters made splendid marriages. By an earlier agreement between Philip the Fair and her father, Jeanne was married in 1307 to the king's second son, Philip. Her younger sister, Blanche, reputedly very beautiful, the following year married Philip's younger brother Charles, who was Mahaut's godson. Unfortunately in 1314 a serious scandal erupted and Philip the Fair had his three daughters-in-law arrested. Blanche and the wife of Louis, the heir to the throne, were both accused of affairs with knights at court, and Jeanne of having known of their immorality without making a denunciation. The court was scandalised and two knights were immediately executed. Jeanne succeeded in proving her innocence at an inquest on her conduct, but Blanche, despite all her pleas of innocence, was imprisoned in the great fortress of Château-Gaillard and repudiated by her husband. After her marriage had been annulled, she was allowed to retire to the abbey of Maubuisson as a nun, and died there in 1326. Although Jeanne frequently figures in her mother's accounts, there is no single mention of Blanche after her disgrace.

The scandal had a bizarre sequel. Mahaut was attacked by certain enemies at court who accused her of high treason, sorcery, and assassination. They claimed that Mahaut had made use of a well-known sorceress to create a potion which would encourage Jeanne's husband to forgive his accused wife, and that the countess herself had arranged for him to drink it. Her enemies further accused her of responsibility for the sudden death of Louis X, before he had heirs, in order to bring her son-in-law to the throne and make her daughter queen, as well as of trying unsuccessfully to free Blanche. In a period when magic and sorcery were much in the public mind and the case touched the royal family so intimately, King Philip felt it necessary to hold an inquiry in which Mahaut confronted her accusers. The case fell apart for lack of evidence, and a solemn judgment of October 1317 definitively proclaimed her innocence and that of her officials, supposedly her accomplices.[20]

Her relief at this verdict must have been overshadowed by the death of her only son during September. Young Robert of Artois was probably eighteen, a lighthearted and curious boy who found pleasure in inspecting a boat at Calais, being shown the belfry and bells of Troyes by the watchman's wife, and visiting the king's lion and leopard. He enjoyed minstrels and a tight-rope dancer and played an early form of tennis. His stricken mother had his death cried in the streets of Paris for two days, sent pilgrims for the benefit of his soul to various shrines including distant Compostela, and gave the Hôtel-Dieu, the great hospital of Paris, his bed and its furnishings as a final charity.

Although Mahaut kept the courtesy title of countess of Burgundy after her son's death, the actual possession of the county passed to her daughter Jeanne and thereby to her husband, the king of France. However, Mahaut maintained her possession of her own inheritance of Artois against an aggressive nephew and when he took his case against her to court in 1319 she fought hard for her rights. The argument became so acrimonious that she appealed to the king:

> Oh, dear sire, have pity on me who am only a poor widow, chased from her inheritance and without counsel . . . You see how your officers press me, one howls on my right, the other barks on my left and I do not know what to respond in the trouble I am in. For God's sake give me time to deliberate, my enemies have had many interviews with your men in my absence and without my knowledge and I cannot have any delay to deliberate. Nevertheless, I wish to swear all that you wish.[21]

Whether or not her rather incongruous pose of the poor widow helped her in court, Mahaut prevailed, for the king judged that the county of Artois and the right to be considered as a peer of France belonged perpetually to Mahaut and her successors. It was a judgment which also ensured his own future rights as the husband of her daughter, its heiress. After the king's decision the countess made a triumphant entry to a pacified Artois where she ruled undisturbed for the next ten years.

Countess Mahaut took an active part in the government of Artois. Firm and severe with recalcitrant vassals, she expected her officials to maintain both her rights and the public order, but if too many complaints were raised against them they might be called before the countess and her council for a reckoning. Her relations with the powerful towns of the county were generally friendly – she rarely interfered with their administration and was generous in building the hospitals they needed. Particularly after her son died, Mahaut's alms were extensive. She made general distributions among the charitable institutions of Artois and also provided 500 livres a year for clothes and shoes for the poor. This last had her personal attention, for the countess insisted that the distribution should be made before 1 November to

20 Such a finely carved ivory cover for writing tablets might well be the prized belonging of a rich fourteenth-century noblewoman

anticipate the cold weather and also ordered that the same persons should not be recipients two years in a row, for clothes and shoes should last longer than that. In her will she left 1,000 livres for the provision of dowries for poor young women who otherwise might not be able to marry.[22]

The Hôtel d'Artois in Paris, built against the city wall close to the road north, was her principal residence but she usually visited her county twice a year. There Hesdin was her favourite stopping-place, with its various elaborate machines designed to drench unsuspecting visitors, cover them with powder or hit them with a stick but also well designed for comfort with beds, bathtubs and chaises-percées. Many of the small comforts of life travelled with her – a small bed (perhaps a kind of couch), silver basins for washing her hands and her hair, as well as the ever-useful tapestries and cushions. The countess's household was modelled on that of the king and consisted of some forty persons, most of whom accompanied her on her travels. The treasurer was the highest official and dealt with large sums of money, for her expenses were rarely less than 4,000 livres a year, and often twice that. Her immediate entourage always included at least one knight, a clerk of some standing, two or three damsels in personal attendance who were often related to other household officials, and her almoner who normally doubled as chaplain. The members of her household were given presents on special occasions, or if they had accidents while on her business. The sick were taken care of, and medicine bought for them at her expense, while elderly servants often got pensions. Several were sent off to hospitals or monasteries with money for their support when they got old and feeble. Her concern for staff went as far as paying for the apprenticeship of two sisters of the clerk who had become her chaplain. Mahaut derived much pleasure from her books and carried many of them with her in large leather bags. When young she bought romances, later her tastes turned to French works of philosophy and religion, although she also had written and illuminated for her use a copy of the chronicles of the kings of France and that new and exciting tale, the travels of Marco Polo.[23]

By 1328 the countess's health had deteriorated and she had lost family and friends. Her erring daughter had died in 1326, her faithful old friend and official, Thierry d'Hireçon, in October 1328, and she had brought in two doctors to care for her little fool Jeannot, a long-time member of her household. On 23 November she spent the day at the convents of Poissy and Maubisson and dined with the king, but fell ill on her return to Paris. Her own doctor was sent for from Arras, but the medieval remedies of a bleeding, a clyster, and pomegranates could not delay her death. A week later Mahaut was buried at Maubisson, the convent where her father, as well as her own daughter Blanche, had also found their final resting-place.

Elizabeth de Burgh was as great a lady in England as Mahaut d'Artois in France and had an almost equally strenuous life. She was the grand-daughter of Edward I through her mother, Joan of Acre, and one of the family of three daughters and one son of Gilbert de Clare, earl of Gloucester. Her brother died at the battle of Bannockburn in 1314 when the Scots shattered the English army. Young Gilbert's death was not only a personal disaster for Edward II, since they were close friends, but also entailed the breaking up of the largest baronial holding of lands and honours in England among the three heiresses who had ambitious and quarrelsome husbands. Elizabeth, the youngest, was born in 1295, and by the age of twenty-seven had already been widowed three times. Her first husband was John de Burgh, heir to the earldom of Ulster, whom she married in 1308, when her brother also married John's sister. John died in 1313, leaving Elizabeth with a very young son. Her second husband, Theobald de Verdon, who had been justiciar in Ireland and was tempted by Elizabeth's wealth, abducted her without the king's consent in 1316, but died himself within a few months. She was too valuable to be left a widow and in 1317 Edward II rewarded Roger Damory, one of his favourite household knights, with her marriage.

Unfortunately the partition of the Clare lands was much delayed – the widow kept insisting for two years that she was pregnant – and caused many quarrels since an older sister was married to the ambitious and greedy Hugh Despenser the younger who attempted to seize more than his wife's rightful share. Elizabeth's husband, Roger Damory, had fallen out with the Despensers and was executed in 1322. Almost immediately Elizabeth and her son were imprisoned in the abbey of Barking at Despenser's command while through threats to her safety and that of her son he forced her to grant him her share of the Clare holdings in Wales. She was again imprisoned at York in 1323 and all her lands seized. It was only after the accession of Edward III that Elizabeth finally got the possession of all the lands to which she was entitled by the original partition. These included widely separated holdings in Wales, Ireland, East Anglia and Dorset. From that time on she spent most of her time at Clare Castle (Suffolk), her administrative headquarters and from which she drew her title of Lady of Clare.

Given the events of her early years it is not surprising that Elizabeth settled happily into a comfortable widowhood, but one marked by piety and good works. Her household accounts start in 1326 and run until her death, providing generous information about the way her life was organised and lived.[24] Because of her wealth and rank Elizabeth had a large household of some 250, and with several hundred horses in her stable. Its luxury is attested by the presence of four goldsmiths to take care of her jewellery and plate. Men predominated. Elizabeth had some seven ladies of her chamber who would each have their own maid servant, plus a laundress (surprisingly described as 'a little clerk') and three others who were apparently chambermaids. Women did much of the brewing and also helped to bring in the hay and the rushes for the castle floors, but they were still very much in the minority. The organisation was very centralised, and her senior officials, such as the seneschal, the wardrober, and the clerk of the chamber, supervised and accounted for the activities of their departments. Her council included her own three leading officials and the administrative heads of the honours of Usk and Clare. It dealt with general administration and matters of more than local concern, while its auditors checked the household accounts.

Clare Castle was sizeable and, though it was never besieged, it was kept in fighting trim. It also had some pleasant amenities – a well-stocked fishpond, vines at the great gate, an enclosed garden with its own little pool, and swans to swim in the moat and, no doubt, occasionally grace a special feast. It was constantly repaired and kept up-to-date, as can be seen from the details in the accounts. There was a great bridge over the moat and a causeway was made from it to the garden gate. In 1347 the Lady (as she is always referred to) had a new chamber built for herself which had a window, a bed frame, and a chair, though the rich hangings, cushions and coverlets that went with the bed would have added some comfort to what sounds rather spartan.

Two things stand out about the Lady of Clare's thirty-plus years of widowhood. She seems to have thoroughly enjoyed visitors, ranging from friends and baronial connections to the royal family, as her grand-daughter married Lionel, one of Edward III's younger sons. Her second distinguishing characteristic was her generous charity. Unlike her clerical uncle, Bogo de Clare, one of the most greedy and high-spending clerics of his time who would only allow 1d a day for alms, the Lady gave a daily allowance to some 800 people even when she was not in residence. In a period of some five months her accounts show some 5,090 people receiving alms. She paid for the education of promising little clerks at school and then sent them on to Canterbury or Oxford, while some also studied law. All continued to draw their usual benefits from the household during their years of study. This enlightened assistance benefited herself as well, for it provided her with her own regular supply of clerks from among people she knew and whose capacities she could estimate. She was generous to the Augustinian friars, especially at Clare, which became the mother-house of the order

21 'Elizabeth, Lady of Clare, stands among her scholars in the seal of Clare College'

in England, building them a dormitory, chapter-house and refectory. They received their habits and sandals from her as well as an annual grant of ten quarters of wheat and ten of malt, while two of the friars regularly came to the castle to say mass. Elizabeth was particularly devoted to the Minoresses, the Franciscan nuns. They visited her and she gained papal permissions to enter their enclosed monasteries, even with a considerable suite, and to spend the night there. In 1355 she invited the Minoresses at Aldgate to her house in London, and it was in their convent that she arranged to be buried.

Her most lasting memorial – and a very unusual charity for a woman at that time – was her foundation of Clare College at Cambridge. The university chancellor, Richard de Badew, originally sought her help for a small and struggling hall. Her benefactions began in 1336 and continued for the rest of her life, providing a considerable endowment.

She appropriated to their benefit the revenues of three churches and got special papal permission to build a chapel in the hall. In her will Elizabeth left her college vestments, service books and vessels, further plate to help their building fund, and £40 in pennies, as well as some of her other books, including two on canon law. In 1359, a year before her death, she had issued the statutes for the college, setting the number of perpetual fellows and scholars at twenty, when funds permitted – an increase of five since 1348 – and prescribing their studies. Six must be priests, two could study civil law and one medicine but the rest were to be enrolled in arts or theology.[25]

Apart from her bequests to her college, the Lady of Clare's will reflects the tenor of her widowhood – generous to charities, to the members of her household (in particular the women of her chamber), and to a great many religious houses, especially the Minoresses. Her surviving daughter, born from her marriage to Roger Damory, got her mother's best bed of green velvet striped with red, a coverlet of miniver, and a fine kerchief, as well as cheerful room hangings of worsted patterned with parrots and blue cockerels. Her oldest grand-daughter and heir, Countess Elizabeth de Burgh, was left the equipment, seed, and animals from the manors which now passed to her. The younger grand-daughters got a supply of valuable plate and an elegant bed each as assets for their marriage. Tactfully, Elizabeth left some items to the king for his college connected to St. George's Chapel at Windsor, and also one or two items to the prince of Wales, but she remembered her friends more warmly. Henry of Lancaster, whose sister had married her son and who died of the plague only a year later, was bequeathed her little psalter with gold fittings, and a reliquary cross in a gold enamelled casket. A gold image of St. John the Baptist in the desert was left to one of her visitors, Jeanne de Bar, countess of Warenne while Marie de St. Pol, widowed countess of Pembroke and a close friend, was left a small gold cross with a sapphire and two gold rings, one with a sapphire and one with a diamond.[26]

This same Marie de St. Pol is a fascinating example of the continuing links between the English and French nobility even in times of conflict. A daughter of Guy de Châtillon, count of St. Pol and Butler of France, Marie was married in 1321, aged about seventeen, to Aymer de Valence, earl of Pembroke, A widower in his fifties and a half-brother of Henry III, Aymer had made a distinguished career in England but had retained the lands and interests of his French father. When he died suddenly in 1324 Marie was left a young, childless and very rich widow with important holdings on both sides of the Channel. She never remarried but spent much of her time in good works, giving away large sums until her death in 1377. At a time when England and France were

22 Marie de St. Pol's psalter includes a miniature of the countess kneeling before St. Claire, suggesting her connection with the Minoress convent at Denny

engaged in war or suspicious armed truce, Marie maintained a cautious neutrality. She resided mainly in England but kept her lands in France and spent some time at her house in Paris. Three of her kinsmen were hostages in England for the French king's ransom, after his capture at Poitiers, and she seems to have had some slight contacts with them and later with King John himself.

The friendship between Elizabeth de Burgh and Marie was very real despite the almost ten years difference in age, for their interests and pattern of life coincided to a considerable degree. There are hints that Elizabeth's connection with Clare College was an example for Marie's similar foundation of Pembroke in 1347 as a Cambridge hall for twenty-four major and six minor scholars. Her natural fondness for her fellow-countrymen is suggested by the inclusion in her statutes of a preference for the election of scholars of French birth already studying at Oxford or Cambridge and she spent her later years seeking privileges for her college.[27] Another similarity between the two widowed countesses was their close link with the Minoresses. Marie was a high-handed patroness, choosing to transfer the Franciscan convent at Waterbeach to her own manor of Denny. Not all the Waterbeach nuns acquiesced in this move and there was a period of active confrontation between the two factions. In the end the abbess forcibly removed twenty nuns from Waterbeach and all except four or five recalcitrants agreed to remain at Denny.[28] Marie de St. Pol was buried there in the habit of the order, leaving bequests to the abbess and each of the sisters.

What sort of woman was this Anglo-French countess? Even after more than fifty years of widowhood she showed great concern that her husband should have a suitably elegant tomb and, in all her charities, requested prayers for both their souls. Both rich and generous, Marie was obviously a forceful and well-organised woman. She had anticipated any problems concerning her will by preparing well in advance sealed schedules of instructions for her executors. Besides providing gifts for every religious house where she had been received, her will also specified that their letters in her archives should be returned to them. Marie knew how to make use of her power and rank, successfully bombarding the pope with requests for privileges for herself, her clerks, or her foundations of Denny and Pembroke College. Her friendships, by the evidence of her will, ran the gamut from Richard II, the archbishop of Canterbury, and the French king and queen to her college and its scholars, many religious houses and two hospitals. Her charity showed a practical turn for she ordered that all the linens, beds, and wool cloths belonging to her chamber should be divided, with one-half going to the men and women of her chamber and the remainder to poor hospitals.[29] Marie lived a comfortable, uneventful life, primarily in East Anglia, and her proximity to Elizabeth de Burgh at Clare, where she often stopped and dined, encouraged this friendship of social equals with similar interests.

The day-book of Dame Alice de Bryene for 1412–13 and her steward's account for the year ending Michaelmas 1419 provide a useful peephole into the more down-to-earth activity of the only moderately well-to-do noble lady.[30] Dame Alice was widowed in 1386 and returned to Acton, Suffolk, probably to be near her kinsfolk as she was related to many of the knightly families of the county. She died in 1435 and was buried in Acton church with a commemorative brass. She succeeded in marrying her two daughters well – one to John Devereux, Richard II's household steward, and the other to Robert Lovell, a wealthy young Essex landowner and esquire at Richard's court. A few letters to Dame Alice survive, including one from the king about the possible marriage of two young girls being brought up in her household although he realised that the countess of Hereford was also in negotiation with her over possible marriages. Such negotiations could be long and tricky businesses. More personal are notes from her sons-in-law from Calais and Ireland. Robert Lovell wrote most affectionately from Ireland, thanking her for her very great tenderness and charity and 'the other innumerable goodnesses' she had shown him, and insisting that he would be glad to do anything he could that would give her honour or pleasure.[31] The correspondence is only spotty but it presages the great letter collections of the Pastons and the Stonors which have made late fifteenth-century gentry so much more intelligible because their letters provide a window on their lives, affections, and interests.

The entries in Dame Alice's day-book and the accounts of her steward vividly bring to mind Christine de Pizan's vignette of how the lady of the manor should rule her servants and all that she should do herself. This household was relatively small and almost totally stationary while Dame Alice was personally involved in its running. She bought her own wine in London, purchased her spices at Stourbridge Fair, and ordered a guard over the meadow in late June, the period of the feasts of Corpus Christi and St. John the Baptist, so that the peasants should not take the grass, needed for hay, 'for strewing their houses therewith'.[32] Although Dame Alice had a steward, most of the money passed through her own hands, including the wages. The clear impression is of a carefully managed estate and a busy social life where whole families would come visiting, and there might be wandering friars or the local rector as well as her own officials, such as the harvest reeve or the bailiff of the manor. The number of meals served might vary from twenty-four to sixty, though during harvest time, when many workers were also fed in her hall and at her expense, there might be as many as a hundred present. Great occasions such as Christmas and New Year called for special festivities. A harper came at Christmas and stayed till after New Year, while the eighteen people present for the Christmas eve fast dinner got not only fish but a hundred oysters. All during Christmas week there were from twenty to twenty-eight every day for dinner while New Year was the high point. Some two hundred people were served a dinner which included 314 white loaves, two swans and twelve geese, as well as the expected pork and mutton, capons and conies the provident Dame Alice had in stock. She also bought beef, veal, five young pigs, and twelve gallons of milk. All in all, it was a splendid feast.[33] Her household appears to have been a well-run and comfortable establishment, though not one of great luxury.

Most of these women had surprisingly eventful lives, facing warlike

23 Service at the high table in a moderately sized household

skirmishes, actual or attempted abduction, vigorous law suits, and even an accusation of treason and sorcery, but there could be petty nuisance as well as serious trouble. William Pykemyle of London found himself in grave difficulties when he falsely declared to the king's daughter, the countess of Bedford, and a royal cousin, the countess of Norfolk, that he was a messenger from the king. He claimed to these royal ladies that the king had invited one to dine with him at Eltham and the other to meet him at Leeds Castle, hoping to be tipped for his message. The countess of Norfolk gave him 40d and somehow the matter came to the attention of the sheriff and aldermen who were sincerely worried about the 'damage, peril, and scandal' that might follow from the disturbance of such great people. His petty fraud was harshly punished. William had to repay the 40d, was condemned to the pillory with a whetstone around his neck as the sign of a liar, and, when finally allowed to leave Newgate prison, had to abjure the city on pain of having both ears cut off if he was ever found there afterwards.[34]

The noble ladies described here are merely a sample of the women of their class and time, some more unfamiliar than others. They show themselves as more or less pious, resourceful, used to command, and as energetic and capable as their fathers and brothers. Their lives remind us that noble society in the Middle Ages was not totally masculine, though most married women could only display their full abilities when they were widowed and thus free from male domination. Far from being merely decorative figures at formal occasions, noble-women lived active lives and held their own in the tough society of their day.

CHAPTER FIVE

Women who Prayed: Nuns and Beguines

In turning from women who ruled to women who prayed, it is important to bear in mind that social class also determined the kind of religious life open to them. The early nunneries were explicitly founded by kings or nobles for their own relatives and those of like status, so that the nuns were often the sisters, aunts, even mothers of the masterful women described in the past two chapters. From the very beginning the involvement of the nobility in the endowment and patronage of houses, the recruitment of religious, and the appointment of superiors influenced the economic, social, even political status of such communities while the personalities of their inhabitants reflected their comfortable sense of their own importance in the society of their day. Links of kinship were strong, particularly between the families of founders or patrons and their own house, which meant that rich and powerful ladies visited convents far more frequently than bishops and reformers liked. Such ladies perceived convents as being convenient inns when travelling, boarding houses in time of trouble or illness, and occasionally schools for their daughters.

The superiors were usually women of considerable social standing, used to power in their own right and enjoying its exercise. An abbess or a prioress was an important person, not only in her own convent but also in the outside world. She had the responsibility of ruling her own community and representing it where necessary on outside business, but she was also seen as neighbour, landlord, employer, and philanthropist in the vicinity of her own house. Some abbeys in the twelfth century were still headed by royal ladies, for example, Cecilia, a daughter of William the Conqueror, was abbess of her mother's foundation of Holy Trinity, Caen. As superiors these women suffered from three major temptations, all of which might weaken their house. They might live with excessive luxury and independence from the common life, for the abbess's lodgings were separate and she could eat there, fed by her own kitchen. They might rule autocratically without consulting the other nuns. In this case, the great danger, frequently referred to by bishops on visitation, was that they would take financial decisions affecting their house without any consultation and not allow their

*24 In pictures of nuns the abbess can be identified by her crozier and
the cellaress by the keys that were her badge of office*

accounts to be audited as was required. Finally, they might poison the
atmosphere of the house by showing marked favouritism to a few nuns.
Even a subsidiary office, such as the cellaress had its own temptations as
well as authority. The duty of the cellaress was to be responsible for
everything concerned with the production and provision of the convent's food supplies. In a large, rich nunnery with many farms and
much livestock the position really required an efficient executive, but
advice to nuns reminded her that she should do all this willingly. The
caution was also added that she should not favour herself or make
private dishes which the rest of the convent did not share[1] – surely a
frequent temptation.

Although women shared in the great religious enthusiasm of the
twelfth and thirteenth centuries, they often had difficulty finding
suitable avenues for its expression. Since the entrance to the established
nunneries was restricted to the upper class and in England, for example,
the average number of religious in each house was just over twenty, the
possibilities were limited. Although some nunneries were much larger
and rich, many were very small and could be poor. Nevertheless, a

woman of social standing who did not, or could not, marry had no other dignified option but to take up religious life. In the twelfth and thirteenth centuries some fathers of no great wealth continued to found small nunneries, looking for suitable places to bestow superfluous daughters, for as founders they could specify this condition. Occasionally a well-endowed widow might set up a nunnery or join, at the very end of her life, one to which she had been particularly generous. Many of the girls destined for religious life, particularly in the earlier centuries, were placed in a nunnery at an early age, received more or less education depending on the quality of the house, and ultimately made a relatively easy transition to being a full member of the community whose life was the only thing they had ever really known. Sometimes the practice worked well. Hildegard of Bingen, who has been described as 'an overpowering, electrifying presence',[2] and was one of the leading intellectuals and mystics of the twelfth century, was offered to the abbey of Disibodenberg in the Rhineland before the age of eight. She was the youngest of a noble family of ten and her mystic bent was apparent at an early age. The protective support of her abbey, which was obviously an intellectual centre, allowed her to develop not only her visionary mysticism, but also her many other intellectual and artistic abilities. However, such an early commitment might be tragically unwise, as in the case of the nun of Watton who was vowed to the convent at the age of four, but grew up frivolous with no inclination to the monastic life. She became pregnant by a canon of the Gilbertine double monastery of which they were both members. When the pregnancy became obvious, her lover was brutally attacked and mutilated by her fellow nuns, and she was imprisoned.[3] These examples represent the extremes, and from the thirteenth century on greater emphasis was put on the free choice of conventual life by the girls themselves. Nevertheless many medieval women found themselves in nunneries for non-religious reasons because there was no other option. They often found the discipline onerous and boring, avoiding it wherever possible, though they did not provoke open scandal. The result, only too obvious in the later fourteenth and fifteenth centuries, was a generally uninspiring mediocrity with an increasingly secular outlook.

Even in the thirteenth century the visitation records by the bishops who were meant to inspect all the religious houses in the diocese and report on their defiencies, suggest that austerity and the pleasures of the world waged a continuous battle. In England pet dogs and cats were frequent, while Eudes Rigaud, archbishop of Rouen, forbade the nuns of Holy Trinity, Caen, to keep larks and other small caged birds. Six years after his first injunction he discovered disapprovingly that the young nuns were still keeping birds and also sang their office with farcical improvisations on the feast of the Holy Innocents. Although the feast was generally considered a time of acceptable religious licence Archbishop Pecham complained of similar amusements at Barking Abbey.[4]

Efforts to keep the nuns enclosed and to prevent them going out were pursued throughout the thirteenth century and culminated in a strict regulation of enclosure by Boniface VIII in 1298, but the ingenious nuns kept finding new excuses for necessary visits and the bishops' fulminations on the matter seem to have had little effect. The greater freedom of the twelfth century was progressively eroded by a clerical mentality which grew more and more nervous about the independent women. The admittedly conservative Gilles li Muisis sums up this line of thought in his poem about nuns. He remarks that 'God and all the world esteem the quiet nun who never quits her cloister', but he then complains that they were always on the road or in the shops. Even he realised the difficulty of enforcing discipline on very noble nuns, for he says resignedly that only nuns of high lineage have some excuse for this behaviour, though they should not stretch it to excess.[5]

However, despite the hope of many ecclesiastics that nuns would be submissive, quiet, and invisible in their convents, the reality was often quite different and much more interesting. A quick view of some of the extraordinary nuns and a few representative houses may suggest the diversity and range of possibilities. Unquestionably the two most notable women in twelfth-century monasticism would have roused comment in any century: Hildegard of Bingen as the most remarkable, and Héloïse as the most famous. Hildegard not only had mystical visions but was also responsible for two very down-to-earth treatises: the *Physica* was a classification of the various natural elements in the world such as plants, animals, birds and fish, but also included precious stones and metals; the other, known as *Causae et Curae*, deals with physiological matters in a fascinating blend of science as it was then known, symbolic applications, and sound common sense based on observed fact. She also composed songs and an early liturgical drama, *The Order of Virtues*. This sizeable body of work, most of which was concentrated in the second half of her long life, was further expanded by her extensive correspondence with popes, emperors, kings, such distant notables as Eleanor of Aquitaine and Thomas Becket, as well as nuns and ecclesiastics of all ranks. Even Bernard of Clairvaux, not inclined to find good in women, accepted the truth of her visions and recognised her influence.

Hildegard was a major intellectual figure of her time. Remarkably well educated in an age when monastic houses still served as lively centres of intellectual activity, she not only knew the expected Latin and scripture, but was also conversant with biblical exegesis, the philosophical study of the cosmos, natural science, and music. A bold and self-confident woman, despite her conventional modest disclaimers of her importance, her trust in the reality of her divine illumination, and her conviction of her rightful place as part of the ruling social structure allowed her to maintain her own position even when she opposed church authorities over matters of discipline. Current scholarship has enhanced her reputation, demolishing the earlier somewhat misogynist conviction that it must have been her male secretaries who really wrote her works. It has been clearly demonstrated that their additions were minor editing and linguistic polishing rather than integral creation. It is striking that at a time when clerical writers were condemning physical passion under any circumstances, and coming close to the manicheistic view that all sexual activities were evil, Hildegard was writing clearly and explicitly about such subjects as the process of conception and the active part taken by the woman, with what has been described as 'an enraptured feeling for the beauty of the sex act'.[6] Hildegard exemplifies the apogee of women's adoption of the Benedictine ideal of great learning combined with a strong religious life. Highly respected in her own day, she provides an extraordinary glimpse of how a remarkably gifted and able medieval woman could transcend the oppressive body of beliefs which labelled women as inferior and evil, and exercise a powerful influence over both men and women of her time.

Héloïse was a very different person and has suffered from excessively romantic attention. Although she spent nearly thirty-five years as a nun, prioress at Argenteuil, and then abbess of the Paraclete, her modern fame rests on her incandescent love affair with Peter Abelard. Abelard was the lion of the Paris schools when only in his thirties – a man who was brilliant, proud of his mastery, and still chaste. The reputation of the intelligence and learning of the lovely young girl of seventeen, who had been educated at the priory of Argenteuil and was now living in Paris with her uncle, Canon Fulbert of Notre Dame, attracted his attention and desire. His success in courting her under the guise of aiding her studies, their passionate attachment, Fulbert's awakening suspicions, the birth of their son, their secret marriage, and Fulbert's final violent revenge by arranging the castration of the man who had betrayed his niece are very widely known. Most illuminating are the series of letters which passed between Abelard and Héloïse after he wrote (apparently to another) his own account of what he called the *History of Calamities*. Since Abelard had no other refuge but the monastery after his mutilation, he insisted that Héloïse, as his wife, must first become a nun. She says very clearly in her first letter that she

ule laurus bien atrinfe
omment helours latrese
liudor piemes almair

*25 Héloïse discussed
with Abelard the
problems of adjusting
the Benedictine Rule
to make it suitable for
nuns*

emes alnlair le confesse
um fuer helours la trese

did so not for love of God, but for love of Abelard, but argument still
rages over whether this continued to be her motivation during her long
years of convent life. It is interesting to note that she not only
maintained her reputation for intellectual brilliance during those years
but that such a respected cleric as Peter the Venerable, abbot of Cluny,
praised her wealth of religion as well as learning.

Whatever her motivation, Héloïse devoted herself to being the best
abbess possible, and the final letters of her correspondence with
Abelard are primarily devoted to the problem of a suitable rule for the
nuns of the Paraclete. She wanted advice on this from Abelard and she
was notably practical in the points she brought to his attention. She
reminded him that Benedict's rule was designed for men not women,
and thus parts of it were certainly unsuitable. She argued rationally and
with careful logic for the changes she felt should be allowed to make it
more appropriate for nuns.[7] It is difficult when reading their correspondence not to find Abelard so absorbed in his brilliance, his
persecutors, and his own troubles that he appears to have had no
emotional understanding or sympathy for the woman whose life as a
nun was undertaken at his wish and out of human love, but was lived out
with dignity and devotion. There is a charming legend in an early
thirteenth-century source, a text of the chronicle of Tours, which
has Héloïse – described as Abelard's true love – asking her nuns on
her deathbed to place her body in Abelard's tomb. When the tomb
was opened to receive her corpse, the chronicler reported that

Abelard, dead for over twenty years, stretched out his arms to embrace her.[8]

Hildegarde and Héloïse were both extraordinary women and not typical of the less rarified levels of most women who sought religious life. The twelfth century saw the development of new religious enthusiasms, and new orders of men and women to embody them, as the Benedictine ideal lost its place in the forefront of intellectual and theological activity and declined into rather mediocre respectability. Hugh of Cluny had founded Marcigny before the end of the eleventh century as a refuge for women whose husbands had become monks at Cluny, though he does not credit them with any more positive spiritual commitment. Marcigny was originally very popular with the upper classes – Adela of Blois ended her life there – but newer foundations soon displaced it. One of the earliest was Fontevrault, the creation of Robert of Arbrissel, a remarkable preacher and charismatic spiritual director. He founded it in 1101 in the forest of Bart, an uncultivated district close to the borders of three important dioceses, Poitiers, Angers and Tours. It began as a kind of collective hermitage but soon blossomed into a mixed community including the Grand Moustier for nuns, la Madeleine for repentant prostitutes, St. Lazare for lepers, and St. Jean de l'Habit for men religious, where the clerks said mass and sang the services while the others did the necessary manual work. Their rule was based on the Benedictine but the abbess, who was to be a widow, ruled over the whole community. This desire for a widow as abbess was reiterated in Abelard's letter to Héloïse in which he discussed the rule for the Paraclete, for he considered it most unfortunate when a virgin was preferred to one who had some knowledge of the world, or the young to the older.[9] Fontevrault was exceedingly popular throughout the twelfth century and, according to the always optimistic arithmetic of medieval chroniclers, had attracted several thousand souls by the time Robert of Arbrissel died. It gradually became more and more élitist in its membership, recruiting daughters of the royal family and the high nobility, and being the preferred burial place of Henry II and Eleanor of Aquitaine, Richard the Lionhearted and Isabella of Angoulême, wife of King John.

With the natural cross-flow between the Angevin dominions in France and England in the twelfth century, Fontevrault sent a colony of its nuns to England to set up the priory of Amesbury. Henry II refounded the house on the site of an older nunnery, endowed it handsomely, and built expensive quarters for its religious. Royal interest continued, for both Henry III and Edward I visited it and gave generous gifts. By 1256 Amesbury had a prioress and seventy-six nuns, a prior and six chaplains, a clerk and sixteen lay brothers. It was well endowed with worldly goods, owning 200 oxen, 23 horses, 7 cows, 4 calves, 300 pigs over a year old and 4,280 sheep. With such large flocks it is not surprising that its income included £40 from wool in addition to £100 from rents.[10] At the end of the thirteenth century when the dowager queen Eleanor of Provence, Edward I's daughter Mary, and his niece Isabella of Lancaster had all entered the community they encouraged royal gifts and accumulated lands and privileges. Such royal patronage also increased the number of nuns to 177 in 1317.

Isabella of Lancaster suggests the life led by such highly born nuns. She had been placed at Amesbury in her extreme youth, under her cousin Mary's protection, and often joined the restless royal princess in her rather unmonastic travels and stays at the royal court. Isabella made her profession as a nun in 1327 and was prioress from 1343 until her death in 1349. While in office she was successful in maintaining the revenues of the house, encouraging her father and brother to become its patrons after the death of Edward I. Apparently she took advantage of her relationship with the royal family to have a separate establishment ten years before she became prioress, was maintained in a degree of affluence by her friends, and spent a considerable time away from the convent. Her tastes seem to have been fairly secular, for in 1335 she was paid 100 marks by Edward III when he bought her book of romances.[11] Amesbury had at least some sprinkling of cultural interests, if no reputation for serious study. Nicholas Trevet, a Dominican friar who was also the son of a chief justice, wrote a popularised version of his *Annales* as an Anglo-Norman chronicle, and dedicated it to Princess Mary. The rather uncomplimentary terms in his prologue suggest a considerable contrast between the ladies of Amesbury and Hildegard's nuns at Bingen:

> Because we are aware of those who are backward in study, that they are vexed by the prolixity of the histories, and that many lack books of these, it has pleased us to gather in brief the tale of the lines which descend from the first father Adam.[12]

Trevet's book is full of picturesque details and anecdotes and includes with rather heavyhanded tactfulness an account of Mary's entry into Amesbury in 1285, as well as a genealogical table showing Edward's descent from Adam.

The motivation of these three women – Hildegard, Héloïse, and Isabella – to enter religious life was not a matter of personal choice. Hildegard's original bent was towards religious life and she was happy and fulfilled in it, but her family placed her in the convent when young. Héloïse obeyed Abelard's wish, rather than her own, but fulfilled her role admirably. Isabella is a characteristic example of the superfluous high-born daughter placed in a nunnery suitable to her social status, and usually becoming its superior because of her external influence. Isabella was a conventional, not very devout nun, but apparently a good administrator. On the other hand, there were also some girls who wanted to become nuns, even against the disapproval and sometimes vigorous opposition of their families, as in the case of Christina of Markyate.

The young Christina belonged to a well-to-do family in Huntingdon but wished to maintain her virginity and made a vow to do so. She was sufficiently beautiful to attract the unwelcome attentions of Ranulf Flambard, the notorious adviser of William Rufus, who had made him bishop of Durham. Her parents were anxious to press their daughter into marriage with a suitable young man, and finally succeeded in effecting the betrothal though Christina firmly refused to consummate the marriage. Her parents tried a series of stratagems to force her acceptance of their decision. At a guild feast Christina was required to serve the wine, a duty which involved taking off her mantle, tightening her garments, and rolling up her sleeves. The parents hoped that the compliments she would receive on her beauty, and the sips of wine which normally accompanied each cup poured, would break down her resolution but Christina fulfilled her duties with icy detachment. Finally they led her young husband into her bedchamber, hoping that he would achieve the consummation of the marriage which would automatically seal the pact, but she managed to dissuade him the first night and then to evade him. Her powerful family were reinforced by the local clergy who did not wish to offend their patrons.

The author of Christina's life describes all this in emotional detail and emphasises that her family recognised their daughter's beauty, intelligence, and practical ability. They were anxious for her worldly success as it would not only enrich and ennoble herself and her parents, but even all her relatives. They could not understand, nor would they accept a daughter who insisted on choosing her own path in life instead of docilely abiding by their wishes. In a vivid picture of what was undoubtedly fairly common domestic violence, her mother pulled her hair out and beat her, while her father was so angry with her intransigence that he stripped her of her clothes down to her shift, took away the keys he had placed in her keeping and – until restrained by a kindly guest – was ready to drive her out of the house at night. She finally fled her family's rage, gained shelter with a recluse and later was protected by a hermit.[13] After living for some years as a recluse, she made her monastic profession, becoming the head of a small Benedictine priory at Markyate where women, inspired by her story, had gathered round her in a small community.

Christina's case was unusual, and because of her close link with the abbot of the rich and powerful abbey of St. Albans, her life was written. Generally in the twelfth and thirteenth centuries it was the current of enthusiasm for the Cistercians that affected women as well as men. The Cistercian general chapter disliked this and made various attempts to disavow any official responsibility for nuns, but nunneries following the Cistercian rule continued to proliferate. Occasionally they were very grand indeed, such as the foundation at Las Huelgas near Burgos made by Alfonso VIII of Castile and his wife Eleanor of England, where one of their daughters became the second abbess. Las Huelgas, like Font-evrault, became the royal burying place for the Castilian house and only accepted nuns of the highest families. The powers of the abbess of this exceedingly aristocratic but not always very devout convent were so extensive that there was a Spanish proverb which claimed that if ever the pope should take a wife he could marry no other religious than the abbess of Las Huelgas because of her pre-eminent dignity.[14] Las Huelgas was an interesting exception to the general rule. Cistercian nunneries in France were of middle rank and although there were a considerable number in England, primarily in Lincolnshire and York-shire, they were generally small, and poor, unlike their populous and rich male counterparts.

The current of anti-feminism which developed in the newer religious orders was most brutally displayed in the late thirteenth century disavowal by the Premonstratensians of any responsibility for their nuns. This new order of canons founded by St. Norbert near Laon in 1120 had caught the religious imagination of many of the townswomen of northern France, and had developed very large female communities, often in double monasteries. The popes tried to protect the rights of these female members, but the men found the nuns an economic burden as well as one which might require them to detach too many of their monks as chaplains and confessors. Abbot Conrad of Marchtal gives the most vivid expression of their misogynistic tendencies and their official excuse:

> Recognizing that the wickedness of women is greater than all the other wickednesses of the world, and that there is no anger like that of women, and that the poison of asps and dragons is more curable and less dangerous to men than the familiarity of women [we] have unanimously decreed for the safety of our souls, no less than that of our bodies and goods, that we will on no account receive any more sisters to the increase of our perdition.[15]

After this extreme example of prejudice it is pleasant to turn to the peaceful foundation of a new nunnery in the thirteenth century in

England. Countess Ela of Salisbury is a remarkable example of what the
wealthy and strongminded medieval widow might accomplish when the
death of her husband opened possibilities for independent action.
Heiress to the title and lands of the earldom of Salisbury, Ela was
married by King Richard to his illegitimate half-brother, William
Longespee, in 1196 when she was under ten. She bore William eight
surviving children and the occasional glimpses of her in the records
show her as quite able to maintain her position when necessary, and to
assert her nobility of birth. When she was pursued by an unfortunate
suitor of lower rank who had acted too precipitously on the rumour of
Earl William's death, she quickly dismissed him with taunts on his
foolishness in even aspiring so far above his station. During her married
life, Ela had been influenced by Edmund Rich, the saintly scholar and
preacher who later became archbishop of Canterbury. After her husband's death in 1226 the vigorous countess, now around forty, first
turned her efforts to ensuring the safe transmittal of the inheritance to
her eldest son, who was still a minor. While she dealt with the problems
of setting up her young family in suitable positions and marriages, she
seems to have cherished the project of founding a nunnery on her own
manor of Lacock, and ultimately entering it herself. With the advice
and encouragement of Edmund Rich she set on foot the lengthy process
of getting the necessary royal and episcopal permissions, and in 1230
the bishop of Salisbury confirmed her foundation charter and declared
the house was to follow the Augustinian rule.

By the date of the formal foundation, 16 April 1232, the first
buildings were probably already under way in Countess Ela's manor of
Lacock on a twenty acre meadow known as Snaylesmead, bordering the
Avon. Certainly the first nuns were veiled there that year. Ela entered
her own abbey in 1237/38, after responsibilities to her children had been
fulfilled, and was chosen abbess in 1239. Until she retired in 1257,
pleading old age, she used her secular prestige and friendships, as well
as her strong practical sense, to advance her well-run and prosperous
house of some twenty nuns. Lacock was an abbey of middle rank with
annual revenues of some £100, most of which came from lands given by
Ela or her family. Essentially, it was a family house, designed to shelter
the countess and any of her descendants inclined to religious life and to
pray for the souls of the countess, her husband and the whole family
connection. This orientation was underlined by the presence in the
community of two of her grand-daughters and by her own burial in 1261
in the choir of the abbey church where she was ultimately surrounded
by the bones or the hearts of her three sons who died in England. Her
female descendants (since her eldest son and grandson both predeceased her – one on crusade, the other in a tournament) maintained the

26 The south walk of the cloister of Countess Ela's foundation of Lacock

family concern and protection for their house into the fourteenth
century. The Lacock annals insist that Ela 'strenuously governed' her
house and nuns and 'served most devotedly . . . in fasts, holy vigils,
meditations, strenuously strict discipline, and in other good works of
charity'. Nevertheless, it seems likely that both Ela and her descendants
would have seen as eminently suitable to her dual position and social
status that her nuns at Lacock should mark the anniversary of their
foundress with the distribution to one hundred poor of a wheaten loaf
and two herrings each, while they themselves celebrated with simnel
cakes, wine, three courses at dinner and two at supper.[16] Unfortunately
we know nothing of the abbey's interior life, since there are no extant
visitation reports, but it continued quietly until the Dissolution.

Wherwell was a much older house than Lacock and Benedictine
rather than Augustinian, but it provides a splendid eulogy of a thirteenth-century abbess and the criticisms of some visitation reports to
round out the picture of female convent life. Euphemia was in every
sense of the word a constructive abbess. She seems to have administered
the affairs of the abbey with discretion and succeeded in doubling the
number of nuns from forty to eighty. Most of her time appears to have
been devoted to building operations which improved its amenities.
Fortunately no nuns were hurt when the old bell-tower above the
dormitory fell down one night, and Euphemia had it rebuilt in stone to
blend with the church and the rest of the buildings. When it appeared
that there was a danger that the presbytery would collapse, she had it
taken down, the damp ground beneath dug out to a depth of twelve feet,
and then rebuilt it safely. She tore down the old abbey outbuildings in
the manor-court and replaced them with a suitable hall, as well as
building a new and better mill, creating new gardens and vineyards
where there had been barren ground. Besides providing an external
chapel of the Virgin Mary near the infirmary, Euphemia made a
pleasant open walk, adorned with vines and trees. While repairing the
abbey buildings she built a new infirmary away from the old buildings,
and underneath it a dormitory with the necessary offices. With great
common sense, and at least rudimentary ideas of plumbing, she
channelled a watercourse beneath the infirmary privies to carry off all
the waste – an intelligent procedure which has also been credited to
the Abbess Hildegard when she set up her new convent on the
Rupertsberg.[17]

When the Abbess Euphemia died Wherwell must have been in very
good repair. Archbishop Pecham's visitation more than twenty-five
years later suggests that it was a moderately observant house, though its
current abbess seemed overwhelmed and he appointed a coadjutrix to
help her fulfil her functions. There were the standard complaints of all

visitations – too much talking by nuns, even entertaining in their rooms, seculars allowed in the cloister and other casual behaviour. Wherwell appears to have allowed merchants to display their wares in the church and to have been particularly plagued by feminine visitors of whom the straitlaced archbishop disapproved. At least, unlike the visitations of Godstow abbey by Pecham and later bishops, Wherwell did not suffer the continuous encroachments of those light-minded scholars of Oxford who claimed in 1432 that 'they can have all manner of recreation with the nuns, even as they will desire.'[18] In the thirteenth century, Wherwell was a far more respectable house, but the general atmosphere does not suggest a high level of fervour or any particular concentration on a life of prayer or study, the original reasons for convents and women's entrance to them.

With the arrival of the friars and their enormous popularity women too tried to attach themselves to these new orders, but with little success. The essentially wandering life of the friars was inconceivable for women in medieval eyes, and the vows of absolute poverty for their houses as well as themselves provided another difficulty, for women were not supposed to beg and might starve. For most church authorities the preferred religious life for women was in an enclosed convent where they could be kept safe from the distractions and temptations of the world, from which they would emerge as rarely as possible, and into which seculars with their disturbing ideas and fashions would not enter. In line with these ideas, both Franciscans and Dominicans had a few convents of women who followed a life of strict enclosure. The most famous and well-endowed of these was the house at Poissy near Paris. In 1297 Philip the Fair transformed an old Augustinian house there into a Dominican priory as his most important project in celebrating the canonisation of his grandfather Louis IX, who had been born at Poissy. By 1304 the convent was ready for occupation and had been generously provided with endowments and privileges. Its church was modelled on that of Louis' own Cistercian foundation at Royaumont, and was decorated with many fine statues and ornaments. It is sometimes stated that Louis' heart was enshrined there, though it seems more likely that it remained in Monreale where Charles of Anjou had taken it after Louis' death at Tunis. However, Philip had his own heart buried there, for he saw Poissy as a monument to the righteousness of Capetian power as exemplified by its royal saint.[19]

Christine de Pizan left a detailed, if somewhat rose-coloured, description of the house at Poissy in a long poem entitled *Le livre du dit de Poissy*.[20] In it she gives all the details of a trip in April 1400 to this house where her nineteen-year-old daughter was a nun. The girl was in remarkably high-born company for the convent, being a royal foundation, accepted only girls from noble families who, in addition, had to have an express authorisation from the king for their admission. It seems likely that when Christine realised that life as a nun was her daughter's dearest wish she used her familiarity with the court and her warm patronage by the king's brother, Louis, to arrange her daughter's admission. The current prioress was Marie de Bourbon, sister of Charles V's queen, who had been given to the convent at the age of four and professed at seventeen. She was elected prioress when only thirty-three and ruled her house for twenty years with wisdom and distinction. Among her community of some 200 nuns was Marie de France, a daughter of Charles VI, who had been sent there at the age of five, and her cousin, Catherine d'Harcourt.

Mentioning these highly aristocratic ladies at Poissy underlines the obvious fact that throughout the Middle Ages there were fashions in religious orders, as there were in dress or in styles of castle building. The Benedictines had pre-empted the aristocratic enrolment until the twelfth century. In the thirteenth century the Cistercians were the favoured order of Blanche of Castile, brought up near the famous abbey of Las Huelgas. She passed on her preference to her son Louis, whose influence also encouraged royal patronage for the Cistercians in England durng the reign of his royal brother-in-law, Henry III. By the late thirteenth and early fourteenth centuries the Dominicans and Franciscans were in their turn the favourites of French and English kings.

The *Dit de Poissy* belongs to the class of spring poems which describes a well-dressed and noble company riding cheerfully through a forest, where the beauties of nature add to their enjoyment. When they arrive at Poissy, Christine's description of the wonders of the convent, its well-ordered but elegant simplicity, and its well-behaved and devout nuns takes up some 700 lines of her poem. She is enthusiastic about the beauties of the place, but admits that they were given such a comprehensive tour that she was unable to remember all the details. However, she was particularly impressed by the cloister with its high dovecotes with their carved stone foliage and the great pine growing in its central lawn. They were invited to meet the prioress, whom Christine praises as a careful, valiant, and awe-inspiring gracious lady, and who had them entertained in a special parlour where the nuns served them with food and wine presented in gold and silver vessels. Convent discipline allowed no stranger to eat with the nuns in their refectory and, although the ladies of the party were allowed to enter the dormitory to see the nuns' beds with their rope springs and hard mattresses, the gentlemen were kept outside.

The visitors went to the nearby inn for their dinner but had been

27 An abbess and her nuns in procession into choir

given the special privilege of returning for another visit in the after-noon. On this occasion they were allowed to talk in the garden near the fountain, were again plied with wine and food, and were given presents of fancywork made by the nuns in their spare time – purses worked with birds in gold and silver, girdles and handsome laces. Christine had rejoiced in the rare meeting with her daughter, and wept when they had to leave, although the company's supper at the inn was enlivened by the wine sent by the prioress and the sugared wafers, apples and pears dispatched by the nuns. The following morning they all heard mass at the convent and, after a final farewell to the nuns, mounted their horses and set off for Paris. They amused themselves along the way with a kind of literary court of love which attempted to judge an amorous debate between an afflicted lady and an equally afflicted squire, both of whom claimed to have suffered most for love. The major part of the poem is taken up with this popular, artificial poetic convention.

Although Christine de Pizan's description of Poissy was rather romanticised, there seems little doubt that her careful account of the excellent state of the convent's buildings and furnishings, and the rule of prioress, was based on personal observation made less critical by the unusual reunion with her beloved daughter. Christine herself retired to a convent in 1418, when she was in her late fifties. It seems quite possible that her choice may have been Poissy, where perhaps her daughter still lived, and where rooms were available for secular women who wished to retire from the world without taking vows. From her own description it was the kind of properly run place which would have met her ideals of how women in charge of establishments should administer them.

The Franciscan nuns, known in France as Clarisses after their foundress St. Clare but in England as Minoresses, had a house in London founded by Earl Edmund of Lancaster, younger brother of Edward I. It was usually known from its location as the Minoresses without Aldgate, despite its rather grandiloquent dedication as the House of the Grace of the Blessed Mary. These first Franciscan nuns were brought to England by Edmund's second wife Blanche, the widowed queen of Navarre, and probably came from France as they followed the rule of the Franciscan nunnery at St. Cloud. Although the original endowment of the London house was not very large, it was given unusual privileges by both king and pope and had a particular attraction for people of rank. Thus, in the fourteenth century it received generous gifts from Queen Isabella, the countess of Norfolk, and especially Elizabeth de Burgh. Her will provided ornaments and furniture for the house as well as the sum of £20. In addition, she left £20 to the abbess and 13s 6d to each of the sisters. The nuns also had important lady boarders such as the widowed countess of Warwick who in 1398 was allowed by the pope to reside there with a suite of three matrons for as long as she pleased. Henry of Lancaster was also a patron of the house and no doubt had a special affection for the Minoresses as his sister (and Elizabeth de Burgh's daughter-in-law), after being twice widowed, had finally come to rest 'for peace of her conscience' in the order of St. Clare.[21]

Although all these houses continued in existence throughout the Middle Ages with varying degrees of devotion to their founders' original idea, they were not part of the newer currents of spirituality which developed in the later Middle Ages. The convents described harboured the daughters and widows of the well-to-do in a pattern of life considered suitable for their social status. Certainly some of their members were inspired by true religious devotion but the general impression, especially for English nunneries, is one at best of comfortable mediocrity. In many cases there were serious financial difficulties, incompetence, and lightmindedness, leading occasionally to immorality. Although in the fourteenth and fifteenth centuries wills still provided bequests for female religious houses, especially where family interests were concerned, newer types of charities, such as the foundation of chantries for the saying of masses for the dead, were necessarily restricted to men. The impression remains that nuns from the fourteenth century on were in a spiritual backwater which merely provided a respectable manner of living for the aristocratic or wealthy whose families had not been able to provide them with husbands, or who sought a suitable refuge in widowhood. Apparently they did little teaching, even of girls; they were not involved in the active works of charity as were the beguines and the hospitals and their members were not as zealous in the performance of the divine office, nor as interested in learning and culture as the commanding female religious figures of the twelfth and early thirteenth centuries.

Beguines

The beguines were a very different, more open religious association of women which responded to the devotional needs of more than the upper class. They are a singularly difficult group to define, for the term was generally applied to a wide spectrum of pious women living quasi-religious lives in a way adapted to their circumstances and location. They were a fruit of urban society, as the great Benedictine and Cistercian abbeys had been characteristic of a society rooted in the countryside. Beguinages sprung up during the twelfth century in the diocese of Liège and spread to the nearby districts of northern France, Flanders, and southern Germany. It was in these areas they enjoyed their most extensive development while England, for example, had no such houses. These women, often referred to as *mulieres sanctae*, were most frequently grouped in a series of houses, sometimes gathered into a kind of community. The movement had begun, however, from individual holy women setting up cells, often near an abbey, a hospital, or a leper-house, where they could pray and render manual service. Since the beguines were essentially a popular grass-roots movement, each centre developed in its own fashion under the control of its mistress, whom the inhabitants agreed to obey, and their spiritual director, normally a friar or, in certain localities, a Cistercian. Beguines promised chastity during their life in the beguinage but maintained their rights to private property and worked to support themselves. Since they did not take solemn vows they were free to leave the beguinage at any time to get married. Obviously such women were not really nuns, but with their extensive devotional practices and common life they were different from ordinary lay persons.

The movement grew spontaneously and was particularly encouraged by the extraordinary surplus of marriageable women in the Low Countries in the twelfth and thirteenth centuries, as well as by a great number of widows. In Brabant, for example, many nobles and men-at-arms never returned home after crusades or military expeditions, but turned themselves into armed bands, either for hire as mercenaries or as outright brigands. Many young women were thus deprived of possible husbands, while others were affected by the growing desire of families to allow only one daughter to marry, in order to preserve almost all the patrimony for the eldest son. A further group of young women was influenced by the great development of lay piety and preferred the single life. While peasants and the urban working class could provide honest means of support for their unmarried daughters with acceptable work on the land or in a craft or trade, such solutions were not open to girls of a higher social class. Since the established nunneries did not have sufficient places and rejected many as insufficiently well-born or wealthy, the beguinages were the answer to a very real need. In England the pious but poor girl could only become a low-ranking lay sister in a more aristocratic nunnery.

Marie of Oignies stands as the mother of the beguine movement, not only because of her own sanctity, which gave her a great local reputation, but also through her influence on Jacques de Vitry. He was one of the great preachers of the early thirteenth century, the bishop of Acre, friend of popes, and later a cardinal and member of the curia. Vitry not only wrote Marie's life but also did a great deal to bring successive popes to an appreciation and acceptance of the new form of spirituality exemplified by the beguines. Marie was born of wealthy parents at Nivelles in Brabant in 1176 and her parents arranged her marriage to a very suitable young man when she was fourteen, despite her strong leaning to the religious life. Her influence over her husband was extraordinary, for she not only persuaded him that they should live as brother and sister but also carried him along in her passion for personal poverty. They served the outcasts at the nearby leper-hospital of Willambroux for some seven years, using their own revenues to pay the expenses of the sick. In 1207, with her husband's consent, Marie chose complete poverty, took up residence in a cell near the Augustinian priory at Oignies, and earned her living by manual labour. She appears to have been instructed in the scriptures and kept near her a little book from which she could recite the hours of the Virgin. Her strong devotion to the eucharist and to apostolic poverty foreshadowed two of the important new currents of thirteenth century piety, while a passion to teach others led her to expound in the vernacular on basic dogmas and some of the canticles. Marie lived a life of asceticism and holiness which gave the area of Nivelles, Willambroux, and Oignies an outstanding reputation as a centre for lay piety. During the last five years of her life, Vitry came to Oignies from Paris, where he had heard of Marie's holiness and affiliated himself with its canons. When he wrote her life, which is the source of most of our knowledge, he insisted that his ordination as a priest and his success in preaching were due to her guidance and prayers.[22] Marie died in 1238 but Jacques de Vitry's biography and his generous encouragement at the papal court for the recognition of the form of religious life she had exemplified helped the beguines to achieve acceptance.

Unfortunately most beguines did not have the advantage of such a convinced and highly placed advocate to smooth their way among a suspicious hierarchy, nor did the movement have the unity or regularity which would appeal to conservative ecclesiastics. The hardening of church structures during the twelfth and thirteenth centuries encouraged distrust of those outside the accepted categories and the Lateran Council of 1215 forbade the institution of any new religious orders, although a few loopholes allowed occasional exceptions. Since beguines had neither formalised rules and establishments like nuns, nor were always subject to the parish clergy, they were easily suspect. Their lack of status and amorphous organisation made them vulnerable except when they had such powerful and orthodox patrons as Louis IX of France and the Countesses Jeanne and Marguerite of Flanders. The growing hierarchical suspicion of the extreme poverty preached by St. Francis and the early Franciscans, the desire to control rigorously all forms of lay piety especially among women, and the fear of possible heresy all worked against the beguines. Quite often, when heresy could not be proved against them, they were then accused of laziness or illicit begging. Ecclesiastical displeasure reached its peak at the Council of Vienne in 1311 where Clement V, influenced by French and German action against heretical beguines, condemned the movement under pain of excommunication. However, he added a saving rider which asserted that he did not wish to forbid certain pious women, i.e. faithful beguines, from living together in their hospices and directing themselves to penance, whether or not they had made vows of chastity.[23] This saved the orthodox who were the great majority. John XXII, Clement's successor, shared the real enthusiasm for the movement of the ecclesiastical authorities in the Low Countries, and made himself the beguines' fervent champion.

The orthodox beguines were firmly entrenched in their urban communities. They supported themselves by rendering useful services such as teaching and nursing, although the latter was occasionally used as an ecclesiastical weapon against them, since it was considered to encourage seduction. They also often worked in various branches of cloth-making, an occupation which could bring them into conflict with the town guilds, anxious to maintain their own revenues. Guilds often looked askance at the beguines' economic privileges which allowed them to buy and sell freely and to avoid apprenticeship. Perhaps the special emphasis by beguines on the subordination of their secular activities to their spiritual practices was intended to avert quarrels with the local trade by providing a way to limit production. Apart from their earned income,

*28 Engraving suggesting the appearance of a beguine, who did not wear
a specific habit but dressed discreetly and simply*

beguines occasionally received gifts or legacies, often contingent on
providing prayers or taking an important place as mourners at funerals.
Two thirteenth-century beguines suggest the possible extremes of
praise and censure. Mechtild of Magdeburg spent most of her life as a
beguine and was one of the outstanding mystics of the century. At the
other end of the scale, Marguerite de Porete, a beguine from Hainault,
also wrote in the mystical tradition of Hildegard and Mechtild, but her
unbridled language and vigorous denunciations of weaknesses in the
church roused ecclesiastical enmity. She was accused of heresy and
burnt in 1310 in Paris.[24]

The great memorial of Ghent, drawn up in 1328 for the bishop of
Tournai in hopes of rehabilitating the local beguines, put the argument
for the utility and continuing existence of the beguines most forcefully.
It commented on the concern of the two countesses of Flanders for the
large number of unmarried women who could not find husbands or
preferred to live in chastity, describing how they had set up beguinages

with the advice and approval of diocesan authorities. In these women could preserve their chastity 'by vow or without vow and provide themselves with food and clothing without embarrassment to themselves or the convenient conniving of their friends'. The memorial then went on to insist how beguines are no burden, even in the poorest houses where their only possession may be a bed and chest of clothes, because they work with their hands, not only earning a modest livelihood but also giving alms. They lived in obedience to their mistress and within a regular pattern of religious observance and ascetic practice. In a statement which recalls the activities of Liutberga several centuries before, the memorial declares that:

> they are so circumspect in their manners and so learned in household matters, that great and honorable people send their daughters to them to be brought up, hoping that to whatever state of life they are afterwards called, they will be better prepared than others.[25]

Beguines gained considerable respect in France as well. Not only did Louis IX set up many beguinages throughout the kingdom, he was accused by Rutebeuf, a contemporary satirical poet, of making it almost necessary to be affiliated to a beguinage to gain preferment or consideration. One could not speak ill of them because the king would not tolerate it. Philip III seems to have inherited his father's respect for these women since he sought a judgment from a beguine of Nivelles, who was credited with supernatural gifts, when his chamberlain brought a serious accusation against his second wife, Marie of Brabant. The queen was alleged to have poisoned the king's eldest son by his first marriage and to have conspired with enemies of the state. The beguine finally reported that Marie of Brabant was innocent and in thanksgiving the queen founded a hospital for poor beguines which is believed to have been the original foundation of La Royauté at Nivelles. In the late fourteenth century, from the evidence of the Ménagier de Paris, some bourgeois householders found a beguine useful as combination governess for a young wife and executive housekeeper.

The ideal existed in various forms throughout the rest of the Middle Ages. Jean Gerson, the distinguished chancellor of the university of Paris and leading representative of the French church at the Council of Constance in 1414, came from a very pious family in the Ardennes. He encouraged his sisters to live a quasi-religious life at home, much in the spirit of the early beguines. The sisters were generous to the poor, counselled and taught their neighbours, and devoted themselves to prayer. Their brother served as their spiritual director, sending them some of his writings and composing for their special benefit treatises on meditation and the contemplative life. As the French countryside became more dangerous during the latter part of the Hundred Years War, with marauding bands and the occasional military campaign devastating the countryside, such isolated retreats were no longer safe. The sisters seem to have left their home for the security of Reims, and probably entered a convent there.[26]

The ambivalence that dogged the beguines throughout their useful but contentious history is well described by the same thirteenth-century abbot, Gilles li Muisis, who was so dubious about the travelling habits of nuns. He wrote that he only knew beguines from hearsay but had heard that they were elderly, wise spinsters. He believed they were governed by a superior under a rather severe rule, but admitted that some said the severity had been relaxed. In a final rhetorical flourish he asks if it can be believed that young men visit these women and dance, feast and sing? Almost four centuries later, the artist Dürer, attending a religious procession in Antwerp in 1520, mentioned the presence of a large troop of widows, many of high estate, who kept themselves by the work of their hands and lived by a special rule.[27] Despite the many doubts and complaints the beguines seem to have filled a very real need for women during the later Middle Ages. The peaceful atmosphere of the well-known beguinage at Bruges has survived to suggest how such a life might provide a useful, respected, and necessary refuge for many women over the centuries.

CHAPTER SIX

Women who Prayed:
Recluses and Mystics

The communal life of nuns and, to a lesser extent, beguines was not the only possible pattern for medieval women anxious to lead a life centred on religion. There was also the accepted option of withdrawing permanently to an individual cell in order to devote one's self to prayer and ascetic practice. Such women, as well as men, were known as recluses or anchorites (the women were occasionally also referred to as anchoresses) and their life provided neither the supports nor the problems to be found in a community. The last group of women who prayed, the mystics, cut across the whole spectrum of religious life and may be found among nuns, beguines, or religious but they too emphasise the individual, since their mystic visions were the result of a personal relationship with the divine. It is tempting to see the growth of these individual vocations and the widespread flowering of mysticism in the fourteenth and fifteenth centuries as linked with the growing place for individual endeavour in so many aspects of medieval life, while simultaneously providing an outlet for a personal piety which sought a more intimate relationship with God.

The medieval recluse drew on a long tradition, since the idea of going out into the wilderness to escape the sinful world, to pray and do penance had biblical roots and appealed enormously to the early Christians. Its fascination lingered through the centuries, although the wandering hermit was more and more discouraged by the official church as being difficult to keep under ecclesiastical supervision. In time of invasion and frequent war the more settled, but still solitary, life of the recluse gained favour and was always far more suitable for women. Such men and women were well accepted figures in medieval religious life in many parts of Europe. More is known about recluses in England, but they were also common on the Continent for the thirteenth-century monk, Cesarius of Heisterbach, describes several. One, known as the Lady Heilige, whom Cesarius describes as 'truly holy as her name', was supported by the dean of St. Andrew's church in Cologne from the revenues of his prebend, while another was established near the castle of Vollmarstein in Westphalia.[1] In the Low

Countries Jutta of Huy, a slightly older contemporary of Marie of Oignies, provides a typical example. The daughter of a noble family, she was forced into marriage by her parents when very young, but she much disliked married life. When she was only eighteen her husband died and left her with three children. Her father was very anxious for her to remarry, but the young widow managed to enlist the bishop's support in remaining single though, since she was very pretty, she was pestered by suitors who caused her considerable distress. For some years she devoted herself to nursing the lepers in the leper-hospital in her birthplace of Huy near Liège but then decided to devote herself to contemplation. She had herself enclosed in a cell adjoining the leper-house and spent more than forty years there before she died in 1228,[2] An association of men and women grew up around her cell in a kind of beguine-beghard double community, attracted by her reputation and her sanctity.

English recluses have left many more traces in secular records than their continental equivalents. Their cells could be seen in many parish churchyards as well as at such unexpected places as the Tower of London, lesser castles, city walls and gates, and occasionally remoter places in the country. It is amusing to note that they were so taken for granted that the index of one of the volumes of Henry III's Liberate Rolls lists them under 'trades and occupations'.[3] The physical conditions under which these women lived were not as harsh as the term 'cell' suggests. In reality the cell, or anchorhold, was normally made up of two rooms, perhaps only divided by a curtain – one a parlour, the other a bedroom. There were two windows, one looking towards the church or chapel where the recluse could follow mass and occasionally receive communion; the other a parlour window, discreetly covered by a curtain, where she could talk to those who sought her advice or counsel. When Katherine, the widow of W. Hardell of London, wanted to build an anchorhold for herself near St. Bartholomew's chapel and hospital in Smithfield, Henry III duly granted her for the purpose a piece of land twenty feet square.[4] Given the small size of medieval city houses or peasant dwellings, this area would have seemed generous.

Two sensible and influential treatises were written by Englishmen as guides for female recluses: one in the twelfth century by Aelred of Rievaulx, addressed specifically to his sister but with much general advice; and the other, known as *Ancrene Riwle* or *Ancrene Wisse*, composed in the thirteenth century and making considerable use of Aelred's earlier work as well as newer material.[5] Both Aelred and the author of the *Ancrene Riwle* wrote with warmth and common sense and espoused a high, but not unattainable ideal of sanctity. Aelred described three reasons for becoming a recluse: to escape the dangers of life in society, to avoid its troubles, or to adhere more closely to Christ. He believed that many of the recluses of his own time had forgotten this and felt that it was sufficient to enclose their bodies within walls, but to let their minds wander abroad. Such recluses were fatigued by cares and worries and spent hours at their windows acquiring all the latest gossip (much of it lewd), or satisfying their indefatigable curiosity, or getting too involved in the buying and selling of their beasts. Aelred was positive that none of these activities was suitable for enclosed women and insisted that they should either make their own living by acceptable handiwork, or arrange their revenues before they were enclosed so as to have just a sufficiency. Even though he disapproved, Aelred painted a charming picture of the recluse who taught little girls and got so wrapped up in them, sharing their laughter and trying to control them with vain threats of punishment, that she had no time for thoughts of God.[6]

Nevertheless, Aelred was no wild-eyed ascetic. He saw the proper life of a recluse as one of silence, suitable self-supporting labour, and reading and prayer, all adjusted to the different seasons. His suggestions about the details of everyday life are sensible and restrained. A recluse's clothing should be simple and plain, but it should include heavier cloaks and inexpensive furs to repel the winter chill. Her food should generally be bread and vegetables, with a little butter and oil and some milk, as well as a measure of beer or wine. This diet could be amplified on non-fasting days with fish, fruit, and salad if these were available.[7] Aelred rounded out his treatise with some moral directives on remaining chaste and avoiding pride but, as seems suitable for those whom he wished to guide in the footsteps of Mary rather than Martha, he concluded with a long meditation on the life of Christ and the Virgin, suggesting ways for the recluse to develop a personal sense of having been present at events with Christ and his mother. The sister to whom the treatise was addressed was older than he was and had been a recluse for some years. She had importuned her brother for some time for such advice but, as a Cistercian, Aelred had been inhibited by the growing Cistercian unwillingness to undertake direction of or responsibility for female religious. His sister's cell was probably in the north near Hexham or Durham, an area where there had been a long tradition of the solitary life from the time of the seventh century St. Aidan. This was currently exemplified by Aelred's good friend and contemporary, Godric of Finchale (the pedlar and merchant turned pilgrim and hermit), whose sister was also a recluse. Aelred's advice was certainly meant for a wider audience than his sister and the treatise continued to have a long and fruitful history.

The *Ancrene Riwle* has no known author, though the most detailed study of it has suggested with considerable authority that it was written by an Augustinian canon located at Wigmore Abbey, which was under the protection of the great marcher lord, Hugh de Mortimer, baron of Wigmore.[8] The author seems to have been a member of the Anglo-Norman feudal society of the Welsh Marches, and the original English version appears to belong to the first quarter of the thirteenth century. The slightly later translation into Anglo-Norman may have been done for Annora de Braose, the widow of Hugh de Mortimer, when she was planning her own enclosure as a recluse around 1230. The treatise was originally written for three ladies living as recluses who were supported by a nearby great house (probably Wigmore Castle) and, like Aelred's guide, emphasises contemplation, but not necessarily mysticism. It is, in fact, singularly characteristic of the early thirteenth century in its heavy emphasis on confession and penance. These matters were much on ecclesiastical minds after the Lateran Council of 1215 which required every Christian to confess and go to communion at least once a year at Easter. The effect of this church statute was to inspire the compilation of a large number of guides to confessors which could serve to instruct them in the problems which they might face with penitents. Besides this newer matter *Ancrene Riwle* also borrowed extensively from Aelred and has the same balanced and common sense approach to the ways in which mortification and austerity should be interpreted in a recluse's life. Recognition of human needs shines through the text, including the delightful comment that, unless there was some compelling need, a recluse 'must not keep any animal except a cat'.[9] The permission may have been inspired by the need to keep down the mice

29 Church embroideries, such as this altar frontal, could aid a recluse to follow Aelred's advice and picture events of the life of Christ and the Virgin

but the pleasant suspicion arises that the cat was a very welcome inhabitant of the anchorhold. A considerable number of manuscripts in Anglo-Norman, English, French, and Latin have survived, which suggests that the treatise continued to be popular as a basic guide for recluses throughout the Middle Ages. It gave sound advice, although later recluses tended to lay much more emphasis on contemplation culminating in mystical visions than was true in the twelfth or thirteenth centuries.

It should be remembered that a recluse did not live totally alone. She was expected to have a discreet elderly female servant to seek her daily provisions and do her errands, and might also have a young girl to do the heavy work. The recluse could entertain visitors in her parlour for good reasons, though normally not men, but most of her contacts with others were through her window, and even there she was constantly advised to use restraint and discretion. There is considerable evidence that many of these recluses were sought out for advice and counsel, and probably knew a good deal of what went on in their neighbourhood. Cesarius of Heisterbach has a cautionary tale of the abbot who went to ask a highly respected recluse whether it would please God and be expedient for him to remain abbot. The recluse withdrew briefly to pray and returned to tell him that if he remained abbot he could not save his soul, for he had gained his office by simony. The astonished abbot protested his innocence but she reminded him that when the previous abbot died he had been so anxious for election that he had advised many of the simple brothers of the house that to choose anyone from outside would cast aspersions on the competence of their own members. All the while he knew that he was certainly the one who would be elected from within the community. The abbot admitted the truth of this and went off to seek the abbot of Clairvaux and ask for absolution.[10]

The life of a recluse could not be taken on casually. The permission of the bishop of the diocese was required before a woman – who could be a maid, a widow, or a nun – could be enclosed. The candidate's character and estate had to be investigated, as well as the suitability of the place chosen for her cell. Some cells were occupied by a series of recluses over long periods of time, others were newly constructed. It was also the responsibility of the bishop to make sure that her maintenance had been arranged. The prospective recluse might have a patron who would be responsible for her upkeep – Henry III was a great patron of recluses and so were some bishops. A woman who lived in a cell dependent on a monastic house would normally be provided by the monks with an arranged allowance of food and clothing. Other recluses might have substantial revenues and arranged for executors to provide them with a suitable yearly income from their own lands and rents. Although they were against trading or teaching as incompatible with their vocation, they could augment their income by some needlework. As well, they often received gifts from their neighbours and by the fifteenth century were so popular that a recluse could often live very well and even help out her family from the alms given her. As always in the Middle Ages, hard statistics on their numbers are not available, although an effort has been made to draw up a table of all known recluses in England and their locations.[11] The greatest concentration seems to have been in Yorkshire and Norfolk.

Only a few recluses can be differentiated as individuals, either because of their exceptional holiness or their previous importance, but even a few such out-of-the-ordinary examples may help to explain the nature and appeal of the life. The best known recluses of the thirteenth century are a pair of sisters, Loretta and Annora de Braose, who turned to this life in their widowhood. The two girls were among the youngest children of the large family of Maud and William de Braose, a powerful marcher lord who had energetically supported King John and appears to have been associated with the king in the murder of Arthur of Brittany at Rouen in 1203. At the time of the papal interdict on England, John turned against William, confiscated his lands and pursued the family to Ireland. William managed to escape to France where he died in 1211 but his wife and eldest son were captured and died in Windsor Castle, it was rumoured by starvation. Loretta had been married to the earl of Leicester, probably in 1196, and was a childless widow by 1204. The Leicester inheritance was divided between the earl's two sisters and their husbands, but Loretta duly received her own dower lands and those of her marriage portion, although they were all confiscated when King John moved against her father. Her sister Annora, wife of Hugh de Mortimer, baron of Wigmore, was imprisoned. Loretta may well have gone to France to join her father, and it is not until 1214 that the two sisters reappear. Annora was released from prison at the request of the papal legate because her brother was bishop of Hereford, and Loretta regained her dower lands, swearing that she was not married, and would not marry without the king's consent. Loretta had no plans for marriage. By 1219 she had made some arrangements regarding her lands that would provide for her support as a recluse, and by 1221 she had been enclosed in a cell at Hackington, a village only a mile or so from Canterbury Cathedral by the old path across the fields. Since Archbishop Stephen Langton would have had to agree to her enclosure and had presided at her father's funeral in France when both men were exiles, it is reasonable to suppose that there was a link of acquaintanceship between them. In addition, Simon, the archbishop's brother, returned from Paris to be archdeacon of Canterbury some six years after Loretta's enclosure and came to live in Hackington in a house close to her cell in the churchyard. Loretta would have had powerful ecclesiastical friends and protectors.

The widowed countess may have adopted the life of a recluse out of devotion but it seems likely that she also regarded it as a stable refuge from a world which had treated her harshly, one of Aelred's acceptable motives. The difficulties and dangers of Loretta's first fifteen years of widowhood, and the knowledge that as a childless widow, and member of a family in disfavour she lacked natural supporters, seem valid reasons for her decision while her high social status, and perhaps disinclination to accept another's rule, explain her choice of the recluse's cell rather than a convent. Her sister Annora seems to have had a more spiritual approach when she too became a widow. She also was childless and had probably been on sympathetic terms with the recluses for whom the *Ancrene Riwle* was originally written. Once Annora was enclosed at Iffley, some ten years after her sister, she dropped almost totally from view except for annual royal gifts to the 'recluse of Iffley'. Loretta, however, was not the usual anonymous recluse whose existence can only be tracked through royal or episcopal grants of money, firewood, or a warm robe. Gifts to Loretta were more generous, for her friend Alice, countess of Eu, sent her annually two quarters of wheat, two of barley and one of oats, and two sides of bacon. After Alice's death King Henry continued the grant and added lambs, cheese and eggs – rather luxurious fare for a recluse.[12]

More surprisingly Loretta continued to exercise public influence from her cell, as well as interceding with the king and his officials for her neighbours. In 1224 she furthered the cause of the first Franciscans to come to England and was described by their early historian as one of their special patrons. He wrote with enthusiasm that 'she cherished them in all things as a mother her sons, sagaciously winning for them the favour of magnates and prelates by whom she was held in highest regard'.[13] Although Annora probably died in 1241 or soon after, Loretta lived on for another twenty-five years, still active and respected. In April 1265, she received a letter from Henry III, then under the control of her great-nephew, Simon de Montfort, earl of Leicester. It asked her to expound to her neighbours, the abbot of St. Augustine's and the prior of Christchurch, all she knew about the rights and liberties of the stewardship of England as they pertained to the earldom of Leicester.[14] At this time Earl Simon was searching so desperately for a way to legitimise his baronial government he would even attempt to get reinforcement from an aged recluse whose connection with the earldom of Leicester was sixty years behind her. After more than forty years as a recluse Countess Loretta had not totally disentangled herself from her secular concerns. Aelred might well have disapproved of the amount of time she spent at her parlour window.

Another noble lady some fifty years later inspired both a legend and one of Wordsworth's more forgettable sonnets, an unlikely combination. Katherine of Ledbury had married Nicholas, Baron Audley, who died in 1299, leaving her a widow in her twenties with two young sons and a daughter. By 1312 she appears to have fulfilled most of her obligations towards her children and been planning her life as a recluse, for she then gave away much of her maternal inheritance in a deed witnessed at Ledbury by the bishop and the local vicar. By 1322, when she is referred to as Katherine de Audeley, recluse of Ledbury, she was receiving £30 yearly from the sheriff, no doubt a previously arranged pension from the lands in the custody of her husband's executor. The legend celebrated by Wordsworth asserted that she and her maid wandered from Worcestershire to Herefordshire, following the footprints of her stolen mare, looking for the town where she had been warned by a vision the bells would ring untouched by human hands. This duly happened at Ledbury and there she settled until, as Wordsworth writes, 'she exchanged for heaven that happy ground'.[15]

Occasionally, noble widows attempted the life of a recluse and then changed their minds. In the fourteenth century Maud of Lancaster had first married Elizabeth de Burgh's son, the heir to the earldom of Ulster, but after his murder in 1333 she then married Roger de Ufford. After Roger's death in 1346 she retired to a convent of Augustinian canonesses at Campsey, leaving her brother, Henry of Lancaster, to manage her estates. Maud found the Campsey priory 'very lean' and took an income of 200 marks from her estates to relieve its poverty. She also endowed a chantry there with five chaplains to pray for the souls of her two husbands, herself, and her daughters. However, she was not satisfied with Campsey as a place of retreat, for she was continuously sought out by various nobles. She then had herself enclosed as a recluse, but this did not prove successful either, so she finally transferred to the Minoresses.[16]

There is a fifteenth century account of a nun wishing to lead a stricter life and getting episcopal permission to have herself enclosed as a recluse. Beatrice Franke had been a nun of the Benedictine priory of Stainfield and Bishop Gray of Lincoln commissioned the abbot of Thornton to deal with her request. The bishop had heard that:

> she had dwelt laudably in the said priory for many days under the discipline of regular observance, not recklessly nor light minded to the damage or loss of her order, not of pretence but in truth to win the fruit of a better life, to change her condition to a stricter life under the

rule or order of an anchorite, and to be shut up closely in a building adjacent to the parish church of Winterton.

The abbot duly examined Beatrice at Winterton and found her 'well-founded in her desire', released her from her vow of obedience to her prioress, and then accepted her new profession and promise of obedience and chastity made to the abbots of Thornton, who thus took responsibility for her. The commission appears as merely a final formal acknowledgement of negotiations which had been carried on earlier. The ceremony of enclosure proceeded, reinforced by the consent of the people of the parish where she was to abide, and when the symbolic locking up had been completed, the abbot concluded 'we left her in peace and calm of spirit'.[17]

The case of Beatrice Franke illustrates the process by which a particularly devout nun might move from her nunnery to the recluse's cell. Perhaps Julian of Norwich, the best known and most distinguished of all English recluses for her influential *Revelations of Divine Love*, made the same sort of move. Her recent editors, who are impressed by her very considerable learning and deep knowledge of scripture, suggest that she had entered a religious house when young, received her visions there, and may not have become a recluse until after the completion of the longer text of the *Revelations*. This was only finished in 1393, some twenty years after the visions and her earlier short account of them.[18] Whatever the truth of this suggestion, the range of her knowledge makes it evident that she had benefited from some scholar's devoted teaching of the current learning of the schools. The terms of a bequest in 1394 to 'Julian anakorite' is the first reference to her as a recluse, and is corroborated by a brief trail of bequests over the next twenty years. There is also Margery Kempe's description of going to seek Julian's advice during a visit to Norwich in the early years of the fifteenth century. Margery's report is particularly convincing since it echoes Julian's own language as well as thought. Although Julian's attractive personality shines through her great work, she says almost nothing about herself or the events of her life.

Mystics

The basically regular and ascetic life of the twelfth and thirteenth century recluse became in the following two centuries more and more oriented not only towards contemplation, but towards the hope, and even expectation, of mystical experience. Julian of Norwich is one of the most brilliant examples of just how far that mystical experience could lead and provides a natural introduction to the group of medieval women mystics. Mystics tend to be perceived by the majority of people

as rather inexplicable and uncomfortable individuals, uninterested in
either everyday people or things. A sober definition of the nature of
mysticism may help to clarify its essential elements and suggest why the
wholly secular find such individuals daunting. Mysticism has been
described as

> an immediate knowledge of God attained in this life through personal
> religious experience. It is primarily a state of prayer, and as such
> admits of various degrees from short and rare Divine 'touches' to the
> practically permanent union with God in the so-called 'mystic mar-
> riage'. It issues in an increase of humility, charity, and love of
> suffering.[19]

Neither the experience nor the virtues resulting from it are easily
achieved and are frequently misunderstood by detached or unsym-
pathetic observers. Nevertheless, these medieval female mystics were
historically important because their visions reflected some of the
deepest spiritual currents in the life of their day and made them
respected interpreters of ideals to which medieval secular society gave at
least lip service. Because their lives were naturally uneventful, clues to
their personalities normally come from their visions, as they themselves
wrote them down or had them recorded by others.

During the twelfth and thirteenth centuries the mystical current was
particularly strong in Germany and the Low Countries and most of the
best-known mystics in these areas lived happily within the established
conventual tradition. Hildegard of Bingen, who joined mystical gifts
to her many other talents, found emotional and moral support in
the convent of which she was abbess. Her three books of visions – the
Scivias, *the Liber vitae meritorum* or *Book of Life's Rewards*, and the
Liber divinorum operum or *Book of the Divine Works* – were all products
of the second half of her life, written in obedience to a divine
command.[20] Her mystical power was recognised almost from the
beginning, for she received papal ratification of her visionary writings
even before the *Scivias* was completed. This rapid ecclesiastical acceptance of her role as a prophet helped to account for her prestige among
the great of her world, secular as well as religious. Her works provide a
consistent world view which sums up eloquently and in visionary terms
the early medieval theory of the microcosm and the macrocosm, a
theory inherited from the Stoics. Man the microcosm reflected the
macrocosm, the world that lay around him, and man's fate was determined by the interplay of the surrounding forces. This theory, whatever its scientific shortcomings, provided a framework for organising
life and thought which, it has been suggested, was as influential for early
medieval thinkers as Darwin's theory of evolution for the late

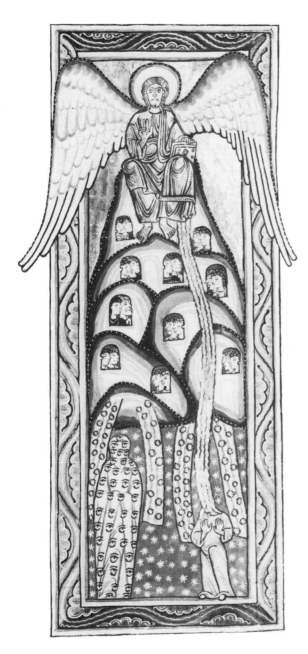

30 This miniature of Hildegard of Bingen receiving light from heaven marks the beginning of her mystical treatise Scivias

nineteenth and twentieth centuries.[21] One of Hildegard's extraordinary abilities was to visualise this conception in quite remarkable detail. Some of her early manuscripts are magnificently illustrated with amazing fidelity to the text and may have been supervised by Hildegard herself.

Her public reputation as a mystic was so high that it allowed her to speak authoritatively and with impunity to her wide range of correspondents, and to those whom she admonished on her journeys, without arousing ecclesiastical suspicion at her adoption of a male role. Hildegard considered that women played a positive role within the church, but their function was contemplative rather than clerical. She argued, unlike her male contemporaries, that women were less concupiscent than men and there is a delightful chapter in *Causae et Curae* in which she insists that the world should be grateful that it was Eve who succumbed to the lures of the serpent rather than Adam. Original sin initiated by man would have been so strong and incorrigible, and man so obdurate, that he would neither wish nor be able to be saved.[22] Hildegard had a serene self-confidence in her message and in herself as a divine messenger. She felt her responsibility to obey the divine command to instruct others, despite the prohibitions and suspicion which generally fell on a woman in such a role. Her position is well expressed in a letter to Elizabeth of Schonau, a younger German mystic who had written seeking her advice and prayers. Hildegard – and this was always her safeguard – insisted that she did not speak from her own power, since she was only 'a poor little earthen vase', but from the 'serene light' of inspiration by God. She emphasises her own weakness and her position as merely a mouthpiece of the divine in the famous last paragraph of her letter:

> But I who am prostrate in the feebleness of fear, occasionally give forth a small sound of the trumpet from the living light, whence God aid me that I may remain in his ministry.[23]

Female mystics in the Low Countries, including Marie of Oignies, appear to have been numerous, but their visions were less often committed to writing and rarely circulated, so that their influence was primarily on their immediate milieu. On the other hand, German piety had a strong current of acceptance and respect for female mystics and in the thirteenth century the convent at Helfta was a noteworthy spiritual centre with sufficient prestige to exercise a wide authority. Its abbess from 1251 to 1291 was Gertrude of Hackeborn, daughter of a powerful noble family whose brothers provided the nuns with land for expansion when their quarters at Rodarshof had become cramped. During Gertrude's rule the house was large and prosperous, further endowed with land by the archbishop of Magdeburg, and protected by the counts of Mansfeld and the abbess's relatives. The nuns were recruited primarily from the wealthy noble families of Thuringia and Saxony, and their numbers may have reached a hundred by the end of the century. It was a well-run and cultured house with an intense intellectual and cultural life. Some of the nuns were learned, books were collected, and manuscripts both copied and illuminated, though there is no hint that outsiders were responsible for the nuns' active intellectual life. Abbess Gertrude and the respected visionaries of her community counselled and influenced the neighbouring clergy and laity, and spread the intensive eucharistic piety characteristic of Helfta.

Unfortunately the abbess and her three nun-mystics provide us with a typically medieval confusion of names, for there were two Mechtilds and two Gertrudes. Mechtild of Magdeburg had begun having visions at twelve, had become a beguine in Magdeburg around the age of twenty-three, and remained there for some forty years. According to the biographical information incorporated in her book, *The Flowing Light of the Godhead*, she was inspired, when she was about forty and had suffered a severe illness, to write down what God had shown her over the years. Her authorship appears to have constituted of a somewhat haphazard scribbling of odd sheets in Low German, which were later collected and rearranged by a Dominican friar. After Mechtild went to spend her last years in Helfta she became totally blind, but she was encouraged by her sister nuns to dictate the final section of her book. Mechtild belonged to the same school of mysticism as Hildegard, for she too believed herself to have been given a mission by God. Even her phraseology is reminiscent: 'Then, he commanded me . . . that I, a poor despised little woman, should write this book out of God's heart and mouth'. She could be outspoken to both men and women on the dangers of authority and its temptations, on the style of life it was suitable for a cleric to adopt, as well as lamenting the sins of the church and 'the fallen crown of the priesthood'.[24] Such pronouncements made her rather unpopular at Magdeburg, and may have been responsible for her move to Helfta where she became a valued member of the community.

Mechtild of Hackeborn was some thirty years younger than her namesake, and had evinced a desire for the convent from an early age, entering at the age of seven. Because she was Abbess Gertrude's sister she naturally shared in some of the administrative duties of the convent, being responsible for both teaching and directing the singing, as she was renowned for the beauty of her voice. Gertrude of Helfta, the third of these mystics and no relation to the Abbess Gertrude, was first Mechtild's pupil and then her companion and confidante. When

Mechtild, at about the age of fifty, disclosed her visions to two of her sister nuns, they secretly wrote them all down. This Latin compilation was known as the *Book of Special Grace*, which by the fourteenth century circulated widely on the Continent in both Latin and the vernaculars, usually in somewhat abridged form. By the fifteenth century it had also been translated into English.[25] Finally in her turn Gertrude of Helfta wrote of her visions in her *Revelations*, composed in Latin and also known as the *Herald of Divine Love*.[26]

These women have recently been most perceptively studied, their works analysed and their place in the religious life of their time evaluated.[27] Bynum emphasises the security of the nuns at Helfta, recruited from the nobility and living in a highly respected and well established convent, all of which allowed them to be singularly self-confident in their teaching and counselling roles. She points up the contrast between the much more uncertain Mechtild of Magdeburg with her less secure beguine background, and the younger Mechtild and Gertrude, who had lived happily from childhood in a strong female community. They were completely at ease, both about being women and still exercising authority in their role as interpreters of the divine. The Helfta mystics encouraged and assisted the spread of the devotions which were the standard practices of the later medieval piety, especially devotion to the eucharist and to the humanity of Christ, often broken down into such specific elements as his infancy, his passion, his sacred heart, etc. Although Helfta could display 'the splendour and grandeur of female piety',[28] it also suggests the essential importance of the protective elements which it provided its nuns – prosperity, rank, and established religious life.

Thirteenth-century Germany influenced the spirituality of fourteenth-century England, especially in Norfolk where the trade and personal relations with Germany and the Low Countries were particularly strong. The area had a strong bias towards individualistic piety, for it has been estimated that there were some twenty-eight female and forty-seven male recluses in Norfolk in the fourteenth and fifteenth centuries – a much higher proportion than is known anywhere else in England.[29] Julian of Norwich is undoubtedly the best known and most highly respected. As has been evident in the brief reference to her as a beguine, there is almost no solid information about her life, but we do have her *Revelations of Divine Love*, written by herself in vivid Middle English.[30] Her treatise breathes warmth and humanity, as well as the love of God she was so anxious to share with others. Julian has recently enjoyed special attention from feminists attracted by her ability to elaborate with considerable theological sophistication the idea of Christ as mother as a way of expressing the nurturing function of God. The concept was not original, as it had been quite widespread in male Cistercian theology in the twelfth century, especially in Bernard of Clairvaux.

Julian's work was simple in form but profound in substance. Despite her conventional disclaimers of her ignorance she carried lightly a remarkably wide theological learning. Compared to the works of the Helfta mystics, her imagery is much more sober, with less emphasis on regal glory and passionate feeling, as well as less lyrical in its approach. Nevertheless, her vigorous insistence on God's unbounded love for all humans, and the love they should have for him in return, is so straightforwardly and vividly expressed that it continues to speak across the centuries. It is known that Julian was much valued for advice and spiritual guidance during her years as a recluse but, once she had finished the longer version of her *Revelations*, she wrote no more, appearing satisfied that she had transmitted as accurately as possible all it was her responsibility to make known.

Birgitta of Sweden differs profoundly from the mystics already discussed. She was – even more than Hildegard of Bingen – a widely known public figure of political importance in her own day, but she was also a widow who did not lead an officially recognised 'religious' life. The earlier mystics all had one thing in common – their virginity. There was an extraordinary emphasis put by many medieval spiritual writers on the value of virginity in women, of it being the only way in which women could avoid unbridled sensuality to which the clerics felt they were so susceptible. This influence made it normal for the devout woman to feel that total commitment to God required a carefully guarded virginity. The nuptial imagery which occurs in so many mystical visions, the emphasis on total surrender to Christ and being accepted as his spouse is quite often expressed in very physical terms, and suggests the importance that the physical reality and spiritual significance of virginity assumed in their lives. Birgitta refused to accept this premise. She had been married and not found it distasteful, but she put her emphasis on chaste widowhood as a new vocation and claimed to have been taught by Christ that 'a humble widow is more agreeable to me than a proud virgin'.[31]

The circumstances of her life and social position suggest her willingness and ability to speak with authority to popes, kings and queens, as well as lesser mortals. Her wide European reputation and unusual importance in England (where she has been described as 'that most popular of Lancastrian saints'), make her a fascinating fourteenth-century figure.[32] Born in Sweden in 1302/3 she was related to its royal house through both her parents. Her bent for mystical experience began early for, at the age of ten, she had a vision of Christ crucified. At fourteen she was married to a Swedish nobleman of eighteen, and the couple had eight children. In 1335 she was called to the royal court to serve as mistress of the royal household for King Magnus's young bride from Namur, a position she gave up when she found she could have little serious influence. She then returned home to supervise the education of her own children and to share a life of increasing piety and asceticism with her husband. The couple went on pilgrimage to Compostela and her husband died in 1344, soon after their return. In her widowhood Birgitta sought shelter near the Cistercian abbey of Alvastra where the prior became her spiritual director. Birgitta, although not intellectual, had received a pious and distinguished education. Through her father and her husband, she was conversant with the court and with the administration of law, while the births of her children had also made a profound impression on her. When in her widowhood she turned whole-heartedly to a life of prayer and penance and began receiving mystic revelations, they naturally incorporated much of her upbringing and culture.

Her *Revelations* which she wrote down in Swedish and had her spiritual advisors translate into Latin, embodied frank and unpalatable advice to popes and kings, as well as less famous individuals. They naturally gained wider distribution and effect because of her social

31 Birgitta of Sweden receiving one of her revelations from the hands of Christ with Mary's approval

importance in Sweden, which enabled her to assure their forwarding to the distinguished individuals addressed. She was particularly out-spoken to the pope who continued to live in Avignon, excessively dependent on French power, and refused to return to Rome to govern the church. In a vision she had for Clement VI (d. 1352), she declared that Christ exhorted her to urge him to make peace between the kings of France and England, 'who are dangerous beasts and the loss of souls', and then go to Italy, threatening him with punishment for his unworthiness and lack of obedience.[33] Much of the English enthusiasm for Birgitta and her visions came from a message she addressed to the English and French kings, reporting a discourse by the Virgin on the sad state of the kingdom of France and the arguments over its rightful king. The early version, probably written in 1348, declared that the king of England was closer to the French throne than Philip VI, but, as Philip had not taken the throne by violence, he could keep it for his lifetime. However, he should consider Edward III as his eldest son and take him as his successor. This was plausible enough in the flush of English self-confidence after the great victory of Crécy and when Edward was in his thirties. The later version, heavily revised by one of Birgitta's secretaries, emphasised instead that it was Christ's wish that the kings should proceed to peace by way of a royal marriage.[34] This version reflects the changing political picture of the 1370s and, continued to be encouraged in English policy.

Birgitta went to Rome in 1349 and lived there, except for the occasional pilgrimage, until her death in 1373. She was supported by a devoted company which included her Swedish spiritual directors, a retired Spanish bishop who became the prime editor of her *Revelations*, and her daughter Catherine, now a widow. During those years she continued to urge the return of the Avignon popes to Rome – a ground for the French Jean Gerson's opposition to her canonisation. Gerson was also bothered by the frequency of visionaries and private revel-ations in his own day, and was particularly suspicious of any revelations originating from women. He not only felt that these must be examined by suitable authorities, but added that the examination of any woman's teaching must be more rigorous than that of a man's. Although Gerson recognised, rather grudgingly, that women of privileged sanctity might do great good, he feared their emotionalism and blamed Birgitta and Catherine of Siena for the schism in the church because they had encouraged the pope to return from Avignon. He was especially anxious to have Birgitta's *Revelations* censured. It should be added, as one of Gerson's biographers has pointed out, that the learned chancellor did not always abide by his strict categories of judgement when one of his countrywomen was involved: 'he seems to have had no difficulty in making up his mind as to the revelations of St. Joan of Arc.'[35]

Despite such French dissatisfaction, English links with Birgitta continued throughout the fifteenth century at all social levels. An English cardinal, Adam of Easton, a Benedictine monk from Norwich, knew and admired Birgitta during his years in Rome. He became her devoted defender, pushing for her canonisation and refuting criticisms brought against her and her *Revelations*. Her canonisation in 1391 was a source of great satisfaction, although the Scandinavians insisted on having the process repeated in 1415 and 1419 in order to make quite sure of their saint despite schisms in the church. Philippa, Henry V's sister, married King Eric of Denmark and had Birgitta's grand-daughter as the mistress of her household. Probably through her influence one of the two new monasteries set up by Henry V in 1415 was confided to the Brigittine order. Birgitta had conceived the order and obtained approval for its rule, though not for her claim that it had been dictated to her by Christ, but her daughter Catherine was chiefly responsible for its establishment and spread.

English translations of the *Revelations*, described as 'the literary remains of the Swedish princess, whose style had the vigour of a Hebrew prophet and the authority of a royal lady',[36] became fairly common, and retained their place among the spiritual reading of such devout and high-born English ladies as Cicely of York, mother of Edward IV and Richard III. They appealed to the devout of less exalted rank too. Margery Kempe had the *Revelations* read to her by a friendly priest and went to visit Birgitta's chamber, and met her maid, when she made a pilgrimage to Rome.[37] Birgitta had broken the accepted mould of what a mystic should be – she had married, lived by no accepted religious rule and in her own house, and in her *Revelations* had spoken with vigour and passion for the reform of both the church and upper levels of lay society. She was an unusual example of how the mystical thread, so strong in fourteenth and fifteenth century piety, could be expressed in quite different fashion from that of the enclosed and ecstatic thirteenth century nuns of Helfta.

In France Colette of Corbie was a more modest fifteenth-century precursor of the great Teresa of Avila, the sixteenth-century Spanish mystic and reformer of the Carmelites. Colette, after some years of religious seclusion, first in a convent and then in a hermitage, had a vision of St. Francis ordering her to reform the Franciscan nuns by restoring the original rule of St. Clare. In obedience to this command and armed with papal approval, she travelled through France, Flanders, and Savoy. She gained support from leading French nobles and was particularly successful in gaining sympathisers and recruits in

Savoy. After her death in Flanders in 1447 at the age of sixty-six, her life was written by her confessor Pierre de Vaux. A magnificent illuminated manuscript of this life was in the possession of Margaret of York, sister of Edward IV and wife of Duke Charles the Bold of Burgundy. Before giving it to the Poor Clares of Ghent, Margaret wrote on the last leaf in her own hand: 'Votre loyale fylle Margaret d'Angleterre. Pryez pour elle et pour son salut'.[38]

It may be a descent from the sublime to the ridiculous but it seems only right to end this discussion of mystics with a brief look at a most extraordinary English woman of the early fifteenth century. Margery Kempe is an unlikely figure to find in a gallery of female mystics, and her claim to be included as such is still much disputed. Wife of a burgess of Lynn and daughter of its mayor, Margery belonged to the well-established and socially respected merchant upper class of that East Anglian town. It is extraordinary that from this smug and often materialist group should emerge a woman who was not only pious in the accepted and conventional sense, but one convinced that she had received a special religious calling to be exercised outside the normal patterns of religious life. Even more startling is the fact that she dictated her autobiography. The *Book of Margery Kempe* first came to light in the 1930s.[39] Until then she had been known only through some devotional extracts printed by Wynkyn de Worde at the beginning of the sixteenth century, which did not in any way suggest the colour and fullness of the original. They had led to the identification of Margery as an anchorite of Lynn – given her marriage and fourteen children, her pilgrimages abroad and her wanderings in England, this is about as remote from the reality as is possible. Medieval autobiography is a very rare commodity. Usually intimate knowledge of an individual can be only sparsely gleaned through hints and casual references in chronicles or other impersonal texts. Margery, on the other hand, gives a patchy and unchronological but very full description of herself and her activities as she attempts to justify her claim to direct divine guidance. In some of its psychological attitudes it repays comparison with the memoirs of Abbot Guibert de Nogent.[40] He tortured himself with concern about his own sexuality as Margery does in her sometimes unwilling struggle to persuade her husband to agree to forego his marital rights as incompatible with her religious commitment.

Margery's autobiography deals with life among a very different class than the women previously discussed and is written in a much more homespun tone. The picture evoked of Margery and her husband returning from York on a hot day in June – she with a bottle of beer in her hand and he with 'a cake in his bosom' for their refreshment – settling down to rest before a wayside cross, and arguing once more if he

32 The anonymous laywoman in the group kneeling before St. James is a reminder of the extensive pilgrimages by such pious wanderers as Margery Kempe

will give up his marital rights, is a splendid vignette of everyday life among very real people.[41] It exemplifies the fascinating mixture of homely, even commonplace events with rather self-satisfied descriptions of Margery's great devotion, her intimacy with Christ, and the gradual routing of those who opposed or mocked her. In a somewhat incoherent fashion, Margery tells of her life from the time of her marriage and her subsequent mental breakdown at the birth of her first child. Tormented by apparitions of hell, she was finally saved by a vision of Christ which brought her back to sanity. From then on, though with many backslidings, such as her vanity about her fashionable clothes and her absorption in her unsuccessful businesses, she ultimately came to believe that she was being told of a special vocation to pray and weep for sinners, and to go on pilgrimages for the good of their souls. The *Book* details the many obstacles along the way and the successes of which she was artlessly proud.

Margery Kempe was a strange and awkward figure in a century which had convenient pigeonholes for women – either as a maid or widow living a recognised religious life, or as a respectable married woman living with her husband and taking care of her household. Margery fitted neither category. She was a wife and mother, though it is interesting to note that of all those fourteen children only one son is mentioned. She travelled extensively without her husband after he had agreed to their living apart. Her more extreme manifestations of what she claimed was divine grace included tears and sobs, and later loud cries, which made her both noticeable and unpopular with the preachers whose sermons she interrupted and the companions on pilgrimage whom she embarrassed. Reactions to this eccentric varied – some despised her and denounced her as a heretic and a Lollard, other respectable priests and bishops supported her and were convinced of the reality of her divine call. The argument continues to rage, with a recent woman scholar elucidating some of the physical and psychological realities that served to shape Margery's piety and sense of divine choice, while male distaste for female hysteria from whatever physical cause it might justifiably arise and clerical preference for a woman who would fit more closely the accepted stereotype of religious life have sharpened a number of adverse judgements. Nevertheless although exceedingly dubious about the genuineness of her mystical visions, and finding her exceedingly self-centred and often exhibitionist, even her critics recognise Margery's courage, sincerity, compassion for the weak and ailing as well as her real belief that she was doing what God asked of her.[42]

There can be little question that Margery Kempe was strongly affected by the deep current of mysticism in late fourteenth century and early fifteenth century piety which created the large number of visionaries who so worried Gerson. Margery could enjoy a considerable diet of mystical writers as they were propounded in the many popular sermons or as they were read to her by a sympathetic priest – the way in which she discovered Birgitta's *Revelations*. The lives of other such mystics as Marie of Oignies and Dorothea of Montau, an almost contemporary widow who became a recluse much admired by the Teutonic Knights, who were both notorious for their 'gift of tears', may have become known to Margery through her travels to Germany, and perhaps encouraged her to record her own life. Besides her piety, she had a real generosity of spirit. When her husband was old and had a serious fall which seems to have led to rapid senility, she returned to their house to take care of him. She complained of all the washing and wringing caused by his incontinence, and at the cost of the firewood to keep the water hot but she remembered too that 'he was ever a good man and an easy man to her'.[43] She had not led him an easy life, so this was a considerable testimony to his good nature and continued affection for his undoubtedly difficult wife.

Nevertheless, there must continue to be doubt about the genuineness of Margery's mystical visions. There is something very self-centred and naive about her descriptions of them, a pleased satisfaction in her special gifts even when they gave her some difficult times. Unlike the other mystics, Margery Kempe appears to have been a woman of no education whose culture was completely dependent on what she heard. She was fascinating and infuriating, extremely devout but anxious to be noticed and praised, verbose and often self-absorbed. Whether her mystical experiences were real is now an unanswerable question, but her *Book* has left us all in her debt for its vivid, down to earth portrayal of an unusual fifteenth century townswoman and the religious life of her time.

The range from the aristocratic and intellectual twelfth century abbess to the ignorant but shrewd fifteenth century townswoman underlines in purely religious terms the many changes that affected northern Europe's intellectual and cultural life between the twelfth and the fifteenth centuries. In a sense, mystics by their very nature cannot be rationally explained. Nevertheless, since all intellectual activity is influenced by the surrounding culture, this brief glimpse of the religious expression of this group of women mystics may help to suggest how women saw their place and value; how they interpreted in their own ways the religious ideas and practices which were so basic to the medieval intellectual structure; and the nature of their influence within a highly structured male church.

CHAPTER SEVEN

Women who Toiled:
Townswomen and Peasants

Queens, noble ladies, and religious of every kind could catch the eye of their contemporaries and make an impression as individuals. The townswoman and the peasant were of far more economic importance in their family units than their gentler sisters, but they tend to appear only in tax rolls, court cases and the occasional will. Such records identify them as individuals but usually provide only a quick snapshot of a single incident, or hint at a general style of life. The lower classes, when treated in literature at all were touched on with disdain or coarse humour. Chaucer's sympathetic portrayal, as well as his range of characters, including the modest peasant widow of the Nun's Priest's tale as well as that unforgettable townswoman, the Wife of Bath, were unusual even in his day. It was left to Christine de Pizan to attempt to give a sympathetic and realistic portrayal of the activities of the various townswomen she knew so well, as well as the peasant woman whose life she idealised.

Christine's *Treasure of the City of Ladies* paints several vivid pictures of the Parisian women of her day at different social levels. She divided townswomen into three groups: the rich and important, such as the wives of the wealthy merchants or those married to royal or princely officials living in Paris; the wives of craftsmen and tradesmen; and finally the feminine members of the urban proletariat, the servants and chambermaids. She advised the first group to love and take care of their husbands, with the practical suggestion that, even if the men have been unkind during their lifetime, their wives' estimable behaviour will so prick their consciences when they come to die they will leave them all their goods. Awaiting such a happy ending, the wife should administer the household with great care and prudence. She should know how everything should be done and be able to demonstrate the proper methods to her servants. Her children were to be well-taught, unspoiled, and not too noisy, while their nurses were to keep them clean and well-behaved. The house should be so attractive and peaceful that the husband would always be happy to return home with his friends to be entertained. Such occasions allowed her to show off the handsome linen she had worked herself. The great urban lady should not only go early to mass and say her prayers devoutly, but should ensure that nothing was wasted which could be given to the poor, and share her own meat and wine with them. This paragon of all the virtues not only kept on good terms with all her neighbours, she did not even talk too much.[1]

Reality often strayed from this sober ideal, as is obvious in Christine's disapproval of the extravagance displayed by the wife of a very rich Paris merchant when entertaining after childbirth. Christine's account of all the gold and silver vessels, the elegant bed-hangings and tapestries with the wife's device woven in gold thread, the mother attired in fine silk and leaning against silk-covered pillows fastened with pearl buttons, positively sputters with disapproval.[2] The Ménagier de Paris, that solid fourteenth-century bourgeois, would never have allowed his young wife to go in for that kind of display. His advice to her was always practical: how to get rid of fleas in the bedclothes, how to clean the heavy fur-trimmed garments, how to supervise the garden and the required shopping, along with his selection of recipes and menus for special occasions. His reaction to the kind of conspicuous consumption described by Christine would have been, one feels, like his comment on some of the more outrageous and complicated dishes designed for fashionable feasts: 'A great expense and a great labour and little honour and profit'.[3]

Gradations in the social scale were as important in the cities as among

33 The goldsmith and his wife enjoyed considerable social importance

the nobility, although the distinguishing element in the urban environment was wealth and acceptance among the great merchant families rather than ancient lineage. It was normally the most important merchants who controlled city government, but the crafts and trades had their own degrees of social importance. By the beginning of the thirteenth century they began to be organised into guilds or corporations which developed rapidly. The terms of labour, the rights of masters or mistresses, the rules regarding apprenticeship, hours of work, and membership were generally controlled by these groups. Some guilds accepted women, although most often they were the widows of men who had belonged, but others, such as the spinners of silk and the embroiderers, were mainly or exclusively female.

In addition to these regulatory bodies there were a great number of pious confraternities – often confusingly described as guilds – which combined religious observances and regular meetings with a form of social insurance. The funds contributed by the members were used to take care of their fellow-members, men or women, who suffered from illness, poverty, or old age. Loans might be provided to allow unlucky traders to start again, or to help the sons and daughters of members to find employment or get married. These confraternities were sometimes set up on craft lines, sometimes from a specific parish, or for a particular pious purpose, and their social and financial status varied widely. Most had women members, usually husbands with their wives, but, in many cases, single women as well, although a few prohibited female entry. The confraternities encouraged prudent charity while also providing a splendid social occasion at the great feast which always followed the religious observance of their patron saint's day. Their obligations extended to the grave, as it was the accepted duty of each member to attend the funeral of every other, and these requirements were carefully detailed in their own statutes.

Christine de Pizan also had advice for such tradeswomen, whom she takes for granted will be married. She reflects the family nature of all trades, emphasising that the wife should encourage the husband and other workers to start early in the morning, and should learn all the shop details so that she can properly supervise the workers when her husband is away or not paying attention. Her special responsibility was to see that the children, both boys and girls, went to school and then were apprenticed to a trade where they could make a living. She should refrain from running around town, visiting with gossips, nor should she go on pilgrimages unnecessarily as this was very expensive. Christine's emphasis on the wife's financial responsibility is very strong. She was to make sure that her husband did not get involved in imprudent loans, encourage him to live soberly, and make sure that he was so comfortable at home that he did not run off to taverns with drunken companions – all these were 'superfluous and outrageous expense'.[4]

The contemporary advice embodied in the anonymous doggerel known as *How the Good Wijf taughte Hir Doughtir* is even more down to earth and suggests a greater freedom of manners and a lower social status. Apart from such expected precepts as the need to go to church, pay tithes, be polite to all, and avoid any possibility of scandal, the daughter was admonished not to go to wrestling matches and other low entertainment 'like a strumpet or a giggling girl'. She should not haunt taverns and must remember when she shared good ale to drink moderately, since her reputation would suffer if she got drunk often – a generous, if realistic, approach. The English author parallels Christine's remarks on how a wife should manage her responsibilities. She should govern her servants well and wisely, making sure the work was done but also sharing in it when necessary. Above all she must pay them promptly to maintain her good reputation. Such close supervision would allow errors to be remedied quickly and ensure that everything was left in proper order with the keys safely in her keeping, for the wife should not be too trusting. If the children were rebellious, they should be beaten not cursed, for this would help them to improve. A daughter's marriage should be anticipated almost from birth, with her marriage portion being collected and the betrothal arranged as soon as possible, for girls are amiable but unstable in love. If she followed all this virtuous advice, which has a distinctly masculine bias since it lays great emphasis on not beggaring her husband by buying unduly rich clothes, or even borrowing them to create a falsely prosperous appearance, as well as answering him meekly, all would be well. She would surely be 'his dere darlynge' and he would not regret his marriage.[5]

Poor chambermaids and servants obviously led a very hard life, for if a fifteenth-century mistress worked hard herself, she expected her servants to work harder. According to Christine, they had to get up very early and go to bed very late, eat when everyone else had finished, have little or no leisure and not even enough time to go to church. Nevertheless, a maid was expected to be honest and hard-working. She should not take a percentage when she went shopping for the household, nor entertain cronies in the kitchen when the master was at work and the mistress at church, nor take her ease in the baths when she had been sent to the river to do the washing. Some wily chambermaids liked working for a newly married couple. Well versed in flattery and the inflation of costs the maid could also be persuaded by a young gallant to take an illicit message to her mistress for a bribe of a hood or a robe. Christine was shocked at such behaviour and declared that 'the end of such abomination is damnation'.[6] A sober householder like the Ménagier de

Paris was prudent in having a sober beguine in charge of his servants while his young wife learned how to run the household.

These treatises suggest the standards of behaviour held up to townswomen. What was the reality? At the higher level of urban society the legal position of the wife resembled that of the great noble lady: she was in charge of the household, took over when her husband was away, and, on his death, had at least a third of the estate. Quite often she was named executrix and provision might also be made for her support in his absence. For example, when Sir John de Lue of London decided in 1309 to go to the Holy Land on pilgrimage, he assigned to his wife Elizabeth, his 'dear companion', a yearly rent of 40s from a tenement in Seething Lane with full powers in everything concerning the property 'for her own profit, as well as ever I myself could have done in my own proper person'.[7] The grant was a permanent one.

Later the wills of such men often express their confidence in their wives and their affection for them. The 1436 will of Thomas Bracebrig, merchant and once Lord Mayor of York, is long and detailed, full of religious and charitable bequests that read remarkably like those of the country gentry. Thomas did not overlook his family – a complex matter, as he had buried two wives, both of whom had provided him with children, before he married his current wife, Juetta. He obviously set great store by family affection and remembrance, since he left his mother-in-law 20s to pray for his soul, as well as 20s to the relatives in the village of Escrick of his first wife Joan, so they could have a funeral feast for her soul and his. His son John, by his second wife Juliana, had recently died, so that John's daughter was to receive all the lands and tenements which Thomas had acquired from his marriage to Juliana, and 10 marks for her marriage besides. Two other sons, both in religion, were given money, though not as much as their two sisters. His widow, Juetta, was to have all his share in their gold rings, (and an extra 5 marks because they were not very valuable) as well as all the suitable apparel without appraisal in order 'that she may be a faithful Executrix of this my will, because my heart confides in her much'.[8] Family man to the end he wanted to be buried in his parish church next to the bodies of the wives and children who had predeceased him – probably with a place reserved for Juetta too.

City women also made their own wills. Emma, wife of Henry de Preston, also a Lord Mayor of York, got Henry's consent to make her will in 1401 and made him executor. She left 100s each to her son and daughter, 20s to her sister-in-law, and 5 marks to Alice Stede to assist her in marrying, though Alice had to remain a virgin and of good repute until she got a husband to be entitled to all of it. For the rest, Emma was only able to distribute her clothes, and to give some of her own jewels and ornamented girdles to her daughter.[9] A more surprising case is that of Isobel Dove in 1435. Her husband was overseas so in her will she named a female friend as executrix. She was given the guardianship of Isobel's goods with the duty of settling her debts, paying for her burial and carrying out her bequests. The executrix was then to keep the residue until Isobel's husband came home.[10]

Widows at these higher levels of urban society might take over their husband's business on his death, as their less well-off sisters would take over their husband's trade. Philip le Tailor had been one of the great success stories of thirteenth-century London, aided by his brilliant marriage to Sabine, a descendant of the city's first mayor, who had brought a large block of property as her marriage portion. After Philip's death in 1291, Sabine carried on his wine selling business for some time and was one of London's highest taxpayers towards the end of her life.[11] Some of these widows were very shrewd in their own interest. There is the delightful story of the angry fifteenth-century draper who made a proper marriage contract with one Elizabeth, the well-to-do widow of a goldsmith. He then spent much of his time in the next three years on her business affairs, thinking it would all add to his own profit in the end. When the draper went to Spain, Elizabeth turned to a rival and refused to have anything to do with him when he returned. She ultimately died unmarried with her fortune of £2,000 still in her own hands. The aggrieved draper not only laid claim to the money, because of the original marriage contract, he also added his account for £45 he had spent on costly rings for her, expensive dainties for her and her friends and gifts to her kinfolk and servants to advance his cause. He even included the purchase of a parrot for the lady which, he dolefully recorded, he could easily have sold at a profit to Lady Hungerford.[12]

The world of the tradeswoman, whether she was a wife working with her husband in the family business or a widow in charge of it, a wife with a separate trade of her own, or a single working woman, was very different from that of her rich neighbour. She was much busier, since she herself worked hard at the trade, often supervised the workshop, but was still responsible for the children and the household. Unlike noble ladies, who were normally companioned by their own damsels, the tradeswoman spent her working days with men – her husband, their journeymen and apprentices in the workshop, and the buying public – and was on a more equal basis. She had to abide by the same hours of work, faced the need to meet the standard of the craft in quality of merchandise and reliability of goods, and shared the same penalties for infractions against guild or corporation ordinances. A married city woman, however, had the privilege of trading with full responsibility as if she was single.

The most comprehensive summing up of trade and craft ordinances is that made by Etienne Boileau, provost of Paris under Louis IX, in his *Livre des Metiers*.[13] This is a register, drawn up in 1268, of the regulations of some one hundred Paris corporations, or trade groupings. It generally makes clear whether the trade was exclusively feminine, one in which both men and women could become masters or mistresses under the same conditions, or one where only a master's widow was recognised as a mistress with the right to carry on the business in her own name. The last group was by far the largest, and a few trades were completely forbidden to women, usually because of the physical strength needed. It is not surprising to discover that women were particularly active in such luxury crafts as silk-spinning and embroidering. Silk-spinning was almost a female monopoly, but male embroiderers became more and more important during the fourteenth and fifteenth centuries, though women often worked for them. In 1369 the father of Alice Catour brought a bill of complaint against Elis Mympe, an embroiderer of London, to whom Alice had been apprenticed for five years, since he had beaten and ill-treated her and failed to provide for her as he should have done by the apprenticeship agreement.[14] It rather sounds as if Elis was attempting to cut corners in what could be a very lucrative trade.

Tapestry weaving was less intimately connected with women because of its much larger scale, but there were women weavers and women patrons. Mahaut d'Artois provided encouragement for the industry in Arras at a very early stage. She bought five cloths, woven on the high-warp loom, for her son Robert from Isabeau Caurée in 1313, and again purchased tapestries from her in 1322. Mahaut also patronised Aghee of London, another *tapisseresse* in 1321. In 1380 Agnes of Avion was paid for a series of tapestries she had woven for Yolande of Soissons. Arras and Paris were great centres of this trade and enough medieval tapestries have survived to illustrate why they were so popular with the medieval rich as 'protection against the cold, decoration for great occasions, and a magnificent pictorial reserve', which could also be carried with them on their travels for instant comfort.[15] Luxury trades, such as tapestry weaving, were particularly affected by the selling of false work, i.e., the use of less expensive materials where they would not be immediately apparent. In 1374 the master of the tapestry trade in London brought before his fellow masters a side piece of an Arras-type tapestry which had been woven on the loom by an alien, Katherine Dochewoman, working in her own house. It was a long piece with linen thread beneath a wool covering, but London regulations called for such tapestries to be made with wool only. The master who brought in the piece wanted it condemned as deceitful. Although

*34 The luxurious tapestries in the queen's bedchamber were designed to
be carried from place to place and rehung as necessary as the attached
rings make clear*

Katherine was warned to appear if she had any response, she was not
present at the hearing. The masters all agreed that the piece was indeed
false and should be burned, but were willing on this occasion not to
execute the judgment.[16] Perhaps the masters had pity on the poverty
and probable ignorance of London regulations by this foreign woman
but it is more likely that the sentence was meant as a warning to the
many aliens who had flocked to work in London during Edward III's
reign. The native-born craftsmen were acutely aware of the danger of
being undercut by so many new skilled artisans.

Apart from luxury trades, small scale brewing and the selling of bread
and poultry were also predominantly female, but women can be found
almost everywhere. The Paris tax rolls identify women as working in a
large number of occupations some of which defy classification. However, it is often difficult to be certain whether the identifying tag given a
woman is merely carried over from her husband's occupation, is

gradually developing into an accepted last name, or truly describes the activity of the woman herself. Despite this inevitable confusion certain things are clear. Women were an important segment of the urban working force, although they were seldom among the very rich unless they had inherited or married wealth. In the series of the Paris tax rolls from 1292 to 1313, the percentage of women among the total number of individuals subject to tax is relatively steady, between 10% and 15%. This number includes not only female artisans but also the widows of rich merchants or officials, and thus includes hereditary wealth. The Paris taxes were payable only by those described as 'merchants of Paris' (a title which in Paris, unlike London, merely meant those who had the right to trade in Paris and were not under direct royal or episcopal control). As well the taxes, depending on the year of levy, had a higher or lower threshold, so many women of the lowest economic strata would not even be listed. Nevertheless, the percentage of women to men does not vary a great deal, although fewer women paid over 20 livres in the tax of 1313 including, to our surprise, Dame Marie the Beguine, assessed at 22 livres. Much the same pattern is visible in the Paris tax rolls of the first half of the fifteenth century. The percentages at that time work out at one woman to nine men in a fairly widespread tax, but only one for sixteen to twenty-one men when the tax was highly selective.[17] Widows were an important majority in the households headed by women, though a small percentage had a living husband away from Paris or lived separately from him.

The records of the English subsidies of 1292 and 1319 are less specific in their identification of women, and women normally paid a far lower tax. Thus, the widow of a vintner, one of the most profitable forms of trade in medieval London, paid a tax of £3, when the highest tax was £8 and the minimum 2s. The subsidy roll of 1319 lists varied occupations for women, such as candlemaker, brewer, girdle-maker, and silk-woman, but their assessments are generally very low. In terms of a subsidy in which a pepperer had the highest assessment of £40, the women do not reach much more than the median, which was only 5s. Two catch the eye: Denise the bookbinder, obviously well-to-do, whose house in Fleet Street had been robbed, paid 6s 8d; as did Mabel Rolaund, who was a lodging-house keeper for Flemings and Brabanters, aliens who often came to London to work in the cloth trade.[18]

The varieties of trades in Paris in which women can be identified was far wider, not surprising since Paris was the centre of the luxury trade for northern Europe. The tax rolls of both 1292 and 1313 show women as silk-workers, embroiderers, old-clothes dealers, pedlars, waxmongers, pancake makers, garland makers, in charge of the baths, clothmakers, spinners, makers of robes, brewers and even the lowly fishwoman, goat-herd, and the woman who shampooed heads. At the very bottom were the great number of chambermaids whose economic wellbeing depended on the wealth of the household they served. Some interesting points emerge from the very full roll of 1313 which, like the other Paris documents, lists its taxpayers by parish. Taxpaying women were concentrated in the parishes of St-Eustache and St-Jacques on the Right Bank. In fact there were about three times as many women on the Right Bank as elsewhere. This was natural, as the Ile-de-la-Cité, and the Left Bank were dominated by the royal court, the bishop, and the totally male university, and were only involved in the city's commercial life as consumers. Women inn-keepers and taverners were fairly frequent – three in the poor parish of St-Denis-de-la-Chartre paid ten percent of all the tax collected there. The parish of St-Severin appears to have been a centre of the book trade, though this often required another supporting trade – even in those days it would seem that literature was no guarantee of a steady income. A woman illuminator, Thomasse, was also a tavernkeeper, as were a male bookbinder, a seller of parchment, and a bookseller, while Master Thomas, another bookseller, had a wife who was an old-clothes dealer.[19]

Women were apparently quite willing to dispute their tax assessments. Genevieve, who dealt in peacock feathers, was assessed at 12 livres, but only paid 7 livres 10 sous, while a woman chasuble maker was assessed at 72 sous, but only paid 60. Other high assessments remained: Perronnelle the pepperer paid a tax of 18 livres, and Marie the felt-maker and her son paid a combined tax of 14 livres 5 sous. Women were to be found in surprising numbers among the coiners who worked at the Monnaie. Only Jeanne is listed by herself, but ten other female coiners lived with their husbands, whose trades ranged from butcher and tavernkeeper to the more respected spicer or draper. In all these cases the rate of the tax varied according to the rank of the husband and the wife paid half. An unexpected figure is Perronnelle the Fleming, described as 'usurer', but she paid only 18 deniers tax and sounds like a very unsuccessful member of a much deplored occupation.[20]

The general impression that emerges from this necessarily fragmented information is that women were active in a wide range of urban occupations, that they were generally considered such an essential part of the family economic unit that they paid half of any tax imposed, and that women on their own were rarely to be found among the wealthiest citizens but that many of them seem to have achieved middle-class comfort. Their access to employment was usually as wife and partner, or as a daughter who could be trained in her parents' craft without reducing the allowed number of apprentices. Some trades had free entry and accepted all who met their requirements. Women who were mistresses in their trades were allowed to take female apprentices under much the same regulations as men, but girls were not allowed in a workshop unless the wife was also there, a basic safeguard for them.

Although information is more extensive for Paris and London, all the important commercial centres had their own methods of regulating the trades within their walls. In Toulouse, where the process began early, control rested in the hands of the city officials, rather than a royal official or the trade itself. The statutes of many Toulouse trades took for granted that women would be accepted on the same basis as men, but the public officials of the guild or corporation were always men. Notarial contracts in Montpellier in the fourteenth and fifteenth centuries show that widows and single women were often involved in a wide range of business activity, though never as numerous or financially important as men. Girls were apprenticed young, usually to such trades as textile finishing, brocading, or spinning silk thread, though they rarely became official guild members. Most is known about the women from the merchant élite, who were often appointed guardians for their children, and such widows, with resources from their dowries and inheritance, as well as single women, were often active moneylenders or traded in property. These were conservative businesses well suited to women's abilities.[21]

Urban fathers and husbands often showed their concern for the proper maintenance of their wives and daughters. The items willed to daughters were usually designed to provide them with a livelihood and encourage a good marriage. In 1378 Richard Groom left his daughter Juliana his brewery in the London parish of St. Botolph for her lifetime. Some forty years earlier Simon of Canterbury, a London carpenter, had left his wife a brewery for life but also bequeathed his daughter Alice a house behind the brewery with free passage through the brewery 'whensoever and as often as she may wish to go in and out of the same like a good and faithful woman'. In 1341 Richard de Bettoigne, a pepperer, alderman, and one time mayor of London, left his daughter Johanna a tavern in West Cheap for her lifetime, and the rest of his rents and tenements to his wife for her lifetime with the usual proviso, 'as long as she remained chaste and unmarried'. Both bequests ultimately fell to his son and his heirs, but provided for the lifelong upkeep of wife and daughter.[22]

Occasionally a careful inventory of goods accompanying the wardship of an urban orphan suggests what a young daughter of a good merchant family might expect to have provided for her. In 1317 two orphaned sisters were handed over to the care of a respected widow until they arrived at the marriageable age. Their trousseau was basic but generous: a featherbed for each plus two complete sets of bedcoverings and a bolster. There were ten ells of tablecloth, as well as fourteen ells of towelling, a heavy brass pot and pitcher, two pewter flagons, a great chest and three silver cups. Another cupboard held twelve pewter dishes, twelve pewter plates and eighteen salt-cellars. The widow was also given custody of the family jewels – rings, loose pearls, silk girdles, and cauls (a kind of coif) – which had been kept in their father's leather writing desk. These were to be divided proportionately between the widow and the two girls, no doubt her profit from the wardship. The expenses involved in bringing up a girl until she could be married are suggested by an accounting of 1380. During his five years of wardship a London fishmonger claimed £8 13s 4d for the girl's board and lodging and £3 6s 8d for her clothes while the miscellaneous expenses, such as shoes, teaching, dressing and doctoring her head (one wonders why?), and other small necessities came to 13s 4d a year. The single major expense was the £4 13s 4d spent in the church courts trying to get her marriage contract arranged. The merchant would have found the wardship profitable as his expenses were repaid and he was allowed one-half of the 20% annual increase in the 100 marks provided for the girl's use.[23]

Our medieval ancestors were not always law-abiding, for the records of the London courts frequently show fraud. A few cases in which women were involved suggest some of the possibilities. In 1327 two female and eight male bakers, were charged with the theft of dough. Many less substantial houses did not then have their own ovens so dough, already formed into a loaf, was often brought to a nearby baker to be cooked in his oven. This group had ingeniously cut a hole in their moulding board with a sliding door concealing it. They arranged to have a servant sitting under the table who opened the door and secretly stole dough from the loaves neighbours left for baking. The matter was considered so serious that it was brought before the full city court and the guilty men were condemned to a full day in the pillory with dough slung around their necks to symbolise their misdeeds. In this case the women had the advantage, for they were not pilloried since they claimed successfully that they bore no responsibility for what their husbands ordered them to do. However, it was not rare for the women to practise their own frauds. In November 1364, Alice, wife of Robert de Coustone, admitted that she had sold ale in an unsealed measure which had an inch and a half of pitch on its bottom, slightly disguised by some scattered sprigs of rosemary. The measure was tested and proved short, so Alice was put in the woman's pillory with half of her false measure. Eight years later Margery Hare, fishwife, was indicted for selling 'stinking, rotten and unwholesome' fish. This was both against the ordinance and a scandal to the city, so she too was condemned to the pillory, and her spoiled fish burnt there. Women who sold their poultry above the price set by the city were put in prison for a day, but warned that a second offence would bring a much heavier punishment.[24] The London authorities did their best to stamp out frauds and short measures, especially in foodstuffs.

It is less easy to uncover equivalent court cases in the French and Flemish cities, but even popular stories and sermons suggest that one of the most obvious characteristics of the city woman was her ability to quarrel with those around her. Patient Griselda seems to have been as rare in the daily life of the Middle Ages as in that of other centuries, and feminine outspokenness can be found at all social levels and is particularly well documented for the late fourteenth and early fifteenth centuries. Alice Shether was brought before the mayor of London as a common scold who molested and annoyed all her neighbours with abusive and malicious words which spared neither rich nor poor, spreading discord and ill-will. She was condemned to the pillory for an

35 A woman poultry seller

hour with the sheriffs proclaiming her offence. Alice, wife of Robert Godrich, came to the house of William Walworth, an important city leader, and raised a hue and cry against him as if he was a thief, claiming that he had unjustly disinherited her of land worth £20 annually, and had unjustly detained her husband in prison. William was appalled at the scandal affecting his good name and asked for damages of £100. His attorney pleaded for Alice's punishment 'so that such scolds and liars might dread in future to slander reputable men'. The jury in the case set William's damages at £40, a very sizeable sum in fourteenth-century London, and both condemned Alice to the pillory and allowed Walworth to recover the £40 from Alice and her husband. It would appear that William was most interested in future deterrence, for he asked the mayor and aldermen to remit the punishment of the pillory and to suspend the money payment during Alice's good behaviour. Some forty years later a similar case involved the famous London mayor, Richard Whittington, and Johanna Hert, jeweller, who admitted that 'for hatred and wantonness and without his deserving it' she had accused Whittington in the king's courts and elsewhere of owing her large sums of money and of keeping jewels of hers worth many thousands of marks. She admitted on oath that she owed him more than he did her, and begged mercy for her defamation of him.[25] Unfortunately no judgment was recorded, and these bald statements make it almost impossible to discover how much the superior position and influence of such men as William Walworth and Richard Whittington were used to intimidate the women. Their willingness even to embark on such accusations against the most powerful men in the city suggests that the London woman could often be aggressive in the maintenance of her rights.

Even these scattered glimpses illustrate the economic stake of medieval urban women in the commercial life of their towns. Despite some legal restrictions and the possible weight of a husband's controlling hand, a determined wife, and certainly a determined widow, could create a satisfactory and relatively independent niche for herself. Although excluded from public office and determination of policy, the work of the townswomen was essential for urban prosperity and they were safeguarded, as well as chastised, by laws meant to ensure peaceful and honest business dealings.

Peasant Women

Christine de Pizan had vowed in the *Treasure of the City of Ladies* to discuss all levels of women's participation in the society of her time so she could not pass over the peasant women who were still in the majority in the primarily agricultural society of the fifteenth century. However her treatment of them is Arcadian and somewhat patronising, for she saw their hard lives through remarkably rose-coloured glasses. She felt that the simplicity of their lives spared them from temptations of vanity or pride while their basic diet of brown bread, lard, and pottage, washed down with water, was more available than the fancier foods of the upper classes. Because Christine recognised that peasant women had less chance to go to church and be instructed, she founded her advice on tenets of basic morality applied to their situation. They should be good to their neighbours and loyal workers for their lords, not mixing less valuable rye with wheat, nor hiding the best sheep and lambs when they had to pay their dues, nor rendering false accounts of the poultry they had in charge. Echoing the manorial court records, she insisted that they should not take wood from the forest without leave, nor let their beasts on to a neighbour's pasture, while their children should be kept from breaking hedges or stealing fruit. Christine ends her brief, and rather unrealistic, summary with the pious advice to go to church when possible, or at least say the Our Father, pay the tithes and keep peace with their neighbours.[26] This final, oft-repeated advice reinforces the impression that medieval women of all classes were easily offended and prone not only to jealousy and angry words but often to physical violence.

Throughout this whole period women on the land had an unquestioned economic value of their own whether they were free peasants or unfree serfs. The working of the peasant holding, whether free or unfree, was very much of a family affair in which women played an important part in providing the necessary manual labour. Thus the woman might drive the plough animal while her husband guided the plough. She had a place in the reaping, binding and haymaking, not only for their own small holding, but often as part of the services owed to their lord, besides being active in such primarily female occupations as the care of poultry, the milking of cows, and the making of butter and cheese. The contemporary treatises on husbandry underline the value of a woman for such labours as she was so much less costly than a man.[27] The basics of a peasant life were similar in the equivalent economies of northern Europe. All these areas were hard hit by the mortality of the plague in the mid-fourteenth century when the scarcity of labour and the rise of wages helped many peasants to buy their freedom. Many other differing factors also applied – major variations in law and custom, the nature of the land tilled which set the local agricultural pattern, the effects of wars and local famines – that general statements are inevitably only flawed approximations of a far more complex reality.

Recently English peasant life has been under the microscope and many studies have dealt with specific manors and villages. As a result we have a far more intimate knowledge of English peasant women from the

*36 Women working
with men in the
haymaking*

thirteenth to the fifteenth centuries than is easily available for their continental counterparts. It is therefore almost inevitable that this discussion relies particularly on English practice. Nevertheless, some general statements do hold good. Peasant women, like all their sisters, were considered subordinate and inferior to men. They normally had no public power or visibility within their manor or village, although the occasional strong-willed woman could exert considerable influence and leadership. Thus, Agnes, the wife of John Sadeler, was identified in court as 'the procurer and maintainer of the rebels' in the village of Ramsley in 1386 and was outlawed when the villagers refused to perform their services and demanded an end to bondage.[28] Women had private rights and could inherit property in default of direct male heirs. They might also have certain customary rights (which varied greatly) in their husband's property after his death. For a peasant, as for other women, her legal status was defined to a considerable degree by the fact of her being unmarried, a wife or a widow.

In England peasant girls were usually married rather later than their upper-class sisters, often between eighteen and twenty-two, although daughters in rich peasant families married earlier than the norm. After 1350 the general age for marriage, especially for girls, fell markedly as depopulation caused by the plague made land more easily available. Peasant marriage was always dependent on the possession of a sufficient holding to provide support, so post-plague conditions discouraged the remarriage of widows. Marrying a landed widow was no longer the only way for a young man to acquire the necessary holding, so younger girls could wed.

Not surprisingly, richer peasants planned for and arranged their daughters' marriages at an earlier age since they had more resources available, whereas the poor girl with no land and not many goods might find no future except as a servant in another's household. Two cases point up the differences. In 1377 Agnes, the daughter of Thomas atte Lowe, took up a holding in Moor which had been surrendered by a former tenant. It consisted of a messuage, that is, a house-lot with its small courtyard, and a half a yardland or virgate, probably around fifteen acres. She was to be responsible for the usual rates and services, and would hold it according to the custom of the manor. Agnes was still a minor, so her father provided surety that the rents and services would be performed until she came of age. He also guaranteed to put a building on the messuage.[29] Such a holding would make Agnes a very desirable bride and certainly encourage her early marriage. Once married, her husband would take over her father's responsibility and become the official tenant, although Agnes might be able to ensure that this holding, which had been specifically presented to her by her father, would pass after her husband's death to her preferred choice of heir. A century earlier, at the other end of the village social scale, Alice de Schishurst of Halesowen is a good example of the poor peasant woman and her marginal situation. Both Alice's brother and nephew were servants for rich peasants, but since she had found no employment she was declared persona non grata on the manor in 1275. For a year she found refuge with two well-to-do widows for whom she probably worked as a servant. The following year, having moved away, she stole corn and peas from one of those who had sheltered her, set fire to the house and then fled.[30]

One financial exaction which was only levied on women, and usually only on unmarried girls was 'leyrwite', a fine on women who fornicated and were cited before the court. These fines were meant to control female sexual activity but involved no permanent stigma, for girls

subject to such fines later married men of equal status. Delay in
marrying often arose from the lack of dowries for the girls, especially in
a family with many daughters, or of land for the young men, a situation
which encouraged illegitimacy. Indeed in some cases when leyrwite was
levied, it was specifically stated that if the man later married the girl, the
usual payment for the marriage of a serf, known as merchet, would not
be required. There is evidence that, in some places at least, by the
beginning of the fifteenth century young women could be sufficiently
independent economically to assume this customary payment themselves, instead of having it paid by their father or, more rarely, their
intended husband. According to the *Liber Gersumarum* of Ramsey
Abbey, which records the payment for the marriages of villein women
in twenty-nine of the abbey manors between 1398 and 1458, the girl
paid her own merchet in 33% of the cases. More of the women required
a guarantor for the amount, suggesting the greater weakness of their
finances and perhaps the likelihood of their having received lower
wages.[31] How far such wage-earning activity by younger women caused
them to delay marriage into their mid-twenties with a resultant drop of
peasant fertility and the size of peasant families is an intriguing issue
which needs more study.

There is slight, but interesting, evidence for some of these young
women having real economic autonomy before marriage. A careful
study of the manor of Brigstock turned up three young women holding
lands of their own and one, Isabella Huet, received income from both
brewing and baking for three full years before her marriage.[32] Another
independent woman, apparently unmarried, was Juliana, the gardener
on the bishop of Ely's manor at Little Downham. In the early part of the
fourteenth century, she commanded a gang of village workers who
owed the bishop several days work a year in his garden as part of their
customary service. Leeks, peas, and beans were planted for consumption on the manor and enough apples, pears, cherries, plums, nuts, and
vegetables were harvested so that there was produce to be sold, either by
the steward or 'in the courtyard' on some sort of local stall. Juliana must
have been a strong woman, for the garden was in such heavy soil that
when the villagers had to dig a new one some years later they broke the
bishop's spades and had to be provided with new ones. Although there
is no record of how much Juliana earned, she must have done reasonably well for she was involved in a number of illicit land deals for
herself, and leased a fishery and several meadows from the episcopal
bailiffs.[33] Still another unexpected economic activity for women on
manors was moneylending. The village moneylender has always been a
feature of rural life and has roused great resentment, since loans were
usually made because of the failure of the harvest and repayment was

difficult, if not impossible, if conditions remained bad. In England
there are law cases concerning women moneylenders, while the monk
Cesarius includes in his collection of edifying moral stories an account
of two women usurers from German manors whose deathbeds were
visited by devils and such evil portents as crows and ravens. The birds
snatched away the body of one of the offending women, only to let it fall
to the ground and shatter into pieces before the eyes of her terrified
fellow peasants.[34]

Peasant wives were full-time workers whose tasks were essential to
their household's subsistence and comfort. They not only shared in the
general agricultural labour, but also worked in the small garden of their
courtyard where they might grow vegetables, have a few chickens and
perhaps a pig to add to their meagre diet, and also gathered herbs and
wood on the common land. There were the domestic tasks of weaving
the cloth for the household, cooking and doing the laundry. Above all,
they bore, nursed, and took care of their children, who were a further
contribution to the household's labour supply, and kept them reasonably close as they went on with their own tasks. The problem of
supervision, as any mother would testify, grew more difficult as the
infant became the toddler, inexhaustibly curious and with no sense of
danger. The coroners' rolls document the frequency of child deaths

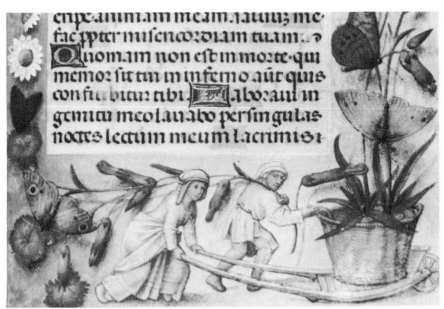

*37 An illustration from a Flemish psalter suggests how hard women
might work in the garden*

38 This active youngster is obviously trying to escape his busy and distracted mother's supervision

during those crucial early years when the children were left alone and copied their parents' activities. Little girls fell into pots or pulled their boiling contents over on themselves; more adventurous little boys explored their surroundings and succumbed to danger at a much higher rate than the girls.[35]

Apart from all these domestic tasks, many wives were involved in such commercial enterprises as brewing and baking, and might even act as butchers. Brewing was the leading economic activity in northern villages where ale was a necessary food source and large amounts were consumed. It also had to be made regularly since hops were not in general use until the late fourteenth century and ale soured quickly. Brewing was an ideal occupation for women as the processes in its manufacture stretched over several days but did not require continuous attention, so they could be fitted in between other tasks. A mash prepared from crushed malt, made from steeped and germinated grain, was added to water and heated in a great pot to dissolve the solids and convert the starch into sugar. Before straining off the resultant wort, or liquid, yeast or spices might be added. The first straining was the strongest and most highly prized. The equipment needed was rudimentary – large pots, ladles, and straining cloths as well as access to large amounts of grain, water and firewood. Some women, especially in richer households, might brew only for home consumption, but poorer peasants found the extra income from selling ale was an economic necessity. As a diet staple, the price of ale was regulated by assize, and our knowledge of the number and importance of female English brewers comes from the fines for offences regarding brewing listed in such profusion in the court rolls. Each rural community had its own appointed ale-tasters, almost always male, who had to approve the measures used, and the quality and pricing of each batch before sale. The expectation, and reality, of sharp practice was so general that the frequent fines were almost considered as licence payments. The story of the honest widow who saved her house from the fire raging around it by lining up all her measuring pots at her door and praying that, if she were honest, God would stop the flames, and so it happened, was considered an obvious miracle.[36]

Although it is hard to be specific, it would appear that women rarely brewed before their marriage, except as sharing in a labour involving all the able-bodied members of the family. Women worked as brewers for varying periods, occasionally for many years, but usually abandoned the work as they grew older, no longer had a growing family to support, nor could count on their children's assistance. However, one indefatigable woman from the Ramsey Abbey manors appeared in the court rolls over a period of fifty-six years, and was fined nineteen times for offences regarding ale and once more when she took to baking, less frequently practised by women. Bakers, both male and female tended to come from the long-established and respected families in their community, and brewing and baking were often combined as compatible activities, although equipment for baking was more expensive and therefore required more resources. Occasionally the court rolls provide a glimpse of as many-faceted a woman as Emma Powel, who was cited over a period of fifty years for brewing ale, baking bread, acting as a butcher and selling pudding (no doubt blood pudding or perhaps sausage).[37] Such cottage industries appear to have been a necessary part of many peasant women's lives.

Not all women occupied their time quite so diligently. The case of Agnes Pole in the Ramsey manor of Houghton-cum-Wyton introduces a lightminded woman whose extra-marital activities caused an uproar in her village. Agnes was the wife of a village juror, thus part of the élite of the manor, but took as a lover one Stephen Note, a peripheral member of the community. Stephen was not only guilty of adultery but of hanging around the Pole home and assaulting Agnes' husband. She paid a fine of 6d for her misconduct in 1308 and when ordered to appear at a subsequent court session was stigmatised as *meretrix*, i.e. whore. Two years later matters had still not improved. The liaison continued and poor John Pole had suffered physical abuse from both his wife and her lover. The court fined her the large sum of 40d and made her promise to act towards her husband with goodwill in the future.[38]

It must not be assumed that the peasant widow was always poor and marginal in her community. Even the 'poor widow' of Chaucer's Nun's Priest's Tale could own three cows, three pigs, and a sheep, as well as her remarkable rooster and his seven hens, and made a sufficient living as a dairy woman. Widows could be a relatively high proportion of the tenants on a particular manor. By common law the English widow was entitled to one-third of her dead husband's holding for the rest of her life, but could not dispose of it, since it normally passed to their issue. On many manors the widow was entitled to more than one-third, sometimes life tenure in the whole holding, more normally one-half to two-thirds. Such widows were not necessarily marginal members of their community but could be responsible for good-sized holdings with all the rights and services that went with them, even though they probably contracted out some of the heavier physical tasks. Two thirteenth-century widows in the manor of Clifford belonging to St. Peter's Abbey, Gloucester, illustrate what was expected of them. Matilda, the reeve's widow, held half a virgate of land for an annual rent of 8s and various customary works. Although still of villein status, it was anticipated that she might brew for sale, and owned both horses and oxen. The other widow was less well-off. Margery held the same amount of land but her rent was only 3s. However, she owed heavy physical services to the lord. These included ploughing one-half acre every week from Michaelmas to the beginning of August, plus assorted manual services during July, August, and September of up to five days a week, including one day a week of carrying goods on her back to Gloucester or elsewhere. She was also required to provide eggs at Easter.[39]

Occasionally it is possible to get a more comprehensive view of a particular widow and how she managed her affairs. Alice, widow of Stephen Sprot, had married him by 1341. Stephen began a career as a reeve, the chief peasant official, in the manor of Woolstone (Berkshire) in 1359 and continued in that office with a few interruptions until 1382. He gained in prosperity over the years and his holding rose from four acres to about fifteen for which he paid 7s 4d in rents and work services commuted, a sum reduced by 2s during his years as reeve. He and his wife appear to have had only one child, a son Richard, for whom in 1371 his father paid a fine of 3s 4d to allow him to leave the manor to go to school and prepare for ordination. Richard was also granted his freedom on condition that he was ordained priest. This rather unusual

39 Easter, with its demand for large numbers of eggs, would encourage such intensive searches as this

choice of career for an only son may have been encouraged by his mother's brother who had taken the same path more than twenty years before. When Stephen died in 1384, Alice paid the required heriot, or death duty, to the lord and took up the holding herself, paying the sum required for the rents and the commuted services for the next two years. By this time she would have been at least sixty and perhaps tired. Since she had no children to consider she arranged to surrender her holding (in a gradual process) and in November 1388 bought her freedom for 30s. Alice and Stephen had obviously been leading peasants in the manor and thrifty as well. Once a freewoman Alice must have left Woolstone for she disappears from its records, but these slight traces of her existence are enough to suggest a very adequate degree of comfort and prosperity over a long life.[40]

Widows with children appeared willing to take into account the needs of their children as they grew up, for they often granted control over some or all of their property to their husband's heir during their own lifetime. Sometimes the process can be seen fairly fully. Thus it is possible to follow the arrangements made by Emma Shephirde, widow of Philip Swetman, in the manor of Brigstock over some twenty years. Almost immediately on her widowhood in 1302, and after having taken possession of her widow's share, Emma transferred part of her portion to Henry Swetman, the son named as her husband's heir. He in turn gave a share of the property to his brother Peter. Twelve years later Emma gave a small house to her two daughters while in 1316 she divided a croft she had kept between Henry and Peter in return for a cartload of hay a year. By 1325 Emma must have been feeling the onset of old age and the need to come to a final settlement, for she then granted to Henry the residue of her holdings, though he was only to take possession after her death. In some cases, when a widow thus resigned her lands, or even before, a specific contract would be drawn up to define what she would receive. In 1281 Thomas Brid, a tenant at Ridgeacre undertook to build for Agnes, his widowed mother, a two bay house measuring thirty feet long by fourteen wide, with three doors and two windows. He would also provide her each year with a generous allowance of wheat, oats and peas and – a pleasure for old bones – five cart-loads of sea-coal.[41]

Widows enjoyed specific rights by virtue of the lands they controlled through their own inheritance, by purchase, or in life tenure of their husbands' property. Since such widows might end up holding a significant portion of village lands at any one time, they could be zealous in pursuit of their rights. In 1442 it was the widows in the manor of Painswick in the Cotswolds who cried out against John Talbot, earl of Shrewsbury, who was the lord of the manor. Talbot had taken sixteen Painswick men with him to fight in France, but only five came back. The widows were angry at losing their lands as well as their husbands, and their clamour forced the calling of an inquest. Feeling the need to pacify their aroused feelings, it was decided that the widows should be entitled to all their husbands' holdings for life, and should also be free to choose a second husband if they so desired.[42] The widows were fortunate in the climate of their times for the other grievances were also settled in the interests of the tenants.

One final point should be made about the possibilities for peasant women. Although a lord's court would push an unmarried girl with a good holding towards a suitable marriage quickly, in the interests of having the rents, taxes, and labour services owed from the holding guaranteed by a male head of household, the girls were not as tied to the land as their menfolk. The ecclesiastical prohibition against marriage within the four degrees of relationship inevitably caused a considerable number to look outside their own manor for a possible husband. Unless the girl was an heiress, it was she, not the man, who moved. Widows too might often move away, possibly to marry again, and some girls slipped away clandestinely to marry or merely go off with a man.

French law and custom varied in different parts of the country, as well as being quite different from the English model but a French study of fourteenth and fifteenth century wills in the Lyonnais is illuminating for that area. Peasant wives were better treated than the noblewomen of the district for the nobles overwhelmingly preferred to name a male heir, even if they had no sons. In over one-third of the peasant cases, the wives were left the guardianship of the children and the usufruct and administration of the family goods, often without having to give inventory or accounting. The widow was also designated as the head of the family. Obviously such provisions were intended to maintain the cohesion of the family as well as its inheritance, and to make the widow's task of bringing up the children easier. The testator often arranged the problem of the widow's independence and maintenance as she grew older and the children had become adult. In one case the husband specifically ordered that when the widow wished to retire she should retain the chamber which they had occupied, receive some twelve measures of wheat a year, twenty sous in money, and a piece of land away from the main holding.[43] The great majority of these peasant wills either included provisions for independent lodging or a lifetime legacy. This might be a vine, a field, or even such moveables as kitchen equipment, with the number of plates or the contents of the coffers carefully spelled out. The wife's pension might consist of grain, wine in the wine-growing district, perhaps firewood, the right to fatten a pig or raise a goat on the heir's land. When the widow, in only one-fifth of the cases, was merely to be given food and lodging by the heirs, with no rights in administration or the upbringing of the children, quarrels were often anticipated. Heirs were specifically enjoined not to shut the door on the widow nor to force her to work as an unpaid servant.[44]

For both French and English peasants the maintenance of the family holding was important, though the French seem to have had less concern for the younger members of the family, and were more worried about maintaining the integrity of the holding for the main heir. The material available suggests that English peasant widows generally fared better from the provisions of their customary law which operated without personal bias. Their guaranteed lifetime interest gave them more continued influence with their children and family quarrels seem to have been more rare and regarded as less of a danger. It is not possible to judge whether the relatively independent economic activity of English peasant women in brewing and baking was parallelled on the Continent. Undoubtedly all peasant women had individual economic value, because of the need for their manual labour, and peasant women could be confident of their importance in the family unit in a way that their nobler sisters might have envied. Such specialised records as court rolls, coroners' rolls, and wills, make it possible to build up a general idea of what their lives were like, thanks to the detailed information quarried by the new brand of historians who are particularly concerned with the accurate portrayal of the everyday. We can now get occasional glimpses of what these women did; it is still difficult, if not impossible, to bridge the gap of centuries and understand what they were like.

CHAPTER EIGHT

Medieval Women as Healers and Nurses

The woman at the head of a household, whatever its size or importance, seems to have been responsible for the health of those within her sphere of influence. At the courts of kings, princes, or great nobles there would be a doctor in attendance or on call, but women in less distinguished households would need to turn elsewhere for assistance. From the twelfth century on there were recognised doctors in towns of any size; in the country help might come from a practised herbalist or the infirmarian of a nearby monastery or nunnery, or perhaps even from a village 'wise woman' with a local reputation for healing skills. With such varied practitioners it is not surprising that medieval medicine was an undigested mixture of ancient knowledge of useful herbs and plants, ideas for treatment gleaned from classical sources, practical experience, and a general, if occasionally shamefaced, reliance on magic and incantations. Nor is it surprising that unexplained deaths often led to unfounded accusations of poison, frequently for political purposes and often blamed on a knowledgeable but deceitful woman. Orderic Vitalis, the Norman chronicler, accused Sichelgaita, daughter of the duke of Salerno and wife of Robert Guiscard, the Norman conqueror, of attempting to poison her stepson Bohemond in order to advance her own son. Since Sichelgaita had been brought up among the doctors of Salerno, already famous for their medical knowledge, it was easy to suggest that she had learned from them how to prepare poisons. His lurid story further suggests that Guiscard found out about this and threatened to kill her so that Sichelgaita urged the Salernitan doctors to keep Bohemond alive, poisoned her husband instead, seized his best ship and returned to her native Apulia.[1] Guiscard probably died of fever, but the suggestion of poison was frequently invoked by medieval chroniclers to explain the unexpected.

The early medical practitioners were little interested in theory, but were essentially pragmatic, relying on their own experience and acquired skills. Until the rise of the universities, medicine was considered primarily as a craft, and surgery continued to be so regarded until the fifteenth century. Both could be taught by husband to wife, father to son or daughter, or master to apprentice in the same tradition as other

40 *Wife making
medicine or an invalid
delicacy for her sick
husband*

crafts. Their success depended on personal prestige and acceptance,
though in many towns the sworn masters of the craft were responsible
for seeing that their members met the required standards of skill
and morals. Although records are sparse, women shared the field,
particularly in Italy where they were well accepted.

The average woman's share in healing began with first aid for those
around her. It was an accepted part of a noble lady's education to know
how to deal with the wounds, broken or dislocated bones, and severe
bruises that her menfolk might bring home from wars, tournaments, or
vigorous hunting expeditions. The romances suggest the suitability of
women being skilled in bandaging, ointments, and the cleaning of
wounds, having acquired these skills as part of their education. Sometimes they describe almost miraculous cures helped along by the
remarkably restorative powers of love. The tale of *Aucassin and
Nicolette* inflates such skill almost to parody. Nicolette discovers that

her lover had dislocated his shoulder, so she immediately manipulates it into place, and gathers suitable herbs and grasses to bind tightly around the affected joint with the hem she tore from her shift. Aucassin's cure is immediate. In the German tale of *Parzival* Gawan, having survived a titanic struggle, was healed of his wounds by the skills and salves of a wise old queen and the devoted nursing of her beautiful maidens. On a more realistic plane, the fourteenth century *Livre de Seyntz Medicines* by Earl Henry of Lancaster suggests the kind of home nursing care members of a wealthy household might expect. Such skill was not just a literary figment. Young Sir John Paston, at the end of the fifteenth century wrote to his wife, asking her to send him her special ointment speedily, along with instructions for its application and use. The king's attorney, James Hobart, had an aching knee and, as it was he who was responsible for bringing John and his wife together, her husband admitted he would give up £40 if her plaster could cure him – a major admission for the money-loving Pastons.[2]

Much medical responsibility fell on the abbesses of convents and their delegated infirmarians, and particular skill in this field was usually emphasised. For example, Hildegard of Bingen had served as infirmarian before she became abbess and her life claims that she was renowned for her cures and her skill. Her two books dealing with natural history and human biology and illness were among the most advanced of her time, and suggest the extraordinary pot-pourri of medical knowledge in northern Europe in the twelfth century before the advances of Arabic medicine had become well-known through translation into Latin. Abelard's letter to Héloïse on the management of her convent underlines the importance put on the wise choice of a skilled infirmarian. She needed to have some medical knowledge to properly dispense the medicines with which her infirmary should be stocked, and she, or another nun, should be trained for bloodletting, that frequent medieval cure-all, so that there would be no need to bring a man into the convent. Even in the fifteenth century a religious of the convent of Longchamps was named to the office of barber, i.e., trained in bloodletting, when she was only thirteen and served her convent in this function for nearly forty years.[3] However, by the end of the twelfth century, medicine and surgery became primarily secular occupations. The church's disapproval of medical studies by clerics or religious tended to deny any external role to infirmarians in abbeys or nunneries, while the growth of the towns with their surging population encouraged new forms of medical organisation.

The divisions between doctors, barber-surgeons, empirics, midwives and apothecaries began to sharpen, as each craft endeavoured to entrench its own specialty, although in practice the lines continued to be fairly fluid. Doctors emphasised their theoretical learning and considered themselves the social and professional superiors of any other practitioners. They took pulses, examined urine, made diagnoses, and prescribed medicines, especially laxatives, and clysters (for enemas). They stood aside from surgery, wounds, bloodletting, or any form of manual practice and, except in the case of very important ladies, had nothing to do with childbirth or gynaecology. Barbers were a much more miscellaneous group, ranging from those who merely shaved and cut hair, through the more or less expert bloodletters, who were so much in demand, to those who treated wounds and actual surgeons. Empirics gained their training wholly from experience and were unacquainted with the academic or the theoretical. Their methods might include medicine, massage, and the use of herbs in potions or salves. Midwives were women who assisted in childbirth and might deal with some of the gynaecological difficulties that often accompanied it.

41 *Woman in labour,
aided by midwives*

Finally apothecaries, then as now, were responsible for the making up of medicines and seem to have also prescribed them, though the doctors tried to stamp out the practice.

In trying to discover the place of women in these fields it is interesting to look at the claim put forward by Pierre Dubois in his treatise on *The Recovery of the Holy Land* that women had a particular aptitude for the study of medicine and surgery. He saw such studies as ideal for noble girls, well educated and attractive, who could be married to wealthy and important Saracen princes to encourage their conversion. Such medical and surgical skills would attract the native matrons to them and make them more responsive to such missionary work. Dubois, unlike many of the learned doctors of his day, saw the necessity of practical experience as well as academic knowledge, and wanted girls to instruct in both the theory and practice of medicine and surgery, as well as the knowledge and handicraft required for apothecaries.[4] His ideas are fascinating but they had no influence on his contemporaries.

However, a small percentage of women were busy in all the branches of healing and their existence is attested by the various ordinances promulgated to regulate practitioners. In 1271, when the medical faculty at the university of Paris was just beginning to gain political importance and trying to assert control, the doctors put on record a number of prohibitions. No Jew or Jewess was to practise medicine or surgery while no male or female surgeon, apothecary or herbalist was to engage in any practice beyond the strict limit of their craft. In 1352 they prevailed on the French king to legislate against 'persons of both sexes, women and old wives, monks, rustics, some apothecaries and numerous herbalists', as well as medical students, forbidding them all to prescribe medicines, laxatives, and clysters 'in which lurks peril of death'. Only masters, or those who had a licence from the faculty of medicine at Paris or some other university, could administer such medicines.[5] At the end of the fourteenth century the master surgeons of London swore to the city officials that they would faithfully serve the people in their care, and promised to supervise both men and women undertaking cures or practising the art of surgery, denouncing any faults to the city authorities. By 1421 parliament was petitioning the English king, in much the same terms as the Paris faculty had used, to ban practice by untrained or on-the-job trained surgeons, apothecaries and their apprentices, but also including in the forbidden categories 'a wise woman, lay sister in a convent and midwife'. The petition was approved in 1423, but, as in France, could not be effectively enforced.[6]

Women healers had naturally learned their craft working with another, usually their father or husband, and were often described as being more skilled than men. However, few women knew Latin or could consult the learned medical treatises of the schools, while the academically trained doctors denigrated their practical experience, except in childbirth, in which they did not wish to assist. As the academics urged the possession of a degree as a necessary requirement for licence – and women could not go to universities – they described all women as illegal practitioners, although municipal authorities continued to license women. There were in addition many truly ignorant women who practised at the poor fringes of society and might practise, or be accused of sorcery by their equally ignorant neighbours. Women healers are elusive, but some evidence can be found to suggest their activities and their growing difficulties.

The first woman officially identified as a doctor in northern Europe appears to be Helvidis, thus described when named as a benefactor of a church in northern France *c.* 1136, but thirteenth-century women doctors can be seen in action. Laurette de St-Valery, widow of the lord of Longpré near Amiens, learned medicine so as to help the poor, after her husband had gone on crusade and died in Constantinople in 1205. She gained local acclaim for her charity despite her terrifying appearance, for she was bearded like a man. Sibille Lissiardi was a Parisian matron of the same period who was eulogised in a mid-century miracle story. It described the cure that she, 'as most learned in surgery', worked on Geoffrey la Chapelle, a household official of Philip Augustus. The unfortunate man had suffered from haemorrhoids since his youth and Sibille was believed to have cured him by a combination of skill and piety. She may have been the daughter of a doctor Lissiardus who had been active in Paris twenty years before, and could have learned her skills from him.[7] Even more distinguished was 'Magistra Hersend physica', who was married to the royal apothecary and herself attended Louis IX and went on his crusading expedition to the Holy Land in 1248. At Acre in 1250, Louis granted her a lifetime pension of 12d a day in return for her services. Although these were unspecified, it seems likely that Hersend may have attended Marguerite of Provence when the queen bore her son, John Tristan, at Damietta, and that it was for this that she was rewarded. Hersend appears to have returned to France in 1250, perhaps with the king's brothers. A few years later she and her husband bought a house on the Petit Pont in Paris.[8]

The situation in England during the thirteenth century appears similar to that in France – few women doctors, but usually respected. These include Katherine the surgeon of London, who was the daughter of a surgeon; Ann the Medica, on the staff of St. Leonard's hospital in York; and Agnes in Huntingdonshire, who was acknowledged as a skilful practitioner.[9] Others less competent might find themselves in difficulties. At the turn of the thirteenth century Margery the Leech in the village of Hales kept appearing in the manorial court records, mostly for petty trespass. On one occasion, however, a perhaps disgruntled neighbour threw her into the river, ostensibly to discover whether or not she was a witch, but Margery raised the hue and cry on her own behalf and the court found against her attacker.[10]

Women practitioners continued to be in evidence in France – the Paris tax roll of 1292 listed two women barbers, two midwives, and five *miresses*, who may have been either doctors or surgeons – but the fourteenth century saw them being vigorously pursued by the Paris faculty of medicine and the passage in 1311 of another royal ordinance against unlicensed practitioners encouraged a number of suits against women healers. In 1312 Clarice of Rouen was summoned and accused of illicitly exercising the art of healing. The usual penalty of excommunication was imposed but when she appealed the sentence, her excommunication was not only reaffirmed but her husband was also condemned as an empiric.[11] The terms of the sentence sound alarming – they were to be denounced in all the churches and anyone who associated with them was to suffer the same penalty – but its actual deterrent force was lessened by the wide, and often frivolous, use of this penalty.

The most famous case involving a woman is that of Jacqueline Felicie in 1322, who lodged an appeal against her original condemnation.[12] The Paris faculty of medicine called as their supporting expert John of Padua, a knight who had been surgeon to Philip the Fair, while Jacqueline, obviously a woman of some social standing, as she was normally referred to as 'the noble lady Jacqueline', had eight witnesses to testify to her work. She also produced a well-reasoned petition against her condemnation. The faculty wanted to prove that she had visited patients in Paris and its suburbs, had used the doctor's technique of diagnosis by examining urine, taking the pulse, and touching the body and its members; had agreed to cure such patients 'God willing', and taken money from them; and had administered potions, laxatives and digestives by mouth. Their concern was not with her ability but with whether or not she had been licensed by the chancellor of Paris, or had been approved by a university faculty whether in Paris or elsewhere. In effect, they were asserting university control over the licensing of doctors in contrast to the general practice of municipal or royal licence.

Jacqueline's witnesses were led by John of St-Omer, a tavernkeeper and citizen of Paris, and his wife Matilda, and also included a brother of the Hôtel-Dieu, a sergeant of the Paris court, and three very respectable women. With the exception of one woman who found Jacqueline's prescribed herbal medicine so horrible that she refused to take it, all the other witnesses were her enthusiastic supporters. They emphasised that she refused to take any money from them, unless and until they were cured, and added that they had previously been visited by several male masters of medicine who had done nothing to cure them. The case of Brother Odo of the Hôtel-Dieu was noteworthy in that it involved Jacqueline working with an approved male doctor – a necessary safe-guard for a woman treating a man, particularly a religious. When Odo had been seized by paralysis several physicians, including Master John of the Tower, visited him but were unsuccessful in their treatments. Master John proved willing to work with Jacqueline in treating Brother Odo with not only herbal medicine but hot baths and massages. In what sounds like the fourteenth century equivalent of a sauna the ailing brother was placed on a bed of heated charcoal, covered with fresh herbs, to induce sweating and was then wrapped in fresh cloths and put to bed. This regime restored him to health and Brother Odo proudly testified to having heard men say that Jacqueline was wiser in the art of surgery and medicine than any master physician or surgeon of Paris.

The case took some weeks and the final arguments on both sides were heard on 2 November 1322. Jacqueline's lengthy petition of appeal included several abstruse and not necessarily apposite legal points, but her arguments concerning the place of women in medicine sum up the feminine rationale for their work. She argued that the original sentence did not apply because the statute used applied only to 'halfwits and ignorant fools, uninformed of the art of medicine and totally ignorant of its precepts, usurping its practice', whereas she was exempt because she was instructed in both the art and precepts of medicine. She claimed that it was better and more decent that a wise woman expert in the art, should visit a sick woman and inquire into her hidden troubles, for she could palpate her breasts and stomach, as well as her hands and feet, which a man should not do. A woman might even allow herself to die out of modesty rather than reveal such secrets to men, so that, even if it could be considered evil for a woman to visit, enquire, and cure, it was surely a lesser evil for a wise, discreet, and expert woman to practise in such cases to avoid the greater evil of death. Jacqueline also argued that those well trained in an art, man or woman, could practice it, unless their lack of skill could be proved. She had demonstrated her com-petence and ability and she emphasised her success where many expert masters of the art had failed and therefore requested the lifting of the sentence of excommunication and the fine.

The response from the medical faculty was intransigent. Its proctors argued that the statute applied to all unlicensed practitioners who were illiterate (almost certainly in this case in the technical sense of having no

Latin) and therefore ignorant of the art of medicine. They added that, since women were not allowed to be an advocate or witness in a criminal case, how much more they should be prohibited from giving potions, food, or clysters to the sick when they did not know the theory or art of medicine. It was much easier to kill a man in this way than to lose a law case by ignorance and such killing would be a mortal sin, thus under the jurisdiction of the church and the condemnation by its officials binding. These points of academic superiority made, they airily swept away her other arguments as irrelevant. It was 'unworthy to reply' to her assumption of the need for a wise woman to visit other sick women, and her claims of curing patients when other master physicians had failed were merely 'frivolous'. She could not know the art of medicine because she had not studied it in the schools.

The verdict was immediate and repeated the original sentence of excommunication and fine not only for Jacqueline but also for three other women, one of whom was a Jewess, and two men. The attack was not so much against women as against those outside the university, male or female. Despite the cases of Clarice of Rouen and Jacqueline Felicie there were at least twenty other women doctors who had no trouble with the authorities. The countess of Artois paid Marguerite, a barber, for curing a boy in her household and consistently favoured women apothecaries. Melinecte, a barber at Rouvres, one of the castles of the duke of Burgundy, was called to cure a wound of one of the ducal grooms, while Sarah of St-Gilles, a Jewess of Marseilles, had such a professional reputation that in 1326 a young man apprenticed himself to her for nine months. She was to clothe and feed him and teach him the art of physic and medicine; in return, he promised to give his teacher all he might earn during his apprenticeship. The academics did not even have it all their own way in Paris. In 1374 parlement decided against the chapter of St-Marcel which had forbidden a woman to act as a barber, despite the fact that royal ordinances did not forbid it, provided that her father had taught her the craft, that she knew it well, and had no other resources. The chapter had argued that the royal acts were not applicable in their jurisdiction but parlement ruled against them, ordering the chapter to give the woman back her tools and allow her to practise her trade.[13]

There can be little doubt that women continued to practise and were popular with their patients. Frequent hints suggest that women charged less, took poorer patients, and, in some cases, practised purely for charity. Because of this the municipal government might give them special consideration. In the 1440s the town government of Dijon allowed Martinette, who had offered to take care of the sick poor of the Hospital St-Jacques, to display before her house a representation of a

surgeon treating a poor person. Such a sign board was necessary after a
city ordinance required sworn barbers to treat the poor for the love of
God. Paris was less open-minded than Dijon, for the surgeon Perreta
Betonne was involved in an ongoing struggle with the masters and
sworn members of the guild of surgeons there. In June 1410 she had
been questioned before parlement, both about her ability to read and
the properties of various herbs and had been found deficient. The
provost called another session to allow her cured patients to attend. On
that occasion Perreta argued that she worked 'for God', i.e. without
pay, and that it was unjust to persecute her when many other women
surgeons worked in Paris and were not investigated. A hearing in
January 1411 heard the masters' complaint that she displayed the
banner or sign of a practising surgeon before her house on the Grande
Rue St-Denis, although she had not been examined or approved. On
this occasion the provost confiscated her sign and forbade her to practise
until the matter had been decided in court. She was imprisoned in the
Châtelet without bail, required to deposit her books on surgery in the
provost's office to be examined by several physicians and the provost's
clerk – a statement which again implies that Perreta was only illiterate in
the university sense of the term, i.e. knowing no Latin. The case was
constantly delayed while Perreta boasted of the cures she had achieved
while the doctors wished to deny them, and both sides blamed the other
for holding up the trial. Perreta righteously proclaimed that she was
ready to proceed and insisted that she should be freed to treat the many
sick persons she had under her care who required her visits and
remedies. The last we hear of this long drawn-out dispute is of the
provost postponing the hearing for yet another month but forbidding
her to practise or to erect a sign outside her house meanwhile. Fifty
years later another woman, Guillemette du Luys was a surgeon in the
service of Louis XI.[14]

English women who served as doctors and surgeons have not been as
carefully investigated as the French, but the few visible do not seem to
have been as vigorously pursued in the courts, probably because neither
Oxford nor Cambridge had a powerful faculty of medicine. The
women, like the men, were described as leeches, and two women, Alice
and Felicie are thus identified in the London subsidy roll of 1319. One
paid tax, at a rate that suggests a very comfortable income. Female
leeches were also used by monastic establishments. Around 1313
Christina the physician appears in the accounts of Jarrow priory as
provided with corn, though whether this was a gift or a payment for
services is not specified. At the beginning of the fifteenth century a leech
named Joanna was paid by the infirmarian of Westminster Abbey for
the medicine she provided for two of the monks over a period of three

years. It is possible that this Joanna can be identified with a petition put
to King Henry IV by Joan, widow of William du Lee who had been
killed during Henry's first military expedition to Wales. Joan wanted a
licence to practise physic about the country 'without hindrance or
disturbance from all folk who despise her by reason of her said art'.[15]

Whatever women's difficulties in maintaining their position in other
fields of medicine they ruled almost without question where childbirth
was concerned. Women were always the midwives and the occasional
references to male doctors presiding at births are limited to the labours
of queens or princesses, and even there are rare. Generally male
doctors felt childbirth and gynaecology were beneath their dignity and
might provoke scandal. The whole process of pregnancy and childbirth
was not well understood. Magical practices to ease delivery, such as the
use of precious stones with magical properties or wonder-working
girdles, were grafted to scanty theory, some practical knowledge, and
the pragmatic solutions gradually worked out for recurrent problems.
Under such circumstances it is not surprising that midwives were felt to
be dangerously close to sorcery or occult practice.

The history of the medieval midwife begins with the school of
Salerno and Trotula, and although the early concentration of medical
knowledge at Salerno was real enough, the existence of Trotula is still
hotly debated. Her name is often attached to two early treatises which
were very practical. Whoever the author may have been – whether there

42 *Illustration from a medieval treatise on childbirth showing some
foetal positions*

really was a Trotula who was an expert midwife who advised doctors in Salerno on the complications of childbirth, or whether she should be identified with the legendary, rather lecherous, old Dame Trot encountered in Chaucer or the *Romance of the Rose* – is not important here. The treatises bearing her name with their emphasis on practice not theory, were widely distributed and long lasting – eleven editions appeared in the second half of the sixteenth century. However, the thirteenth-century Gilbert the Englishman, who may have studied at Paris but probably learned his medicine at Salerno and Montpellier, in his *Compendium Medicinae* dealt fully, and rather more ably, with gynaecology.[16] Such works sparked the vernacular, often illustrated, treatises on childbirth, which were disdained by university doctors but were specifically aimed at adequately informing literate women and urging them to share this information with others. In this way they could help those women who were afraid to tell their troubles to a man

43 Although supposedly a picture of the Nativity, with the ox and ass in attendance, the artist has depicted a comfortable scene of upper-class childbirth

'so that one woman may aid another in her illness and not divulge her secrets to such discourteous men'.[17]

There were a considerable number of midwives. About one-third of all the women identified in the comprehensive compilation of medieval French medical practitioners were midwives (44 out of 121 of those known by name). Many French cities and towns equipped themselves with sworn midwives who controlled access to the profession and maintained its standards. The skill was learned by apprenticeship to a practising midwife and the candidate was then examined by a physician chosen by the local administration. They were to be found in towns of all sizes which might encourage midwives to be available for service, either by giving them privileges, such as exemption from taxes or even a pension on retirement, or by the drastic refusal to let them leave town.[18] Among the favourite midwives of the nobility in the fourteenth century, Asseline Alexandre, though practising in Paris, attended the duchess of Burgundy in childbed on three separate occasions in the 1370s and travelled to Dijon or Montbard, while Jeanne la Goutiere was chosen by the duchess of Orleans, and may also have served Queen Isabeau of Bavaria.[19] Although the evidence is not as clear in England there are various references to midwives who seem to have been well paid, for they are among the highly taxed. A fortunate midwife like Margery Cobbe who attended the queen of Edward IV at a successful birth might receive an annual pension – in her case £10.[20]

Midwives needed to be careful of falling foul of the church authorities. They were warned of their duty to baptise newborn babies in acute danger of death – and informed of the formula and method – but had to be careful not to carry their concern too far and deprive the local parish of its right. Agnes la Chauvelle was fined in the beginning of the fifteenth century by an official of the archdeaconry of Chartres for having baptised an infant unnecessarily. Far more to be feared was the suspicion that a midwife was a partner in sorcery. This became more dangerous in the later Middle Ages as accusations of witchcraft became more prevalent. The midwife Perotte du Pouy was accused of being an accomplice of bishop Guichard of Troyes when he was accused of sorcery in 1308, but she and her son were witnesses at the bishop's trial and escaped personal punishment.[21]

Perette of Rouen, a midwife in Paris at the beginning of the fifteenth century got entangled in such a situation. She was the wife of an elderly, perhaps not very successful, minstrel, the mother of fifteen children and a sworn midwife who had practised for over twenty years and had an excellent reputation. Perette was secretly approached by Jehanne, another midwife apparently quite ready to meddle in sorcery, who wanted the body of a stillborn child and was willing to pay handsomely for it. The idea shocked Perette, but Jehanne continued her importunities and attempted to play on her colleague's sympathies by disclosing that a noble had been forced to leave the court on suspicion of leprosy. The unfortunate nobleman had been promised by a so-called doctor that the fat of a stillborn child had magical powers when used to anoint the face. Against her better judgment, and on the promise of a larger sum, Perette finally acted as go-between for Jehanne and Katherine la Petionne, a midwife who had also been approached. Katherine finally acquired the desired corpse which she gave to Perette to be passed to Jehanne. Perette, who seems to have been both stupid and overly obliging, duly delivered the body to Jehanne and the noble who had urged its procural, but was then defrauded of the money she had been promised. By this time, the affair had become so widely known that it came to the attention of the provost and Perette and Katherine found themselves in prison, though the wily Jehanne escaped scotfree. After a harsh imprisonment of seven weeks, the two midwives were tried, condemned to a full day in the pillory and to the loss of their office as midwives. Perette was fortunate in having devoted supporters who valued and trusted her skills and helped her to petition for a royal pardon. In May 1408 Charles VI granted her both the pardon and the right to resume her work as midwife, on the grounds that her punishment had already been considerable and that she was an honest and virtuous woman who had been led astray by honesty and simplicity rather than malice. For the last three years of her life Perette was again free to practise her profession, no doubt along strictly orthodox lines.[22]

Institutional Care
The twelfth and thirteenth centuries unleashed a great rush of dynamism and vitality in many areas of life, but it is not always realised that these two centuries were so extraordinarily fruitful in works of practical charity, such as the foundation of hospitals of all kinds. Medieval charters and wills tend to describe as a hospital any building specially designed to harbour those who needed temporary hospitality. These might include pilgrims, both sick and well, the wandering poor, the impoverished aged or the ill. The two first categories usually took refuge in what is more accurately called a hospice, designed for the temporary lodging of a wayfarer rather than the more specific care of the sick. A clear-cut separation between hospice and hospital is impossible since descriptions were fuzzy, requirements or goals might change, and one would occasionally do the work of the other, but there was a real cleavage between general hospitals, whose patients might get better and leave, and those restricted to lepers, who expected to spend the rest of their lives in the institution. However, both continue to be described as

hospitals and are combined in the numerical totals. It is these hospitals, rather than hospices, that are dealt with here.

Twelfth-century charity encouraged the foundation of all these institutions. It has been estimated that there were only seven hospitals in England before 1066, fourteen more were built before 1100, but the following fifty years saw the foundation of another ninety-two. Fourteenth-century England had some 700 hospitals.[23] Many of these were very small – the favoured number of inmates was often thirteen, in memory of Christ and the apostles – but even so implied a generous number of beds. Since the medieval well-to-do did not normally use such refuges the availability of care for the sick poor compares very favourably with modern provisions. France had a similar flowering, though in not quite so high a ratio as England, given its much larger population. At the beginning of the thirteenth century Jacques de Vitry described with pride the hospitals he knew personally: Paris, Liège, Noyon, Provins, Tournai, and Brussels, as well as the more remote Roncesvalles, Rome and even Constantinople. This list could be augmented in southern France, where Toulouse provided an extraordinary group of charitable institutions in the period just before and after the Albigensian Crusade. A list drawn up in 1246 mentions some fifteen hospitals in the town, and its suburbs, as well as seven leper-houses.[24]

The medieval hospital was encouraged by the growing emphasis on practical charity which can be observed in sermons and wills. The pattern of its organisation was drawn in part from the Hospitaller Order of St. John, which had originally set up hospitals in Outremer for sick and wounded crusaders. When the order was forced to retire from the Holy Land after 1291 it also set up European foundations, primarily for the care of its own brothers but with such sensible rules for the care of the sick that they were often copied by others. Institutional growth ebbed in the fourteenth century as population declined, especially after the Black Death, and leprosy was less common. Many small hospitals with meagre resources became almshouses or disappeared completely. Naturally it was the larger cities which boasted such important hospitals for the sick as the Hôtel-Dieu in Paris or St. Bartholomew's in London. As well as the leper-hospitals and a few houses for those suffering from erysipelas, or St. Anthony's fire as the Middle Ages called it, some other hospitals also were specialised. There were houses of refuge for the blind, the most famous of which was Louis IX's foundation in Paris, nicknamed the Quinze-Vingt for the number of its inhabitants. Ste-Catherine in Paris was particularly devoted to the care of poor or sick women, but its six sisters also had the unpleasant duty of seeking out the corpses of those drowned, dead in prison, or killed in the streets of

Paris, and burying them in the cemetery of the Innocents. Ste-Catherine also served as a short-term lodging for penniless women coming to Paris to seek work, suggesting a thirteenth century equivalent of the YWCA.[25]

Queens and noble ladies were generous founders and benefactors of hospitals of all kinds. Queen Matilda of England may have been inspired by the example of her mother, Queen Margaret of Scotland who had founded a large hospital in Edinburgh, when she set up the forty-bed leper hospital of St. Giles in Holborn and gave it a yearly subsidy of 60s from the Queenshythe, the great London wharf of which she held the income. Matilda may also have had some connection with the leper-hospital of St. James in Westminster, designed to take care of fourteen leprous young girls.[26] In France Countess Jeanne of Flanders founded the hospital of Notre Dame at Lille in 1237 and provided a generous pittance for founder's day of meat, fish and wine for all the sick and the community in charge. She had it specially written into the calendar of the house's missal so that it would not be overlooked.[27] Countess Mahaut of Artois also concerned herself with the building of hospitals in her county, founding one at Hesdin, the site of her favoured residence, in 1321 and another at Bracon in 1327. Her intimate concern with the welfare of the sick can be seen in her insistence at Bracon that they should have a daily dinner of soup as well as a plate of meat or fish, depending on the day, and a serving of the same quality for supper, as well as a separate breakfast. Mahaut also insisted that the sick and women in labour should have whatever they desired when it was possible for the mistress in charge to provide it. This particular requirement, which appears in many twelfth- and thirteenth-century hospital statutes, was adopted from the original rule of the Hospitallers.

Mahaut's accounts include the building contract for the hospital at Hesdin and provide an idea of what such a building looked like. The main hall was to be 100 feet long, 34 feet wide, inside, with columns on each side 16 feet apart. There were to be windows in each of the bays thus created, while the door was to open in the wall on the cloister side. The walls were to be 16 feet high and 3 feet thick, with foundations that were 5 feet deep and 4 feet wide. This main hall, known as the *salle des malades*, was to be surrounded by other buildings such as a chapel, a kitchen, a lying-in chamber for women in childbirth, as well as a chamber with two chimneys for the mistress of the establishment. Her staff included a chaplain, a doctor on a yearly salary, a midwife paid when her services were required, five women servants, and two men.[28] This was obviously run as a secular establishment.

Mahaut's arrangements illustrate the concern of many hospitals for poor mothers giving birth. At Grenoble the hospital would take them in

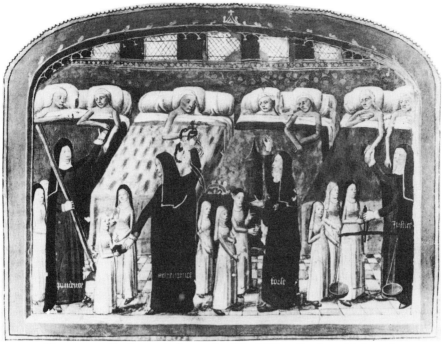

44 The great salle des malades *at the Hôtel-Dieu, Paris, with four sisters representing the virtues necessary for those who cared for the sick – prudence, mercy, strength and justice*

a month before term; at Corbeil, where the hospital had only twenty beds, one room was reserved for childbirth; while at Romans a refuge for twenty-three pregnant women was built on one of the pillars of the bridge over the Isère. The statutes of the various hospitals were equally generous. Poor pregnant women were to be received and given whatever they needed, which at Troyes included thrice-weekly baths. After delivery, the baby was to be baptised by the chaplain and looked after by the sisters. The Hospitaller statutes even specified that cradles should be provided for the babies born to women pilgrims in their hospitals, so that they could lie alone and not be disturbed by an uneasy mother. This laudable practice does not seem to have been transferred to the rest of Europe. Three weeks was the normal hospital stay after childbirth but it was not uncommon for poor mothers to slip away furtively, leaving their babies behind. If the father could not be found, hospital statutes provided that such children should be fed and brought up at the hospital's expense until at least the age of seven. This was also done when the mother died in childbirth.[29]

The intentions were excellent, the results not always satisfactory as a Paris enquiry into the great mortality of infants and children at the Hôtel-Dieu points out. The prioress, drawing on her fifty years of experience in the hospital, described how it harboured a large number of infants – 60 to 70 in normal years, 120 to 140 in one bad plague year. These included not only those whose mothers died or abandoned them in the hospital, but also those infants who were left on the hospital's doorstep. The nuns took them in because of the danger of their being eaten by scavenging pigs or other animals. Because of the scarcity of nursing mothers or wet-nurses the nuns attempted to feed the babies with cow's or goat's milk in an earthenware or tin bottle with an improvised cloth teat the infant could suck. The prioress added that the sisters were so busy with the many grievously ill that they could not devote enough time to the babies or find any place to put them, except among the sick and perhaps ten to twelve to a bed. The unfortunate infants, lacking attention, would do nothing but yell and cry which was 'a marvellous vexation and torment' to the other patients. The children, as well as the infants, suffered from the bad air and the infections and died in great numbers, usually 50 to 60 a year.[30] The prioress was undoubtedly painting a particularly black picture because she was hoping to encourage the foundation of a hospital just for children, but the facts were sufficiently bleak.

Because the major motive behind the lay foundation of hospitals and other charitable institutions was to gain spiritual credit in an age which saw the church as the guardian of the poor, it is not surprising that the men and women who served in them would lead a quasi-religious life. The usual development was for the bishops, whose duty it was to supervise them, to attempt to bring these little communities under a complete religious rule, usually the Augustinian as the most flexible and adapted to such social service. Each institution might have its own variations. Generally speaking, active hospitals developed a community of both men and women (kept strictly apart and with their own prior or prioress) which was totally separated from the hospitalised. On the other hand, the leper-hospitals and some homes for the aged often made their patients members of their community together with the healthy brothers and sisters who cared for them. As well as their religious personnel, hospitals later allowed individuals to buy a preferred place in their house by a settlement made in money, rents, or goods which guaranteed them food and lodging there for life, usually with no responsibilities. Such arrangements, like the equivalent pensions and corrodies in the monastic communities, might encourage a hospital to take on a long-term liability for needed short-term cash, particularly as such pensioners often had exalted ideas of what they required for maintenance and carefully set out their requirements in the original contract. At Chartres in the beginning of the fourteenth century, Isabelle la Chandelière had been received into the hospital for a gift of 100s or five livres, but she had already cost the house more than six livres and gave no service. The social levels of such pensioners continued to rise, for in Paris a century later the sister of the bishop of Meaux was a hospital pensioner.[31]

In order to observe the part women played in these institutions it is usually necessary to turn to the largest establishments whose records are more complete, although some general conditions prevailed almost everywhere. The early communities caring for the sick were more concerned with practicalities than a conventual religious life. They accepted as sisters women who were strong and able, knowledgeable as nurses and able to lift their patients. Occasionally a hospital would specify that no young or pretty woman should be accepted as either a sister or a servant. They did not want women of noble birth, but those who were skilled in manual work and accustomed to it. The development of these hospitals provided another suitable field of activity for women who could not marry and whose social class would not allow them access to the established forms of religious life. However, as the church urged a stricter, more overtly religious rule for those serving in hospitals, they were required to take vows of poverty, chastity and obedience, wear a religious habit, and spend more time on religious exercises. The personnel of a hospital was to be reduced to the minimum necessary, on the grounds that the alms given for the sick should not be used for the upkeep of the healthy, but little attention seems to have been paid to the effect of such restriction on the work of those remaining. The bishops also tried, rather unsuccessfully, to banish those who had bought their places but did not live a religious life. Hospital rules showed various local differences but all included regulations for the religious and rules on the care of the sick, more or less adapted from the original Hospitaller statutes.[32]

Unfortunately the most interesting matter – the actual care of the sick – is the hardest to determine. Bishops had the right to visit all hospitals within their dioceses, but the few surviving visitation reports on hospitals and leper-houses concentrate on such accountable matters as numbers of staff and patients, the physical state of the house and its equipment, and the master's accounts.[33] Given medieval medical knowledge, it is not surprising that their hospitals were primarily places for tending the sick rather than curing them. Regular medical care was rare until early in the fourteenth century and nursing care primarily consisted of keeping the sick fed and clean. For the wretched poor who were their normal patients, even this must have seemed luxury. There was a recognised admission procedure, for the sick person was required to go to confession, then he removed his clothes, which the hospital washed and kept for him until he left, though these goods became its property if he died. A bath followed and then the sick person was put to bed – often shared with two or three others – naked but wearing a nightcap. Hospital regulations specified the provision of sufficient lambswool cloaks and slippers to have one set available for each two patients when they had to go to the communal privies.

One of the most onerous duties of the sisters on duty at nights, in a period when bedpans were unknown, was the obligation to help the sick to the privy. Lamps were rare in the wards and totally absent in the latrine chamber, encouraging frequent accidents among the weak, the confused or the incontinent as they struggled through a shadowy ward to a dimly perceived dark privy. Filth and stench naturally resulted. Even in a hospital as large as the Hôtel-Dieu of Paris it was not until 1487 that a practical-minded royal official, wishing to make the hospital a gift, thought of asking the oldest nuns what would be most useful. They agreed that the greatest need was for a lamp to burn all night in the latrine chamber so that the sick could more easily find the door and not foul the wards.[34] Under such conditions it is not surprising the sisters expended constant labour on the washing of sheets. The statutes enjoined that they should be washed at least once a week, and daily if necessary – an exhausting operation under medieval conditions.

The archives and early accounts of the Hôtel-Dieu of Paris provide a remarkably vivid picture of a specific community of sisters, their duties and the nature of their life. The Hôtel-Dieu claimed to have been founded in the seventh century though little is known of its early days. By the mid-twelfth century it was a busy place responsible to the canons of Notre-Dame. It stood on the southern side of the Parvis Notre-Dame, on the riverbank near the Petit Pont, and its cellars actually opened on the river. The number of chaplains, lay-brothers, and clerks varied from thirty-eight in the thirteenth century to twenty in the fifteenth, aided by some twenty-five paid male servants. During the same period the number of sisters fluctuated between twenty-five and forty, aided by about thirty *filles blanches* or novices who usually entered between the ages of twelve and twenty, and were admitted to the order between eighteen and twenty-five. The canons of Notre-Dame, as responsible for the overview of the house, appointed the master, a priest-brother who was given absolute authority. He occupied himself with external affairs and the work done by the brothers while the prioress, chosen by the canons and the master, had the full direction of the sisters and the female servants, and supervised the care in the hospital. The hospital's door opened on the Parvis Notre-Dame where a sister acted as doorkeeper and examined the sick who sought entry, deciding to which of the four main wards they should be assigned. Men, women, and children were admitted to the hospital without regard to their nationality, only lepers were refused and sent to their own institutions. By the late fifteenth century the staff dealt with a population of 400 to 500 patients and the mortality could be heavy. In 1415 for example, the hospital arranged the burial of 2,077 patients.[35]

The time of many of the sisters was not directly expended on nursing. The general pattern seems to have been that only two or three sisters, and perhaps a couple of maid servants, were actually present at any one time in the wards. However, the duties of the religious included washing the clothes taken from the sick when they arrived and storing them, the massive task of laundering the sheets and the provision of the necessary supplies for the task, the apothecary work, as well as the senior positions of head of service, sub-prioress, and prioress. These offices went by length of service and it would normally take a sister thirty or forty years to rise to an administrative position. The prioress wielded considerable power. She assigned the sisters to whatever

45 The busy life of the Hôtel-Dieu is delineated in the reception of a fille blanche *at one door, the portress greeting a sick man on a stretcher at another, while on the upper gallery the nuns hang out the laundered sheets*

service she chose, gave them permissions for exemptions from the rule, and was responsible for their corporal punishment if they broke it. Apart from supervising the halls which housed the sick and bearing final responsibility for their care, she also managed the linen supply. This was no easy matter: 1,500 sheets were in constant use, and more than 2,000 ells of new cloth had to be bought each year, usually at the great Paris fair of Lendit, to replace the worn out linen. Despite the full-time efforts of some four sisters who mended sheets in service some 500 to 700 new ones had to be made up each year to maintain an adequate supply.

Work in the sheet laundry was constant, exhausting, and occasionally hazardous. The laundry was located in the hospital cellars where they opened on the Seine. During cold winters the sisters might have to break up the ice, in summer their arm of the Seine might dry up, and in time of flood the situation became so dangerous that the hospital had to pay a boatman to patrol the area to retrieve the sheets that were swept away or the religious who fell in.[36] In good weather the sheets could be dried on the galleries or outside, but in winter they were hung in the chamber reserved for sheets or in the women's ward, the Salle Neuve, where there was a wheel supporting a drying rack. Although the sisters took the three vows and lived according to a religious rule their days were so filled with labour that their attendance at religious exercises was limited to matins, high mass, and vespers. The sisters ate their two meals a day together in their own refectory. Like the brothers they were allowed meat three days a week and on major feast days, but they only received half as much wine. The life was a hard one, but the religious averaged twenty-five years of service, and some spent over fifty.[37]

Occasionally it is possible to catch a glimpse of one of these sisters, not as a shadowy figure struggling to help some patient in the wards or taking her turn in the everlasting washing of sheets, but as a remarkably lively human-being. In 1428 Sister Perronelle de Vertjus was sent out from the Hôtel-Dieu to nurse the wife of Me Jehan Bureau, an official of the Châtelet. It was obviously a difficult childbirth for the mother died, but during Sister Perronelle's stay in the household she enjoyed the opportunity to gossip scandalously with the midwife and the official's clerk. She told them that Me Jehan's mother had not always been so great a lady but had been forced to go out to earn a daily wage, carrying her small children on a tray on her head, as was then the custom. Somewhere, she hinted, they had found a cask full of gold and silver and other valuables. She then went on to suggest that Me Jehan and his brothers were all ribalds who had wanted to force their wives to submit to them before marriage. Sister Perronelle's tongue had wagged ill-advisedly about people of considerable social standing. The affronted official, his mother and two of her other children came to the master of the Hôtel-Dieu to complain. In an effort to appease them, Sister Perronelle was summoned to chapter to answer for her injudicious remarks. When it was proved that she was indeed guilty she was required to beg pardon of the mother and her children and ask for mercy. This was granted, but the chapter insisted on its own punishment. Perronelle was not to be allowed out of the hospital for a year, and should do penance every Friday for a month, eating her bread and water on the ground. By the second week the high-tempered nun had again become irrepressible, refusing her penance, calling the other sisters names, and refusing to obey the chapter. Finally the canons of Notre-Dame, as the final authority, condemned her to the hospital's prison cell on bread and water. A week was sufficient to convince Perronelle that repentance was the easier choice, and she was freed.[38] It would be tempting to know if this unhappy experience was enough to bridle what was undoubtedly a very garrulous tongue.

Although some institutions in England had almost as long a history as the Hôtel-Dieu none rivalled it in size or hospital use. St. Leonard's York was founded in the tenth century as St. Peter's, and became one of the great English hospitals with a community of brothers and sisters under the Augustinian rule. It had accommodation for just over 200 poor sick, but there were only eight regular sisters, though in the thirteenth century it had a woman doctor on staff. One sister was designated to care for the babies and delicate children for whose benefit they kept two cows. There was a complement of chaplains and a surprising group of thirty choristers. With these, and twenty-three orphan boys, they also developed a school and had two school masters.[39] St. Bartholomew's in London, like the Paris Hôtel-Dieu, was a medieval hospital which has continued to function in the present. It was founded by Rahere, a royal clerk of Henry I, who became very ill while on pilgrimage to Rome and vowed to build a hospital for the poor of London if he survived. St. Bartholomew appeared to him in a vision and gave him explicit directions for a hospital at Smithfield. Rahere's original foundation was both a hospital for the poor and an Austinian priory, but within ten years the two had been separated and the warden of the hospital became an independent official. The staff consisted of the master, four brothers, and four sisters. Like the French hospitals it also included a maternity ward and made special provisions for the children whose mothers died in childbirth. The early accounts of its history lean heavily on legends, describing miraculous cures at St. Bartholomew's shrine, but refer only incidentally to the fact that the institution was large, well-run, and provided generous amounts of food and drink for its inmates. The early historian of the house was more interested in divine intervention than human treatment, so we know little about the means used, although there are some hints of practical therapy.[40]

Leper-hospitals were also prominent among these twelfth- and thirteenth-century foundations and women were often involved as foundresses, patrons, and in caring for the afflicted. As well as royal and noble foundations, towns also set up their own establishments, which were restricted to sufferers from the immediate locality and were supported by the town itself. They varied in size, but many were quite small, perhaps ten to twelve residents, but their size might fluctuate according to the prevalence of the disease. Because of the permanent nature of entry to a leper-hospital both men and women lepers were incorporated into the religious community, in which the healthy were responsible for the administration but the sick were equally brothers and sisters. Some women devoted themselves to work in leper-houses, a task regarded as the most Christ-like of all works of charity, and took temporary vows. They took care of the female lepers, but did not eat with them and were enjoined not to make the lepers' beds until they had left the room. Other women gave some care to lepers while remaining in their own homes in a pattern suggestive of a modern women's auxiliary.[41]

Although charity was generally shown to lepers, local spasms of terror might still rack a district and lead to real persecution. This was true of Périgueux in 1320–21 when there was a sudden surge of leprosy cases. Lepers were systematically hunted out, their money and goods confiscated, and they were placed in various leper-hospitals or even the city prison. As the epidemic continued for the second year many lepers were burned, but the women lepers were 'immured'. It is hard to judge from the city accounts, which give the details of this expenditure, whether this merely meant that they were completely isolated in some sort of fortress, or, more cruelly, were starved to death instead of burnt. The formula of expenses suggests the latter, as the costs were given to have them guarded and nourished *before* they were immured. In any case, all their goods were confiscated and sold for the benefit of the commune. Unfortunately Périgueux was not an isolated example for throughout France during the years around 1320 general panic and hostility towards lepers replaced the earlier charitable zeal and service. The walling-up of lepers was even enjoined by an ordinance of King Charles IV in 1322.[42]

The late fourteenth century displayed a greater knowledge of leprosy and a less panic-stricken approach to those who suffered from it. Guy de Chauliac, the French doctor who wrote the accepted text on surgery and died in 1368, carefully described seven certain symptoms of leprosy and sixteen equivocal ones. He insisted on the need to have a doctor examine, carefully, all suspected cases so as to catch true lepers but to avoid incarcerating the healthy. In populous regions where there were several leper-houses a certain social stratification often ruled, occasionally bent by the presentation of a large gift. By this time most leper-houses of any size employed paid servants, mostly female, for the care of both men and women lepers. They were paid and lodged, and got the same food as the lepers. Occasionally, as at St-Omer in 1445, they were given a pay raise with the explanation that many people held this form of service in horror.[43] No real medical care was attempted, as no cure was known, but, given the nature of the disease, the sufferers could be well-lodged and reasonably comfortable. The leper-house of Grand-Val at Arras was spacious with good individual provision for each leper, as well as gardens and fields in which to work and rest. The leper house at Falaise followed the usual pattern. It was the responsibility of the town and was officially restricted to the leprous of its three parishes, although they occasionally accepted outsiders when there was space. It was a mixed house and the children born there were tended by

*46 A woman leper
with her warning bell*

a healthy person, and kept until it could be discovered if they were healthy or infected. It is pleasant to discover that they found some amusement for themselves, for the accounts mention frequent repairs to the chapel roof since the sick played handbail against its wall and often hit the roof, breaking its shingles.[44]

Whatever their deficiencies in providing effective health care the medieval hospitals and leper-houses were the fruit of a truly charitable desire to lessen to some degree the suffering of the sick and the afflicted. They attracted the patronage and generosity of many lay people from the rich to the relatively poor. They provided an essential service to the society of their day and, difficult though it is to quantify the number of women who served as sisters and servants within the many institutions, large and small, they certainly provided another, less visible avenue for women's energies and abilities. Although many of these hospital workers were officially regarded as religious they had little in common with the aristocratic Benedictines or the contemplative Clarisses. They were too closely engaged in heavy manual work to derive any social status from their occupation, but the administration of even a small hospital's female community must have benefited from the talents of medieval townswomen, while the prioress of the Hôtel-Dieu of Paris was of necessity a rather burdened executive. Unsung, and often overlooked, such women filled an inglorious but necessary human function in medieval society.

CHAPTER NINE

Women on the Fringe

Women in medieval life were naturally part of the careful ranking of classes and occupations so characteristic of that hierarchical and tightly ordered society. Such a system had little tolerance for those who did not fit easily into its categories or rebelled against its orthodoxies, whether religious or political. The laws of medieval society were made and administered by men who generally considered women not only subordinate and inferior, but also threatening, since it was felt that they easily overstepped the bounds of reason. Thus, these men were more inclined to punish feminine misdeeds as likely to upset public order, and found it easy to cut them off from society when they transgressed its rules. There were different levels of severity in this approach. Prostitutes, for example, were considered as practising a trade that strictly speaking should have no place in Christian society. Nevertheless, they were tolerated as a necessary evil and could be reintegrated into the general community when they gave up their way of life. Female felons were treated as particularly dangerous when their crimes were connected with sexual passion or sorcery which could undermine the accepted order. Heretics automatically put themselves outside the boundaries of the Christian community as the ecclesiastical authorities defined it, and heretical women were regarded with particular suspicion. Since all these types of women offended against society's laws it is the court records of church or state which often reveal beneath their stereotyped formulas vivid glimpses of human chicanery or tragedy.

Prostitution seems to be a usual concomitant of civilisation. In the Roman world it was always regarded as a necessary evil creating an impassable gulf between the good woman and the bad. The ambivalence of so much Christian teaching about women can also be observed in its attitude towards prostitutes. Canon lawyers inherited much of the Roman belief and established a number of restrictions affecting prostitutes. They could not accuse others of crimes, were forbidden to inherit property, and had to use a representative to answer any charges against them. Despite the continuing denunciation of sex and of women who sold their bodies, the moralists gradually came to admit that prostitutes were entitled to keep the money made in their illicit trade. In an early

thirteenth-century manual for confessors, Thomas of Chobham devoted four chapters of an interesting casuistical exercise to the contemporary clerical understanding of prostitutes and their rights. He argued
that prostitutes provide a form of labour, like other mercenaries, in
hiring out their bodies. By the standards of secular justice they do no
evil in receiving its price. Therefore, such a woman has the right to
keep her earnings even if she repents of her deeds, but should then use
them for alms. Thomas echoed the usual clerical disapproval of sexual
pleasure, arguing that if the prostitute derives pleasure from her trade
there is no labour and '"the profit is as shameful as the act"'. Thomas
also took aim at any wiles practised by prostitutes to suggest greater
beauty and seductiveness than they actually possessed, for this deceived
their clients who paid far more than they would have done if they had
seen them as they truly were. He felt that in such a case the prostitute
was only entitled to keep the minimum, and optimistically suggested
she should surrender the rest to the client she had deceived, or at least to
the church or in alms.[1]

*47 Lust is here
portrayed as a
fashionably dressed
woman riding a ram
and admiring herself
in a mirror. In the
background are David
and Bathsheba in her
bath as examples of
the vice*

However there was another strong current of opinion opposed to this utilitarian but negative view. The gospel tradition, based on the conversion of the Magdalene and Christ's approval of her action, was further reinforced by the general medieval identification of Mary Magdalene with Mary of Bethany, the sister of Martha and Lazarus. The two sisters were believed to have landed at Les-Saintes-Maries in the Camargue and both Vézelay and St-Maximin laid claim to the Magdalene's relics, becoming popular pilgrimage spots. This belief in the possible sanctity of the converted harlot was further enhanced by popular saints' legends, such as that of the dramatic conversion and ascetic desert existence of St. Mary the Egyptian, echoes of which appear in many later miracle stories. From this point of view the prostitute could be seen as present temptress and sinner, but also as possible convert and saint. Some preachers made vigorous efforts in this direction. In the early twelfth century Henry the Monk among his other demands for drastic reform, exhorted his followers to marry converted prostitutes. In the 1190s Fulk of Neuilly, another charismatic preacher, offered prostitutes two ways to change their lives, depending on their fervour. Jacques de Vitry wrote that some were so moved by his words that they abandoned their debauchery, cut off their hair, and entered the Cistercian convent of St-Antoine near Paris, which Fulk had founded to shelter them. Those who felt that religious life was more than they should wisely aspire to were given dowries raised from public contributions and found legitimate husbands. The persuasive Fulk managed to collect for this purpose more than 1,000 livres from the bourgeois of Paris and even the impecunious scholars gave 250 livres.[2] It sounds as if Fulk's sermons had touched a number of guilty consciences.

Since Paris was a continuing magnet for both trade and study, it had a large floating population and a great number of prostitutes. These women were allowed a marginal position in the community. Thus they were allowed to offer candles at Saturday vespers but not to bring their offerings to the altar. When they suggested giving a 'noble window' to the unfinished Notre Dame cathedral, the embarrassed bishop refused, 'fearing he would seem to approve the life if he accepted the money'.[3] William of Auvergne, bishop of Paris in the early thirteenth century, founded the Filles-Dieu, a hospice for repentant prostitutes. There they could find shelter, and promised to observe continence until they had earned enough money from legitimate employment to marry. The original foundation was along the road to St-Denis, outside the city gate and near the large leper-hospital of St-Lazare. The house attracted many royal and ecclesiastical gifts of lands and privileges, especially from Louis IX, who added to its buildings and annual revenues as well as permitting it a tap at the fountain of St-Ladre. The king and the bishop shared the right to propose alternatively new candidates to fill the empty places. At the peak of its importance the Filles-Dieu harboured a population of 260 women but began to decline in the fourteenth century. Entry became more difficult as revenues dropped and places were restricted, even though many inhabitants worked as spinners or embroiderers of purses. The Black Death took two-thirds of its members, a devastating blow from which the house never really recovered.[4]

By the fifteenth century Christine de Pizan envisaged repentant prostitutes being dealt with by the charity of the lay community. She argued strongly that such women were not so abominable that they could not be converted, for there was no greater charity than to rescue such a sinner. Given her practical outlook, she saw their salvation coming mainly through self-help and had useful advice for those who might wish to mend their ways. She suggested that a penitent prostitute should leave her old haunts and fancy clothes, live simply and soberly in a small chamber on a good street. There she would have honest neighbours and could take licit employment, though the tasks she envisaged, such as scullion in a great household or watching the sick, were not appealing.[5]

There was a regular structure of prostitution in almost all cities, though it was differently handled in France and England. In France a king of ribalds, of status roughly equivalent to a crossbowman, had a number of miscellaneous duties at the royal court by 1214. By the end of the fourteenth century he was taking a fee of 2s a week from prostitutes who followed the royal armies and had the right to a fee of 5s a year from the Paris prostitutes. In token of this payment he marked with his signet the side of the hoods of those who had paid, and confiscated the hoods of those who had not.[6]

The insistence by royal and civic officials on the regulation of prostitutes arose from two distinct motives. Prostitution was felt to be a male necessity, and was often claimed as a safeguard for decent wives and daughters, but officials also wanted a share in its profits, as well as repressing the petty thievery and violent outbreaks common where prostitutes worked. Towns and cities named special streets where prostitutes could exercise their trade, but such regulations only touched the most obvious brothels. There were always individuals who worked the streets and taverns, as well as small establishments run by a 'maquerelle', a common slang title for a procuress. She might run two or three women under the cover of a legitimate workshop. Naturally these independents were far more difficult to control than the easily recognisable public brothels. French communities often constructed public houses with public funds. They were run by an 'abbess', who recruited the girls, enforced the rules, and saw to it that the inmates had some protection. Some of these establishments were remarkably large and suggest the high percentage of prostitutes in the population. In Dijon, for example, where the population was less than 10,000 in the fifteenth century, despite its importance as the capital of the duchy of Burgundy, there appear to have been more than 100 prostitutes. Some worked in its public house, a large establishment with three sets of buildings with interior galleries centred around a garden; others could be found in the seven public baths, or stews as bath-houses were often called. These establishments had become almost synonymous with brothels by the late Middle Ages so that in the 1440s a bath-house keeper of Avignon felt the need to advertise specially that he had built new baths solely for honest women. They had their own entrance in front of the house of the respectable beadle of the schools, where women could be decently received – and at a good price too.[7]

From the middle of the thirteenth century London issued and reissued a series of regulations insisting that all prostitutes should be housed either in Cock Lane, Smithfield or in the much larger Southwark stews across the Thames on Bankside. During the Middle Ages Southwark was in the hands of the bishop of Winchester. It was his London seat and he had a valuable collection of liberties and privileges in the borough. The supervision of the Southwark stews and the collection of their profits were in the hands of the bishop's estate staff, who seem to have found nothing incongruous in their activity. By the fifteenth century the Southwark stews had recorded the customs in use. These fixed the amount of rent to be charged each woman keeping a chamber there, provided for weekly inspection of all the quarters by the estate officials, and suggested the enquiries that should be made of stew-holders, the prostitutes themselves, and even of the officials, who might be tempted to extortion. The document also set the varying fines, many quite large, to be levied on all the listed infractions.[8]

Occasionally a theologian had a tenderer conscience about prostitutes. When Clement V established the papal curia at Avignon it was customary for the pope's marshal to raise a tax on prostitutes, but at the Council of Vienne in 1311 William Durand demanded the abrogation of this custom. He insisted that public prostitutes should not be established near the chambers of the curia, nor the residences of prelates, nor should the pope's marshal or his officers receive gifts or bribes from prostitutes or their procurers. More than a century later the prohibition against clerics entering the notorious baths of the Pont Trocat in Avignon was still being repeated, the penalty by this time being excommunication and a fine of 10 to 20 marks. On their side, the

Avignonese prostitutes also felt the need to band together. When Queen Joanna of Naples was in Avignon in the mid-fourteenth century she gave permission for the prostitutes to have their own association and statutes. These included a requirement for each member to wear a red braid on her shoulder.[9]

Almost all regulations concerning prostitutes insisted on their wearing a special mark on their clothing and tried to forbid them jewels, furs, and silks, as well as confining them to a particular part of town. The women seem to have paid little attention to these sumptuary regulations and occasionally carried their opposition to the highest level. In 1389 the prostitutes of the Toulouse brothel known as the Grande Abbaye felt aggrieved by the city officials' regulation that they had to wear white hoods and ribbons as distinguishing marks. They petitioned the king for the right to dress as they pleased, and royal permission was granted them to wear clothes and hoods of any desired colour, but still insisted on an identifying armband of a different colour. The various sumptuary regulations must have been frequently flouted for they were constantly repeated, often calling for fines and the confiscation of clothing and ornaments which the city fathers declared should be reserved for honest women. London passed such an ordinance in 1351 objecting to prostitutes being clad 'in the manner and dress of good and noble dames and damsels of the realm in unreasonable manner', and insisted they should

48 A prostitute beckoning to a travelling merchant

have only an unlined hood of striped cloth. The ordinance was repeated in 1382, after the upheaval of the Peasants' Revolt. Where London was satisfied to ban furs and silks generally the Avignonese officials went into great detail in their prohibitions. They forbade furred mantles, especially if adorned with vair or fine cloth; bonnets with gold, silver, or silk; rings of gold or silver; or chaplets of amber, coral, crystal or silver. In addition to confiscation of the article, the fine each time was to be 50 livres. In 1459 the provost of Paris confiscated from an elegant, and perhaps pious, prostitute not only a shoulder cape of satin furred with miniver and a silver-gilt belt but also a coral rosary with a silver *agnus dei* and a book of hours with a silver clasp, because these were the marks of an honest woman.[10] It is obvious that prostitutes could profit from their trade and sport the current fashions – no doubt to the fury of more honest and less wealthy matrons.

Other regulations for prostitutes clearly dealt with sanitary precautions and tried to regulate hours. The Southwark collection of customs, provides the fullest account. Hours on religious feast days were to be minimal and not at the time of church services. As well the women were not to occupy their chambers at night during sessions of parliament, under pain of a fine of 6s 8d every time. Stewholders were forbidden to keep single women against their will, to accept married women or religious, the pregnant, or those who had signs of the 'burning sickness'. They should not charge the women more than 14d a week for their chamber, should not force them to eat at the stew, nor could they sell any victuals. The prostitutes were not to drag a man in by his hood or gown, but should let him choose freely whether to enter or not, nor could they take his money and then refuse to lie with him. They were not allowed to have a paramour of their own or, rather surprisingly, to wear an apron. Only a man, or a husband and wife could run a stew. If a single woman kept her own establishment, she broke the custom of the manor and was to be fined 20s at every court, until the matter was rectified.[11]

Prostitution flourished in the cities and larger towns, where it can be easily observed because it was more organised, but there can be little doubt that the rural areas and villages also had their share of less visible prostitutes. Generally the parish priest would be considered responsible for guarding the behaviour of his parishioners – a vain hope if many were like the lecherous parish priest of Montaillou.[12] He could summon the owners of houses inhabited by known prostitutes to order their expulsion and had the power, if the owners disobeyed, of excommunicating them. Rural prostitutes could be aggressive, for in 1387 at Châteauneuf-Calcernier they took over the church pew of the local royal official. The residents were so appalled by this profanation that they

broke up the pew and the commune was required to build the official a
new one at their own expense. Towns and villages more commonly
restricted prostitutes or women vagabonds by forbidding them to stay
in a location for more than one night and by laying an even heavier fine
on anyone who kept such a woman over a longer time.[13]

The most usual reasons for women becoming prostitutes were
poverty and male violence. The poor widow with small children, the
servant or chambermaid used as a concubine by her master and then
discarded, the alien unable to get legitimate work; all had no money and
no skills. Prostitution was almost the only way open to make a living,
and was by far the easiest and most profitable if a woman was young and
good looking. Rape was frequent, particularly of the poor and ill-
protected, who had neither strength nor influence. In south-east France
groups of young men often practised sexual violence – what would now
be called gang rape – on lower-class women between fifteen and thirty,
either innocent girls or young wives whose husbands were temporarily
absent. In those communities this was considered acceptable amusement for the young men who felt frustrated by their inability to marry
before they were sufficiently established, and treated these women as
legitimate prey. Their victims, in a society which put an extraordinary
premium on the chastity of women, found themselves generally rejected and were easily recruited by a maquerelle. Lawless English gangs
frequently turned to rape, and were particularly inclined to the abduction and rape of a young woman of some wealth since often such a deed
could be turned into a marriage after the fact and the heiress and her
money safely acquired. Many Flemings were prostitutes in the cities of
France and England, having emigrated and found no employment. In
Dijon a procuress was hauled before the court on charges of spying,
since she had Flemish girls in her house and Burgundy was at war with
Flanders. There were frequent complaints of a Flemish monopoly in
the Southwark stews and in 1381, during the Peasants' Revolt, the
insurgents actually demolished a stew there.[14]

When prostitutes passed thirty they were likely to be less in demand.
If they had been careful to avoid theft and brawling, both of which were
heavily punished, they might return to respectable society. There were
the houses of repentance, such as the Filles-Dieu, but many prostitutes
appeared to have saved their earnings and were able to provide a dowry
sufficient to encourage marriage with legitimate tradesmen. Some
professional corporations discouraged such unions, for the butchers of
Paris threatened any member who married a prostitute without the
authority of the masters or the *jurés* with complete exclusion from the
established market and banishment to a stall on the Petit Pont.[15]
Despite some prejudice, it appears that prostitutes, although officially

deplored by the moralists, were still considered a normal and integral part of the social fabric and could re-establish themselves after abandoning their illicit trade.

The major problem for a prostitute was the danger of running foul of the law by dabbling in theft, violence, or sorcery. The 1391 case of Marian du Pont suggests the temptations and dangers. Marian was first a servant in Paris and then a prostitute and robbed both her masters and her customers. She took a small silver girdle from the house of Me Marcal Saumur when she spent one night with him. On a trip to Rouen she took a cup from a local man when she spent one night with him, and even managed to steal a large piece of gold from a pig merchant while he was absorbed in the purpose for which he had hired her. Theft was a major crime if prostitution was not, and the unfortunate Marian was condemned to be buried alive.[16] Procurers might find themselves in court if their practices became flagrant, although the sexual charge was usually prompted by other offences as well. Elizabeth Moring, for example, was brought before the mayor, aldermen, and sheriffs of London in July 1385 on the charge of being a procuress and common harlot. Elizabeth had pretended to follow the craft of embroidery and had retained one Johanna and several other women to serve as her apprentices. Instead of teaching them embroidery she urged them 'to live a lewd life and to consort with friars, chaplains, and all other such men as desired to have their company'. Elizabeth used to provide space in her own house for this purpose, hiring her girls out at a sum she and the man decided on and which Elizabeth kept for herself, and also sending them out on the same errand. One night in May Johanna was dispatched with a lantern to light a certain chaplain to his chamber, Elizabeth having arranged with him that Johanna would spend the night with him. The serving woman claimed she knew nothing of the arrangement, but she did spend the night. When she returned in the morning her mistress was eager to know what she had received for her trouble. As she had gotten nothing she was scolded and forced to go back the following night and take whatever she could lay her hands on. On the second occasion she crept out early in the morning, removing the chaplain's breviary while he slept, and giving it to Elizabeth who pledged it for 8d.

This particular occurrence is the only charge detailed but the court record accuses Elizabeth of having received many gains from Johanna and her other women by acting in the same way. Elizabeth pleaded not guilty and was imprisoned for a day until she could be tried by a jury. The jury found her guilty as a common harlot and procuress who was a scandal and peril to the city. As a warning to other women she was condemned to the pillory at Cornhill for an hour, with the reason for her punishment being publicly proclaimed, and then she was to be taken to the city gate and made to forswear the city. She was enjoined never to enter London again on pain of three years' imprisonment and punishment by pillory as often as it pleased the current mayor and aldermen.[17] Reading the record it would appear that Elizabeth's original mistake was to use a decent craft and proper apprenticeship agreement as a cloak for prostitution, for such a misuse threatened the commercial propriety of the city's trades, and then to involve her apprentices in thefts. Although denounced as a harlot and a procuress, it was almost certainly these two other elements which accounted for the harshness of her sentence.

Prostitution leads almost inevitably into the question of female felony and the particular situation of women before the secular courts where crimes were tried. Much of our specific information about women and crime comes from the assorted court records which become much more complete from the thirteenth century on. In an era when violence of all kinds was prevalent throughout society and poverty endemic in the lower classes, the criminal record reflects what was going on. Both petty delinquency, usually inspired by poverty, and crimes of violence were frequent. However, it is notable that far fewer female than male criminals appear in the records. From the partial quantitative studies that have lately been done, the ratio of indictments might be as low as one woman to nine men.[18] In many of the cases where women were charged it was frequently as instigator or accomplice, and when they were involved in personal crimes of violence it was usually towards husbands or children. It must be remembered that a wife could suffer from a brutal spouse, for it was always the husband's privilege to beat his wife, although he was not supposed to inflict death or permanent damage. His right was so generally recognised in medieval society that the facts might be covered up when he went too far. In the early fifteenth century a Hampshire man assaulted his wife with a staff, struck her in the stomach and chest, then kicked her, causing such internal injuries that she later died. The jury which heard the case acquitted him and reported that the unfortunate wife had died of the plague.[19]

The position of a woman before the secular courts depended, as in so many other aspects of her life, on her marital status as well as the local law. Normally a single woman of full age or a widow could answer for herself, but a married woman, officially under the jurisdiction of her husband, had to have his assistance or at least authorisation. In some cases this restriction could be turned to her advantage, for she could escape punishment if the misdeeds proved to be his. There is the rather unusual case of Bernarde, the widow of the usurer Pierre de

Chansenor, who was herself accused in 1330 of complicity in usury. She had continued after his death to take the profit on usurious contracts he had made but was absolved on the grounds that she could not be prosecuted for a crime imputed to her husband. Nevertheless, it is more than likely that she knew what her husband was doing and may even have been an accomplice. At a lower level of trade, the London bakers' wives managed to dissociate themselves from their husbands' wrong-doing and punishment.[20]

In the early days, women, like men, could be submitted to trial by fire, water, or red-hot iron to prove their innocence, but they were not exposed to trial by battle. On the Continent women, like men, were tortured as part of the legal process, but with the cold comfort that if they were mutilated and later proved innocent, they could claim compensation. The penalties inflicted on women varied somewhat from those for men. At the lowest level of minor civic disturbance or infraction of trading regulations, a woman was usually punished by some kind of public physical shame, especially if she could not, or her husband would not, pay the required fine. In northern France there was a special humiliation imposed on quarrelsome and over-talkative women. Clothed only in their shift, they were required to carry around their neck a stone of considerable weight while walking around the church on Sunday in presence of the whole congregation. In Verdun in the fourteenth century the penalty could be extended to several Sundays, depending on how serious the quarrel had been and whether the woman had also assaulted physically the one she insulted.[21] England favoured the cucking stool for the quarrelsome woman, a kind of chair in which the guilty one could be tied and displayed in a public place, but a London prostitute who caused an uproar in the street was immediately put in prison. Beatings were common for accomplices in minor cases, and both Paris and London used the pillory, set up in a central location, to increase the guilty person's exposure to public ridicule and even attack. This punishment was so common that London even had a pillory known as the 'thewe' reserved exclusively for women.

It has already been pointed out that breach of the trading regulations, especially in regard to the sale of foodstuffs, could lead to a period in the pillory for women offenders, but it also served as a punishment for a variety of crimes. A trial in London in 1373 sent Alice de Salesbury, described as a beggar, to the pillory for an hour because the previous Sunday she had abducted the daughter of a grocer and then stripped her of her clothing. She hoped to make the girl unrecognisable by her family and thus force her to go begging with her abductor who would profit thereby.[22]

The punishments for the more serious crimes seem to have been

49 A woman shares the stocks with a cleric

applied equally to men and women. A first theft might be punished by
the loss of an ear, if the amount stolen was not too great, but hanging
was common for frequent thievery or large amounts. Women were
hanged for their crimes all during this period in England but in France
in the thirteenth and fourteenth centuries they were more usually
condemned to be buried alive, apparently for fear that the corpses,
which were always left on the gallows as a horrid example, might be
profaned. By the end of the fourteenth century, however, women were
also hanged. Burning was reserved for the most serious offences, such
as treason, sorcery, and infanticide, though it was considered petty
treason for a wife to kill her husband, her natural lord, and it was thus
punishable by burning. Women could attempt to escape the death
penalty by claiming pregnancy, since a pregnant woman could not be
executed until after the birth of her child. This was the somewhat more
limited escape route for women that claim of benefit of clergy was for
men. Occasionally a king might grant a pardon because of pregnancy,
and sometimes banishment was substituted for execution, but there
seems little evidence that any greater compassion was exercised toward
women criminals than towards men.[23]

The range of crimes in which a woman might be involved was fairly
large, but the usual female felony was theft. Women favoured stealing
small portable objects which could be easily disposed of, since much
petty theft was due to economic misery. When women in rural districts
were involved in the theft of livestock they usually worked with a male
accomplice. The lowest class woman often suffered unjustly because it
was so easy to accuse a female servant of theft. When Sir Nicholas de
Babutz, a Teutonic Knight, fell seriously ill in a London inn in 1357 he
was forced to keep to his bed for some time and hid his money, a sizeable
sum of 400 gold écus, in his bedstraw for safety. The first day he rose

from his bed and ventured out of his chamber his money was stolen. He made public complaint in court, believing that the domestic servants and the old woman who had nursed him during his illness were responsible, so they were arrested and put in prison. The court suggested that the knight's own servant and that of his companion should also be imprisoned under the same suspicion. Sir Nicholas agreed but his companion did not. The jury examined the local servants and the old woman and found them guiltless but instead proved the theft against Sir Nicholas's travelling companion. He was then imprisoned, rather to the dismay of his friend who had not expected such a result. Sometimes a woman thief like Desiderata de Toryntone was caught red-handed. In 1337 she stole thirty silver dishes and twenty-four salt-cellars, worth some £40, from John Baret, (the property of his mistress, Lady Alice de Lisle), while John was staying in the town house of the bishop of Salisbury. Fourteen of the dishes and twelve of the salt-cellars were found in Desiderata's possession – she had probably succeeded in disposing of the others – and she was condemned to be hanged.[24]

Women occasionally indulged in what would now be called white-collar crime. They rarely counterfeited documents, a favourite clerical failing, since women normally had neither the opportunity nor the skill for this. They were involved in crimes against the coinage: sometimes in the actual counterfeiting, but more often in clipping or in helping to circulate false coins. In Paris in 1390, Alipo, the wife of a moneychanger who had provided the materials necessary for making false coins, accepted the counterfeits in payment and mixed them with good money before she circulated them in the hope of misleading her clientele. Even at the lowest level a woman could be active in such an enterprise, for Florence Swalve was indicted in the early fifteenth century for making two counterfeit copper coins that resembled good royal money and then passing them in Great Torrington.[25]

Crimes of violence like murder or arson were not as frequent among women but did occur since high tempers and a recourse to physical violence were characteristic of both men and women, and such quarrels easily ended in tragedy. In 1391 Agnes, the wife of Jean le Poulain, became so infuriated with her Paris neighbour who refused to speak to her that she deliberately set fire to his house. Since fire was a constant and extreme danger in crowded medieval cities her penalty was brutal but not surprising – she herself was to be burned as an incendiary. Murder by a woman, especially of a husband, often arose from an illicit affair where the wife urged the murder on her lover and sometimes assisted him, as did Katerina of Farnborough in 1422. She had been abducted by Richard Eton, an Augustinian friar, who was charged with raping her several times. Three months after this, suggesting a clandestine affair rather than rape, the two joined in murdering Katerina's husband and hid his body in the woods. She was found guilty and sentenced to be burnt, while Eton, although also found guilty, pleaded benefit of clergy and escaped execution.[26]

Infanticide was almost invariably a woman's crime and, in some cases at least, seems to have been the result of acute depression verging on insanity. Thus Matilda, a peasant widow, tried to commit suicide on Valentine's Day in 1329 by throwing herself into a water-filled ditch. Her neighbours rescued her, but the unfortunate woman then went home and killed her two sons and a daughter. The terse entry in the English gaol-delivery rolls gives no reason for her act, but it is legitimate to wonder if the impossibility of maintaining herself and her family had driven the distraught widow to her drastic action.[27]

Women were not often indicted for treason but occasionally had to answer to such a charge. During the period of the Hundred Years War French judges could be very harsh with anyone suspected of aiding the English and women who served as accomplices of a father, husband, or brother would share in their male relative's punishment. In England, Alice Emson was more personally enterprising. At the end of the fourteenth century she was accused of lighting a warning beacon for the benefit of the Scots. Since an English fleet was to be launched on a punitive expedition to counter some earlier Scottish raids, Alice provided the enemy with useful information and spoiled the surprise manoeuvre. Quite remarkably the jury seems to have excused her action. Although they had no doubt she had acted as charged, they informed the justices that Alice had been for many years a subject of the king of Scotland before she married an Englishman and came to live in England. In this case of divided loyalty she was let go.[28]

Women might also have to appear in the ecclesiastical courts as well as in the secular ones, since all cases regarding marriage came under church jurisdiction. They also dealt with sexual immorality, especially when a cleric was involved, and in such cases the women were treated far more harshly than the men. Thus the register of William Gainsborough, bishop of Worcester at the beginning of the fourteenth century, records the punishment of a subdeacon and the woman with whom he had lived for some years and by whom he had five children, a clear case of clerical concubinage. The man was required to fast on bread and water for twelve months and, as public disgrace, to stand by the church font on seven successive Sundays while thirteen poor people attended to pray for him. His unfortunate partner was condemned to be beaten with nine strokes of the birch on nine Sundays and nine market days.[29]

Heresy was naturally a matter for the ecclesiastical court though, if the death sentence was involved, the guilty person was handed over to the secular officials for execution. Pockets of heresy were endemic throughout the Middle Ages. Their beliefs expressed dissatisfaction with the social structure of medieval society as well as disaffection with the increasingly hierarchical and legally structured church, which had little understanding or sympathy for popular or emotional currents of piety. Pious women especially could fall foul of church authorities as they moved into the depths of mysticism suspected by canon lawyers and rational theologians. This distrust is most clearly demonstrated in the case of the mystic and beguine, Marguerite de Porete. On one hand, her language was so extreme that a suspicious theologian might easily find it heretical while on the other, she consistently distinguished between the church on earth, with its sacraments, structures, and unworthy clergy, and an ideal community of 'simple souls'. She felt that this community, to which she hoped to belong, should be the guide and judge of the institutional church. This immediately alarmed the ecclesiastics of her day, already concerned about the growth of heresy and witchcraft in France. Marguerite's writings were first condemned at Valenciennes c. 1300, but she continued to write in the same vein. Some seven years later she was again arrested and sent to Paris for interrogation where she refused to answer her accusers. Ultimately she was accused of heresy on the basis of selective quotations from her book, *The Mirror of Simple Annihilated Souls*, made by a rather prejudiced commission of theologians. The credibility of the case against her is further weakened by the fact that it was conducted by the inquisitor responsible for the accusations against the Templars, in which politics were more important than religion. Because of the previous condemnation of Marguerite's writings, she was considered guilty of relapse and burned at Paris in 1310. *The Mirror* was unquestionably a remarkable religious testimony for, despite its condemnation and the official insistence on the destruction of all copies, it continued to circulate anonymously in orthodox religious circles during the fourteenth and fifteenth centuries.[30]

Because heresy questioned the authority of the established social order it was perceived as an enemy of the secular government as well as the church. The two major heresies of France and England – that of the Cathars, or Albigensians, so widespread in southern France in the twelfth and thirteenth centuries, and that of the Lollards in England in the late fourteenth and fifteenth centuries – had very different doctrines but both were pursued by royal justices as well as ecclesiastical inquisitors. The Cathars flourished in the large area of south-east France then under the overlordship of the count of Toulouse. Mainly dualist in their basic doctrines, Cathars believed that only the spiritual world was subject to God, while all material things, including the soul while imprisoned in the physical body, were evil and subject to Satan. Recent scholarship suggests that most Cathars had little concern for the theological underpinnings of their belief but were primarily concerned with promoting the highest moral and ascetic standards and gained much consolation from their religious practices. Languedoc, as that part of southern France which spoke Occitan was known, had been christianised very early but had been lukewarm in its religion for several centuries. The local church had been unaffected by the earlier movements of reform, so that when the twelfth century revival of popular piety finally made an impact on the Occitans, their lack of respect for the mediocre and worldly leaders of the church in the region and their disinterest in, and ignorance of, orthodox doctrine made heresy more appealing than reform.

The spread of Catharism was made easier by the simplicity of its organisation and the holy lives of its leaders. Cathars had no churches, only 'houses', sometimes merely a large room where their adherents gathered. Although there was a bishop for each area and a deacon in charge of each community, the real labour of preaching and conversion was in the hands of the 'perfect', who led most ascetic and edifying lives. They publicly renounced the world in a ceremony known as the *consolamentum*, gave up their property and all sexual intercourse. They also refused to eat meat, cheese, eggs, or milk, which they felt were the products of animal intercourse. They were bound not to lie, nor to take an oath, nor to renounce their faith. The great mass of Catharist followers were not required to obey the strict regulations of the much-admired perfect, and most only aspired to that status on their deathbeds. By the beginning of the thirteenth century the Cathars, although a minority, had become an alternate established church in Languedoc, for they were tolerated by the lay Catholic majority and their ministers respected. The strength of the Cathars arose from their success in making converts among the greatest families of the region which resulted in a high level of protection and toleration. When public disputations were held between Catholic bishops or theologians and the leaders of the heretics, they were frequently presided over by local knights or burgesses who expressed no alarm at the often intemperate language of the heretics.

Women were among the earliest to turn to Catharism, which offered them a higher status than the Catholic church, for they were not only accepted as full members of the sect, they could also join the ranks of the perfect. As such, although they could not be bishops or deacons, they were recognised for their holy lives, and could lead the prayers if no male perfect were present. They took precedence in any gathering over all mere believers and were even entitled to the respectful greeting these vouchsafed to the perfect. Since this included a three-fold genuflection it was rarely given to women by status-conscious nobles, but it was performed by others. Women perfect of some wealth or standing often used their own houses as centres for other women who were drawn to this rigorous life of prayer and fasting by social and economic, as well as religious, forces. As with the beguinages of the north, surplus women could live decently and with respect in such a community, supporting themselves either from their own inheritances or by engaging in trade or cottage industries. These houses also served as a focus for missionary work and for hospitality to the wandering perfect on their missionary journeys. Some were used as boarding schools for young girls who were then influenced into heresy by the good example of such pious women.

The more respected position of women among the Cathars was merely relative, for the female perfects were less active than the men. Any women involved in preaching or debating were usually upper-class, like Esclarmonde of Foix, the widowed sister of Count Raymond-Roger. Esclarmonde was the mother of six children but, as a widow, became a perfect and was active in the debate between the Catholics and the Cathars at Pamiers in 1207. On this occasion, according to the chronicler William of Puylaurens, the Cistercian envoy who was upholding the Catholic cause was so upset by her arguments as well as her presence that he remarked dismissively: 'Go to your distaff, madam, it is not proper that you should speak in such a gathering'.[31] Despite his contempt, Esclarmonde had apparently been an effective preacher for the Cathars, for the bishop of Toulouse held her responsible for many conversions to heresy in his diocese.

Matters changed, especially for Cathar women, when the Albigensian Crusade attacked the south. This expedition, sponsored by Pope Innocent III, was meant to extirpate heresy but was primarily a political force dedicated to implanting the power of the French king in territories over which he had not previously ruled. It was a harsh and brutal affair which ruined much of the south's cultural and political life and destroyed the leading families who had harboured the heretics. The clerical force of the Inquisition followed the army and harried individual suspects. The combination of political and ecclesiastical force was sufficient to drive the Cathars underground and to bring about their practical disappearance by the middle of the thirteenth century. As the vigour of the Inquisition increased, the larger houses of the women perfects, which so resembled orthodox convents and, like them, had been founded, supported, and ruled by members of noble families, were forced out of existence. The remaining women perfect were driven to a wandering life where they were liable to capture. It has been argued that women were particularly prominent in Catharism in Languedoc. There can be little doubt that women were devout members of the sect but the evidence does not seem to support the statement that women were a predominant percentage among the heretics or that they were more active than men.[32] Nevertheless, Catharism undoubtedly provided an adequate and respected outlet for the religious passion of many Occitan women who were alienated from the rigid and unreformed Catholicism of the south.

The religious sect of the Lollards in England also developed political overtones and was similarly pursued by both church and state. In the late fourteenth century the name was originally applied to the followers of John Wycliffe, the Oxford reformer who preached against the temporal power and possessions of the church as well as the power of the papacy, and denied a number of church doctrines, especially that of the priestly power to consecrate the eucharist. Wycliffe was also responsible for the translation of the bible into English and those who followed him put much emphasis on bible reading and preaching, rather than the mass and the sacraments and the many popular pious practices, such as pilgrimages and the veneration of images. Wycliffe himself was protected by John of Gaunt, Edward III's son, and was never formally tried for heresy although his teachings were condemned in 1382. He had originally attracted followers among the nobility, as well as the urban craftsmen and lower clergy, but the Lollard knights who had been influential in the reigns of Richard II and Henry IV had no successors. The ignominious rout of the rebellion led by the Lollard, Sir John Oldcastle, who had hoped to seize and dethrone Henry V, his final capture and execution for treason and heresy combined to ensure orthodoxy among the nobility. Nevertheless, Lollard doctrines retained their appeal among the skilled artisans and their families, as well as parish clergy in the mid-fifteenth century. As a newly literate class, hard-working and independent, this urban group found the Lollard emphasis on the bible and personally directed piety most congenial.

Although the bible in the vernacular had been available for some time on the Continent, the general thrust of Wycliffe's teaching made the use of his translation suspicious. The Augustinian chronicler Knighton remarked in a Latin pun that Wycliffe had translated the bible into the English not the angelic tongue (*in Angliam linguam non angelicam*), and regretted that it was now more open to laymen and even women who could read, instead of remaining the preserve of well-educated clerics. He complained bitterly that 'the previous jewel of clerks was turned into the game of lay people'. Some years later the poet Hoccleve was equally unhappy about all those outspoken women who insisted on quoting scripture and even arguing with men:

> Some women eek, thogh hir wit be thynne,
> Wile arguments make in holy writ!

He insisted it would be far better for them to sit and spin and cackle of something else, for their intelligence was all too feeble for such a dispute.[33] It was one of the most interesting characteristics of the fifteenth century Lollards that they produced a fair number of women well versed in the bible and other pious works. Many had the bible read to them and some became well-known as memorizers of scripture, like Alice Colyns, who was part of a literate family and whose husband owned a number of devotional books. Alice had developed such great skill in reciting scripture that she was frequently sent for when Lollards held their meetings.[34]

The record exists of the trials of fifty-one men and nine women suspected of heresy in the diocese of Norwich in the years 1428–30.[35] The Norwich trials were relatively humane for torture was not used and the penances imposed were relatively light considering the penalties elsewhere. Some were required to fast on bread and water on Lenten Fridays for seven years and others, in cases considered more serious, were condemned to a specified number of beatings around their local church or marketplace. Even these could be mitigated, for in the case of Isabella Chapleyn, who had already been excommunicated and was absolved when she recanted, the twelve beatings assigned as penance were reduced by the judge to three because of her old age, misery, and unimportance.[35]

In this group Margery Baxter and Hawise Moone emerge as leading personalities. Both provided long lists of their beliefs which followed the usual Lollard tenets, opposing the sacraments, pilgrimages, the swearing of oaths, and the veneration of images and claiming that every man or woman of good life was as much a priest as any ordained, even the pope or a bishop. Both admitted that they had harboured some of the best-known Lollard priests who were later condemned. Margery Baxter appears to have been the more practical character. She argued that oaths could be sworn before a judge if it was necessary for one's reputation, and insisted that it was legitimate to eat meat on Fridays and fast days. She felt it was better to eat the leftovers of Thursday's meal than to go to the market and go in debt to buy fish. Margery was an active proselytizer, discussing her beliefs with a local recluse, whom she thought sympathetic, and encouraging one of her neighbours, and her two servant girls of sixteen and fourteen, to come to her chamber at night to hear her husband read from the law of Christ. She also threatened to denounce them if they betrayed her. [37] Hawise Moone could not have endeared herself to the tribunal in the bishop's palace since she stated firmly that secular lords and men could lawfully take all the goods and temporal possessions from men of the church, as well as bishops' and prelates' horses and harness, so that they could be given to the poor.[38]

Many Lollard women were anxious to share in a preaching ministry to all believers but only the occasional eccentric at the end of the fourteenth century went so far as to suggest a place for women even in the celebrating ministry. Walter Brut argued that women could have other priestly powers because they had the right to baptise. At his trial his supporters based their case on the preaching function of women described in the Old Testament and claimed that they had a right and duty to preach if they were virtuous. On the other side, the orthodox fell back on Aristotle's remarks on the incapacity of woman and her imperfect nature which proved that women were created for subjection and unfit for authority. They grudgingly allowed that abbesses might be allowed to preach to their nuns and housewives to their children and other women, but never to men or in public.[39] There is the occasional report of a woman saying mass, but omitting the words of consecration. The chronicler Knighton reports one case of a mother in London who taught her only daughter to celebrate mass in this fashion and built an altar in a secret cubicle of the house for the purpose. This went on for some time until the mother and daughter's secret was divulged by a neighbour who had been most confidentially invited to join them. Called before the bishop they were convinced of their error and required to do penance.[40] It is impossible to be sure whether this was merely a gossipy rumour circulated by the chronicler or a real case, but it does not seem to have reflected a common happening.

One cannot talk of female heresy and its link with political as well as religious forces without mentioning what has become, in retrospect, the most famous heresy case of the Middle Ages, that of Joan of Arc. Joan's trial in 1431 came at a time when France was deeply divided by the factions of the Burgundians and the Armagnacs in the midst of the Hundred Years War. There can be little doubt that her trial in Rouen by the English and their Burgundian allies, including the influential clerics of the university of Paris, her rehabilitation in 1456 by a reunified and victorious France, and her twentieth century canonisation were all strongly political events. The effort to disentangle her historical importance as seen by her contemporaries, the placing of the burden of responsibility for her condemnation to the stake, and the extraordinary story of her gradual transfiguration into a French icon have all sparked continuing, prolonged and often acrimonious arguments. Here it is impossible – and would be unfair to the wealth of available material – to do more than point out the complexity and enduring fascination of the puzzle posed by the actions of the peasant girl from Domrémy who became indisputably the most widely known of all medieval women.[41]

If sorcery is considered as the use of traditional magic practices, such as the spells and potions so often connected with the winning of a lover, fertility, or childbirth, it is not surprising that women often found themselves under suspicion. These were areas of life where female activity was taken for granted but was regarded dubiously by men, who saw them as outside the proper rational and ordered structure. During periods of peace, prosperity, and social calm the incidents of accusations and punishments for sorcery were relatively few. Witchcraft added a further element to the sorcerers' magic, for it not only dabbled in borderline matters but rejected every aspect of Christianity and developed the antithetical worship of Satan. It tended to thrive in the areas and at the times when heresy flourished, and like heresy, indicated an alienation from the rapid changes and many disasters of later medieval civilisation. The inquisitors of the fourteenth and fifteenth centuries pursued witches as they rooted out heretics, although the medieval judges did not display the hysteria about witches which

50 Witch worshipping the devil in the shape of a black goat. The broomstick which had carried her to the sabbat lies on the ground

characterised the seventeenth century. Many of the medieval trials for sorcery, and occasionally for witchcraft, were heard in the secular courts rather than before an ecclesiastical tribunal, though there seems little difference between the lay and clerical approach. Both led to unsavoury political manoeuvring, often at the highest level, for such an accusation was an effective way to destroy the reputation of the one accused, even if later proved innocent, while the charge itself was sufficient to entail the immediate seizure of the accused's goods.

Two French cases in the fourteenth century – one tried in a clerical, the other in a secular court – suggest the development from simple sorcery to devil worship. In 1335 Anne-Marie de Georgel was tried at Toulouse by an ecclesiastical tribunal which was also pursuing heretics. When the middle-aged woman was tortured she confessed that for twenty years she had been a member of the devil's army and had frequently attended the witches' sabbat where she had found many men and women. She told how, through fear, she had submitted to Satan – vividly described as a gigantic black man with eyes like burning coals – and later had ritual intercourse with him in the shape of a goat. This provided her with the power to transport herself to sabbats and to learn how to make poisons and ointments by digging up bodies in graveyards or taking hair, nails, and fat from the bodies of criminals left hanging on the gallows. The inquisitors were eager to equate her beliefs to those of the Cathars, for they asked if God ruled only in heaven while the devil ruled on earth and was now in the ascendant. Anne-Marie claimed to be penitent but was burnt. A case heard before the parlement of Paris in 1390 involved two women and illustrates how sorcery could shade into witchcraft. Margot de la Barre, called Coingnet, was a woman of the lowest class who wandered from village to village, often travelling with prostitutes, but reputed to have magical powers. Marion la Droiturière, who was rather better off, had been jilted by her lover for another woman. In her desire for revenge she had asked Margot to work such magic that he would be impotent. After torture, the two women added to their confessions. Margot admitted that she had called up the devil by conjuring with the name of God, but when asked to describe him she had to fall back on a familiar image – he looked like the demons in the passion plays but had no horns. Both women were burned by order of the provost of Paris.[42]

The English accusations of witchcraft touched far more important women, but none of them was burned. Alice Perrers, the mistress of Edward III in his old age, was accused of being in league with a magician whose potions roused the king to sexual excitement, but this was gossip from the unfriendly St. Albans chronicler, and never led to a charge. However, in 1419 Henry V had his stepmother, Queen Joan of

Navarre, imprisoned on suspicion of treason by witchcraft. It was charged that her confessor, a Franciscan friar, had accused her of attempting to compass the death of the king by sorcery and necromancy. Despite the serious nature of the charge and the fact that the friar was kept in the Tower until his accidental death some ten years later, no investigation was ever made nor was Queen Joan ever tried. Instead she was kept in exceedingly polite custody for nearly three years and provided with every comfort, including a new bird cage for her parrot and the repair of her harp. In July 1422 Henry, when ill, became conscience-stricken and restored her dower, her beds and all her moveables. She was to be allowed to choose her own officials, have five or six elegant new gowns, and horses for eleven chariots to move herself and her belongings wherever she wished to go. Scholars generally hold that the real reason for Henry's original charge was that Queen Joan's dower was as much as 10% of the general revenues of his government at a time of great financial stringency. In 1419 Henry needed money for a dower for his own prospective new queen as well as for the financial demands of the war with France. The charge of witchcraft allowed him to sequester all the dowager Queen's revenues to his own use until her trial. If a trial was not held, there was no question of her being proved innocent and entitled to the return of all her goods. His almost deathbed repentance suggests that he had more need of her wealth than any belief in the pretext he had employed to sequester it for his own benefit.[43]

Eleanor of Cobham, the second wife of Humphrey of Gloucester, Henry V's youngest brother, was less lucky. An exceedingly ambitious woman, neither discreet nor popular, she was known to have an interest in witchcraft and necromancy as well as keeping a number of suspect priests in her household. Under such circumstances it was not difficult for her husband's enemies at court to take advantage of the whiff of heresy to destroy her and discredit Duke Humphrey. Eleanor was condemned by an ecclesiastical court after she admitted some items of the indictment brought against her, and was first imprisoned at Leeds Castle. The ecclesiastical sentence of November 1441 required her to abjure her heresies and do public penance which involved walking bareheaded, clad in black, on three separate days, through the busiest streets of London. She was to bear a lighted candle to be offered at each of the churches – St. Paul's, Christchurch Aldgate, and St. Michael's Cornhill. Eleanor was then imprisoned for the rest of her life, though members of her household were executed, and was finally moved to the Isle of Man where she died, long forgotten, in 1457, having outlived Duke Humphrey by ten years.[44]

Medieval society's tolerance for female crime varied greatly. Prostitutes were accepted, if they avoided theft and brawls. Deeds of violence, whether by men or women, were punished alike but charges of witchcraft and heresy against women were often politically inspired. In such a situation a woman needed extraordinarily powerful support to escape unharmed, though Mahaut of Artois showed it could be done.[45] In a society fundamentally based on force, women were always at a disadvantage and could easily be driven outside the accepted boundaries of their society.

CHAPTER TEN

Women's Contributions to Medieval Culture

One of the problems in discussing medieval culture is that it does not fit comfortably into present day categories. We now draw sharp divisions between religious and secular art, between fine arts and crafts, and between oral popular culture and serious literature in a way which medieval people would not have understood. Such divisions only gradually came to apply in a society thoroughly impregnated by religious forms, moving slowly from an oral to a written culture, and where our judgment of what the age achieved is based on the accidents of survival. Much of medieval culture was ephemeral by its very nature – the fine embroideries and elegant cloths, the seldom written down popular music, and the fabulous spectacles of luxurious courts. These survive only in accounts, matter-of-fact inventories, or chroniclers' descriptions. In such circumstances it is even more difficult to identify specifically feminine contributions, since so many of these cultural productions were the anonymous product of many heads and hands. A number of powerful women can be perceived as patrons and benefactors of individual authors, illuminators, musicians and embroiderers, but it is much more difficult to uncover the relatively few women who practised these arts. Culture and the arts have always required leisure and resources beyond daily needs for their development. Most women had little leisure, and less control of wealth, during the greater part of their lives, but female religious can appear more frequently than their secular sisters as contributors to culture because the conditions of their life favoured such activities.

The established religious houses of women had both time and opportunity for intellectual and artistic activity, and some resources, though usually less than the richest abbeys of men. During the later twelfth and thirteenth centuries the intellectual and artistic possibilities for nuns declined as the schools and universities (both closed to women) became the new centres of intellectual vitality, and the growing towns emerged as centres of artistic production. Nuns gradually lost touch with the scholarship, intellectual challenge, and artistic ferment which had been open to them when monasticism was at its peak of power and influence. In one area of literature, that of mysticism, women continued to hold their own even beyond the end of the Middle Ages. Nunneries also provided a reason and a need for women's practice of several arts. Embroidery was required for the beautifying of church vestments, copying and illuminating for manuscripts in use in the convent, and the composition of music to help the nuns in their daily duty of singing the liturgical offices.

Occasionally nuns were involved in more secular literature. The new flowering of lyrical poetry in the early twelfth century also touched religious women, although they wrote in Latin and used classical models. A recent study has brought to life the poetic exchange between Baudri de Bourgueil, the cultured cleric who eulogised the beauties of the chamber of the Countess Adela of Blois, and Constance, a young nun at the convent of Le Ronceray in Angers. Constance was well-educated – besides her knowledge of the bible, she was steeped in Ovid's *Heroides*, that imagined exchange of letters between Paris and Helen. Like Baudri, she transformed the classical expression of erotic love into a brilliant literary exercise, skirting the boundary between vowed chastity and real feeling. Constance was not the only young woman to be involved in such correspondence. There are a number of similar, but perhaps less effective examples from the young nuns and female pupils at Regensburg.[1]

The twelfth-century convent also provided more intellectual fare. The work of Hildegarde of Bingen as nun, scholar, and mystic has already been cited but it would underestimate the talents of that extraordinary woman not to draw attention to her other contributions to the culture of her day. Her extensive correspondence with her most powerful contemporaries, the literary power of her mystical treatises, and her wide-ranging intellectual activity in so many fields: all entitle her to a distinguished place among twelfth-century authors. In addition, she was a musician and even wrote a play. Her songs and poems are gradually being discovered by dedicated scholars of medieval music, and some of the finest are now available on records. Her *Ordo Virtutum*, an early morality play with musical sections, was written for the nuns of her convent, and it too has now found a place in the repertory of early music.[2] As well, the earliest illuminated copy of her mystical treatise *Scivias* was done under her direction and her creative imagination is responsible for the remarkable miniatures which illustrated her visions. Hildegarde not only contributed to many facets of medieval culture, she did so in specifically feminine terms and with a recognition and appreciation of woman's rightful place in society. Unlike most medieval thinkers, she saw the roles and gifts of men and women as being complementary to each other, both were needed for the proper functioning of society.

Unlike Hildegard, Abbess Herrad of Hohenbourg is scarcely known and yet her *Hortus Deliciarum* is one of the most remarkable manuscripts of the twelfth century. The Benedictine abbey of Hohenbourg was founded by a duke of Alsace, probably in the eighth century. The duke made his daughter Odile the first abbess and she was so highly regarded for her holiness that after her death pilgrimages to her relics ensured the prosperity of her abbey until the eleventh century. Emperor Frederic Barbarossa, anxious to ensure Hohenstaufen influence in Alsace, restored the abbey and installed Relinda, who ruled as abbess from 1147–1162. She was followed by Herrad who was abbess until at least 1191. Nothing is known of Herrad, except that she came from a local noble family and obviously enjoyed an almost inexhaustible energy, for she was a vigorous organiser with a strong sense of what was necessary for the spiritual and material wellbeing of her nuns. She founded a Premonstratensian priory near the abbey to ensure the presence of priests to say mass daily, and later added an Augustinian establishment, which included not only a church and convent for the twelve resident canons but also a farm, a hospital for the poor, and a hospice for pilgrims. The canons also shared the duty of providing the services at the abbey.

The *Garden of Delights* was designed, Herrad wrote in her introduction, for the information and delectation of her nuns, to help them advance further in the service of God. It is possible that Relinda may have conceived the original idea but the governing mind behind this encyclopedic work was that of Herrad. The manuscript, with its complex and integrated series of illuminations applying specifically to the text they surround, was probably executed in a professional workshop in Strasbourg within a few years after Herrad's death but it remained in the abbey of Hohenbourg throughout the Middle Ages. It came into the hands of the bishop of Strasbourg after a major fire in the mid-sixteenth century but unfortunately was totally destroyed when fire broke out in the Strasbourg library during the German bombardment of the city in 1870. Luckily a nineteenth-century scholar had realised the value of the text's many illustrations and had traced most of them. Modern co-operative scholarship has recently succeeded in providing a two volume study which includes facsimiles of the early nineteenth-century copies and as much of the text as can be reconstituted, so we have at least a suggestion of its splendours.[3]

The *Garden of Delights* is particularly interesting as a *florilegium*, literally a culling of flowers but in essence an anthology. It serves as a religious encyclopedia grouping nearly 1,200 texts of various authors. Although there is no attempt at synthesis, the direction is implicit in the choice of texts. The *Garden* is not an original work but Herrad provided the editorial design, drawing on material she had available. Apart from extracting from the Old and New Testaments, she relied particularly on two popular twelfth-century theologians and philosophers, Honorius Augustodunensis and Peter Lombard, but also included many other authorities. The work reproduced some sixty-six sermons, mostly anonymous, and about fifty-five poems. Herrad was probably the author of four of these, though her poetry is more didactic than inspired. Apart from the literary and editorial work she certainly supervised the scheme of the illustrations, and possibly did some of the outline drawing, though she is no longer believed to have shared the actual painting.

The work, even in the fragmentary form which is all that is available, suggests its function as a brilliant and luxurious teaching aid for instructing the nuns of Hohenbourg abbey. Its final illustration is an extraordinary group picture of the nuns and lay-sisters of the abbey – forty-six women's heads, not distinguished as portraits but each ident-ified by name. The most interesting of the large miniatures is Herrad's conception of a popular theme, the ladder of perfection leading from earth to the rewards of heaven, illustrated almost completely in terms of religious life. Charity stands at the top of the ladder, ready to present the crown of salvation to the successful, while accompanying angels attack the demons who try to destroy the climbers. The devil is pictured as a ramping dragon and the temptations which can ensnare even the good are graphically drawn. The hermit, almost at the top of the ladder, is dislodged by his passion for his garden, the recluse by his attachment to his bed and lazy sleep. The monk is seduced by riches, and the nun by clerical gifts, worldly pomps, and rich relatives. The cleric falls into gluttony, lust and simony, while the poor layman and laywoman at the lowest rung are tempted by worldly ornaments, fornication, pride and avarice.[4]

It is a vivid, if discouraging, rendering. Herrad's work seems to have exercised no influence outside her own house but it is a fascinating example of the considerable level which feminine intellectual and artistic ability could attain in an abbey blessed with security and riches which drew its personnel from the wealthiest and most cultured level of the population.

A few English nuns were recognised as authors during the twelfth and thirteenth centuries, although their works were pedestrian. Barking Abbey produced Clemence and an anonymous 'nun of Barking' in the twelfth century. Each wrote a saint's life in Anglo-Norman verse, primarily to serve as translations of the Latin originals which many nuns had become unable to read. The results were so appreciated that the works were known on the Continent. The thirteenth-century work that survives is a life of St. Audrey by a nun from the convent of Chatteris, correct but monotonous and uninteresting. Beatrice of Kent, who succeeded Countess Ela of Salisbury as abbess of Lacock, is reputed to have written the life of her foundress-predecessor which is mentioned until the sixteenth century but has since disappeared.[5] If English nuns were not distinguished authors, they had a better reputation in other artistic fields. Christina of Markyate embroidered a mitre and sandals for her friend Abbot Geoffrey of St. Albans to send to the newly elected English pope. It gave Matthew Paris (always anxious for the honour of his house) great pleasure to report that Christina's embroidery was the only gift Adrian IV would accept. The magnificent St. Albans Psalter, one of the great works of English manuscript illumination, was made specifically for Christina, though why and how is still a mystery. It may have been a return for her spiritual advice, prayers and friendship for the abbot and the monastery.[6]

The most important literary activity by women in the thirteenth century and much of the fourteenth was religious, flowering in the writing and dictation of mystical treatises. The great centre for such works in the thirteenth-century was Germany and the Low Countries where the current of mysticism was particularly strong. Mention has already been made of the three great mystics at the convent of Helfta – Mechtild of Magdeburg, Mechtild of Hackeborn, and Gertrude of Helfta. Unlike Herrad of Hohenbourg's *Garden of Delights*, which seems to have had no influence outside her own monastery, the works of these female mystics were widely known, both to religious communities and devout lay people. They struck deeply answering chords in the developing popular piety which sought emotional as well as rational stimulation. The tradition continued in France with Marguerite of Porete, although her extreme and often ambivalent statements, her lack of a solid base of institutional support, and the contemporary French suspicion and distrust of anything even mildly unorthodox resulted in her condemnation, though her treatise still circulated. In England the *Revelations* of Julian of Norwich, one of the most famous of all English mystics, provide an early and masterful example of vernacular prose. Her book has had long-term influence as a classic of English piety and is marked by a balance, serenity, and compassion which are not only distinctly feminine in their approach but universal in their vision.

Finally, at least a few of the women's religious houses, especially in Flanders and Germany, continued to exhibit some scholarly and artistic activity in the fifteenth century. A Dominican friar, writing at that time about the reform of his order, brought forward encouraging examples of the work of Dominican nuns, and there seem to have been a dozen Dominican convents with active scriptoria. Two nuns at Colmar were skilled in writing, especially the choir books for divine service, and one could paint as well. There was another such nun at Nurnberg, but his prize example was Sister Lukardis of Utrecht who kept herself so busy that his eulogy has a note of astonishment:

> Never idle, she busied herself with reading, prayer, nursing or writing, which she had truly mastered as we may see in the large, beautiful, useful choir books which she wrote and annotated for the convent and which has caused astonishment among many fathers and priests who have seen the missal she prepared, written in a neat, correct script. She was an artistic person in many kinds of handwork and she knew how to use grammar and Latin at table.[7]

Somehow, the impression of the bustling Sister Lukardis is one of earnest effort, rather than outstanding gifts. By this time too, the printing press was already beginning to make this kind of artistic activity unnecessary, except as a specialised craft to mark extraordinary occasions.

The shadowed picture of gradual decline in the cultural level and achievements of the nunneries in the later Middle Ages is balanced by a corresponding growth in the cultural activities in secular society, which affected women as well as men. Although queens and great noble ladies are easiest to identify as patrons and benefactors of the artists and authors of their day, many women of the lower nobility, and what in England came to be called the gentry, helped to ensure the transmission of medieval culture by their particular interest in, and attention to, music, embroidery, and literature. These women were often left in sole charge of castles and manors while their husbands were away at court, on crusade, or at war. During the long periods when they actually presided over the household, supervising their administrative officials, keeping their damsels and maid servants profitably occupied, and taking the responsibility for the education of their young children, it was such cultural pursuits which provided important and acceptable ways to fill their leisure.

Music, although it always benefited from wandering instrumentalists who frequented royal courts and noble households, was also an activity most men and women valued as a pastime. Some literary evidence suggests that at one time queens and noble ladies listened to songs of heroic deeds while working at their time-consuming, perhaps tedious embroidery, but by the thirteenth century they seem to have preferred dance songs. It was considered suitable for noble ladies to sing and dance for their own pleasure in their own quarters, and they might have a female instrumentalist. This sort of entertainment varied in elegance according to the household and was merely a pale approximation of the

51 The medieval timbrel, much like the modern tambourine, was a favourite musical instrument for women

*52 The artist
depicting the female
acrobat modestly
provides her with a
long skirt she would
not in reality have
worn*

music and entertainment at court, which grew in splendour from the
thirteenth century on. The great majority of musicians and entertainers
were men, for in Northern Europe women playing instruments or
acting as minstrels were likely to be suspected of sorcery or of being
Saracens. The religious community disapproved utterly of minstrels,
male or female, because of their essentially secular nature as a question
in Herrad's *Garden of Delights* suggests. When asked about their
possibilities of salvation the answer is overwhelmingly negative – they
have no hope because they are intentionally ministers of Satan.[8]

*53 Matthew Paris drew these dancing girls from Richard of Cornwall's
descripton of Emperor Frederic II's court*

Women occasionally appear as singers, normally attached to a noble household. When Louis IX paid twenty-five minstrels in 1239 the only woman mentioned was a singer of the countess of Blois, while five years later Henry III granted 5s towards the funeral expenses of the singer Lorea.[9] Mahaut d'Artois rewarded a woman who sang for her at Christmas 1319, and also had a woman who played the organs, while her grand-daughter, a princess of France, had three female singers and a woman bellringer.[10] Young women acrobats and tumblers occasionally formed part of a troop of minstrels. Sometimes these had Saracen connotations, like the girls at the court of Frederic II whose balancing on balls so fascinated Richard of Cornwall and whose act was carefully illustrated by Matthew Paris. A female English acrobat was popular at the court of Edward I and his son. Matilda Makejoy appeared at the Christmas feast of 1296 'to make her vaults' for the amusement of the young Edward, and fifteen years later she was amusing his young half-brothers with another performance.[11] The routine of such an acrobat would resemble what we now see as the floor display of gymnasts. It was a hard life, and inevitably a short career for women, and our only traces of their skill are the occasional grotesques which enliven the border of an illuminated page.

Through the twelfth century embroidery was particularly a female art. Because of the high cost of the fine materials used as its base and the gold, silver, and pearls used in ornamenting them, embroidery was originally an occupation for rich and noble ladies. The wife of Edward the Confessor gained legitimate praise for the quality of her embroidery and weaving with gold thread, but the story of Queen Matilda and her ladies embroidering the Bayeux Tapestry, which glorifies her husband's conquest of England has not survived learned scrutiny. Clerics, who benefited most from such work, were enthusiastic about this handiwork. The eulogy of Queen Margaret of Scotland claimed that her chamber could be called 'a workshop of heavenly handicraft' since the queen gathered around her irreproachable women of noble birth to turn out ecclesiastical vestments and hangings, while the twelfth-century moralist, Etienne de Fougères, praised the countess of Hereford for her eminently suitable conduct in presenting churchmen with elegant vestments made with her own hands. Sometimes they would angle for such gifts. Baudri de Bourgueil did not hesitate to remind Countess Adela of Blois in a begging poem that he had made her name immortal and thus deserved his reward, a cope she had promised to embroider.[12]

Medieval church vestments had a better chance of surviving wear, decay, and change in fashions when secular garments, though as richly adorned, perished or wore out. There is one magnificent treasure-trove of thirteenth-century secular clothing at the abbey of Las Huelgas outside Burgos. It served as the royal mausoleum for the Castilian royal family in the Middle Ages and the clothes were rescued unspoiled from the royal tombs. One of the richest is the ceremonial cap of the Infante Ferdinand de Cerda, which displays his heraldic arms of the lions of England and the castles of Castile. They were worked in red and silver thread on a quartered background of coral beads and small pearls, and the cap provides visual proof of the elegance so prosaically described in inventories and contracts.

English embroidery, known as *opus Anglicanum*, was sought-after all over Europe and can be found in many countries. Matthew Paris has a characteristic anecdote of Pope Innocent IV being so impressed by the gold embroidered copes and mitres of the English prelates that he decided to require such embroideries as a 'free gift' from each of the Cistercian abbots in England – a command which delighted the London merchants who profited from it.[13] The English ecclesiastical vestments which have survived such as the Clare chasuble, the Syon cope, the vestments at Sens cathedral believed to have belonged to Thomas Becket, and a cope at St-Bertrand-des-Comminges, are only pale shadows of their original magnificence. Time and use have dulled their threads and faded their silks. The matter-of-fact statement that the chasuble given by Abbot Geoffrey of St. Albans to his monastery was so loaded with precious stones and gold that it was burned by a succeeding abbot to extract the gold – a process also employed on Lanfranc's copes at Canterbury in 1371 – brings home the immense richness of such work.[14]

Embroidery was not only a pastime for great ladies, it was also a skilled trade. Some women embroiderers were patronised by the English court during the early part of Henry III's reign, such as Katherine, who accompanied the king's sister Isabel to Germany for her marriage to Emperor Frederic II, and was one of the two English attendants allowed to remain with her. However, by far the best documented and apparently highly skilled embroiderer was Mabel of Bury St. Edmunds, whose name, especially between 1239 and 1244, frequently appears in the royal records. She must already have been considered an expert when, in November 1239, she was given £10 to make a chasuble and offertory veil for the king's use. The king consistently allowed further amounts for expenses, especially when she had to buy pearls and gold for its ornamentation. By late summer 1241 the work appears to have been completed, for it was to be lined with cloth of gold and appraised by 'discreet men and women with knowledge of embroidery'. It must have been found satisfactory for, two years later, Mabel was given another major royal commission – a banner of red samite embroidered with gold and images of the Virgin and St.

John. Although Henry specified the subjects he was content to leave the actual design to Mabel's superior knowledge. The banner was completed in November 1244 and Mabel was paid £10 for her labour, in addition to what she had received for her expenses. She then disappears from the records as an active embroiderer. She may have retired to her native town, for when King Henry was in Bury St. Edmunds in March 1256, he gave her six measures of a cloth agreeable to her and a robe of rabbit fur 'because Mabel of St. Edmund served the king and queen for a long time in the making of ecclesiastical ornaments'.[15] King Henry was a generous patron, even to those no longer in his service.

The king also bought embroidered cloths from the great London merchants, suggesting the growing importance of commercial workshops, particularly as there is no named successor to Mabel. Women continued to embroider but appeared less often as individuals. Isabella,

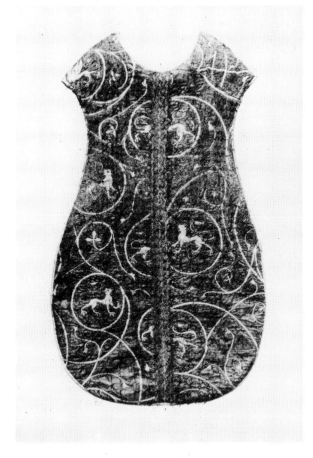

54 The Clare chasuble is one of the great survivals of the opus anglicanum

Edward II's queen, personally paid Rose, the wife of a London merchant, 50 marks as half the amount owing for an embroidered cope which the queen had purchased as a gift for Pope John XXII. Aleyse Darcy, an embroiderer from a leading London family, seems to have had a kind of partnership with a merchant of Lucca, in which he provided the rich cloth, she embroidered it in silver and gold, and they divided the money when it was sold to a rich noble.[16]

What little is known of French embroidery suggests that it was similar to the English, and that in Paris too men took over as masters of the more important workshops. Queen Isabeau of Bavaria's contract with Jean de Clarcy, the king's embroiderer, suggests the parallel. In 1410 the queen ordered a 'chapel', namely, hangings for the walls, a canopy, a chasuble, five copes, a tunic and dalmatic, as well as a cover for the episcopal chair, the lectern and the missal. A ground of azure velvet was to be worked with the queen's arms, the story of Christ's passion, gold sun rays and knots of stars, all ornamented with pearls. The extraordinary richness and intricacy of the work required, and the luxurious cloth, thread, and precious stones make the cost of 4,500 livres seem unsurprising.[17] The less well-to-do or extravagant might indulge in embroidered purses or book-covers.

As the production and illustration of books moved away from a monastic monopoly to become part of urban workshops the process was gradually broken down into highly specialised functions. An illustrator might create initials, or borders, while the most skilled provided the large miniatures which began to decorate the most luxurious manuscripts. It should be remembered that the Middle Ages did not make any sharp distinction between 'fine art' and 'craft'. Illuminators and embroiderers used many of the same motifs as painters and sculptors, while the term 'painter' might often refer to those who spent their time decorating royal banners or elegant saddles. This practice makes it difficult to estimate the status of men and women described as painters, illuminators, or that almost untranslatable term *imagier*, which might refer to a painter, a sculptor, or even an architect. The tax rolls of Paris from 1292 to 1313 have been analysed to extract all those described by any of the three terms, and it is interesting to note that the percentage of women in these trades is considerably lower than in other fields.[18] No woman was described specifically as a sculptor, but it is also true that a widow carrying on a family workshop until a son was old enough to take over would be described as *imagière* or illuminator. She may not have exercised the trade personally but she certainly directed the workshop and ensured its continuity.

Some of the specific cases are interesting. Perronnelle d'Auteuil *imagière* appears in each of the tax rolls. While she is described as an *imagière* in her own right, her husband Me Ernoul de Nuce was also an *imagier*. They paid 5s tax in 1292, 8s in 1296, 10s in 1297, and 12s in 1298. In 1299 Perronnelle is described as his widow and pays 10s, but by 1300 she is again listed as *imagière* and by 1311 her tax has increased to 24s. This suggests that she was quite capable of keeping the workshop going profitably. Another such competent woman was Jehanne whose husband had paid 16s tax in 1292 and 24s in 1296 as an *imagier*. In 1297 she is listed as an *imagière* and pays 36s tax in both 1297 and 1298. A somewhat similar case, where the wife also had a further interest on the side, is that of Ameline de Berron, wife of Jehan de Laingny, illuminator. Ameline is described as illuminator but also *libraire*, that is, one who acted as an agent for selling books left on deposit but who also might rent out master copies from which other copies might be made. Her husband paid 18s tax in 1292, and 12s in 1296 and 1297 but probably died in 1298, when Ameline paid only 3s. By 1299 and 1300 her business appears to have returned to the level of profitability attained when her husband was alive. There were apparently a few single women on the rolls (at least no current or past husband is mentioned) of whom the most successful seems to have been Thiephaine.[19]

Occasionally we can find a female illuminator who actually signed her own name. There is the amusing case of an Augsburg psalter which appears to have been the work of a group of students learning the arts of illumination and illustration. The initial Q of one of the psalms is enlivened by a tail made of the figure of a young girl, swinging on the body of the letter, and signed Claricia. She is obviously not a nun for her head is uncovered and her hair in long plaits, while she is wearing fashionable twelfth-century dress. The same young woman is believed to be responsible for two more pictures and another initial within the psalter. Although Claricia was the only secular woman who signed a drawing, occasionally the scribe will identify the team, as in the case of the husband and wife whose work was signed 'Alan the scribe and his wife the illuminator'.[20]

In the fourteenth and fifteenth centuries the dukes of Burgundy and Jean, duke of Berry, were passionate collectors of the finest and most luxurious manuscripts of their day and the occasional woman contributed to these elegant items, including Bourgot, the daughter of Jean Le Noir. She worked as an illuminator while her father was a famous miniaturist and the father and daughter were popular with both royalty and the nobility. They seem to have begun their career in the service of Yolande of Flanders, the countess of Bar, as they did a fine Book of Hours for her soon after her marriage in 1353. Charles V persuaded them to move to the French court, giving them a house in Paris and rich cloths. After the king's death in 1380 the duke of Berry established them in Bourges where they illustrated several manuscripts for him.[21] Christine de Pizan drew attention to the talents of Anastasia, one of her own contemporaries and acquaintances. Christine praises her for her great skill in painting manuscript borders and miniature backgrounds and insisted that her reputation was as great as any of the ancients for she surpassed everyone in Paris and was universally talked about.[22] Since she worked in one of the more anonymous specialties into which manuscript illumination had become divided, no work by Anastasia has ever been identified, and it would appear that her reputation was local and transitory and perhaps inflated by friendship.

Nevertheless, it is to this period and to a French manuscript of Boccaccio's treatise on famous women that we owe the extraordinary miniature of a female artist painting her own self-portrait. As described by Boccaccio, Marcia was a pagan virgin who devoted herself to the study of painting and ivory carving. She confined her work to portrait heads, at which she was highly skilled, because her modesty forbade her

55 Marcia painting her self-portrait from a mirror

to depict nude figures in the pagan custom. The picture itself is fascinating, for Marcia is dressed as a fifteenth-century woman using her mirror to create an easel self-portrait. The background suggests what might be found in a contemporary artist's studio, including a very early representation of a palette, the artist's tool which became so essential as oil paints became more and more common.[23] Paris and the Low Countries had become the most important centres of manuscript copying and illumination in northern Europe and seem to have recognised that women could be talented artists. The artists' guild at Bruges, dedicated to St. John the Evangelist, admitted women to the guild with full standing in the fifteenth century. It has been calculated that the female members of the guild increased from about 12% in 1254 to 25% in the 1480s, and eighteen women paid their dues in 1461–62.[24] The English workshops were less active and less famous, and there appears to be no proof of a woman sharing in their activities.

These elegant manuscripts, the products of the important fourteenth- and fifteenth-century workshops, inevitably lead us back to the courts, rich clerics, and noble households who were the only possible purchasers of such luxuries. The Books of Hours, the popular prayer-book of the laity, were very much in demand and many of their incidental drawings and ornamental borders of grotesques and scenes of daily living must have considerably enlivened long and tedious services. However the wealthy nobility were always interested in more secular literature and looked eagerly for exciting novelties. In the twelfth century, at a time when the ideas of courtly love and the songs of the troubadours were so generally popular among the upper classes, women emerge among the creators as well as the patrons. We know little of the countess of Dia who was part of the Provençal outburst of lyric poetry, but she has left unabashed and touching love poems for which she also composed the music.[25] Marie de France, however, was recognised in her own time as one of the great writers of her day, second only in popularity to Chrétien de Troyes. In fact, a late twelfth-century courtier wrote of her that her *Lais* were much praised by counts, barons and knights, who loved the text and had it read and retold because they found such delightful stories banished anger and troublesome thoughts.[26]

No one doubts Marie de France's literary skill but no one as yet has been able to prove her identity conclusively. From her work, and the occasional clues she includes in her prologues, it is obvious that she was from the upper class and familiar with the English Court. She was born in France, lived in England and dedicated works to Henry II and a certain Count William. The favourite, but unproved, hypothesis is that she was Mary, the illegitimate daughter of Geoffrey Plantagenet (and thus a half-sister of Henry II), who was abbess of the royal nunnery of Shaftesbury in the late twelfth century. Whoever she was, Marie was well-educated in Latin and English, as well as her native French, and was aware of the oral as well as the written literature of her time. Her most important works – the *Lais, Fables,* and the *Espurgatoire Saint Patriz* – mirror the popular interests of her day and were designed for the growing audience for vernacular literature. The *Lais* were romances with their emphasis on love and adventure. The *Fables* drew on the popular religious allegories and were translated from an earlier Old English text, while the *Espurgatoire* was a didactic religious treatise, translated from Latin, but with miracles and marvels to enliven it. Marie still manages to rouse her readers to enthusiasm, for a recent biographer writes that: 'Marie's breadth of learning, her charming, subtle literary style, sagacious mind and sensitive spirit are captivating', and is convinced that she is a literary figure of permanent importance.[27]

Literary culture requires a reading – or at least a listening – audience. It is an interesting fact that apart from clerics and such bibliophiles as Charles V and his brothers, the dukes of Berry and Burgundy, the secular interest in books, and even possession of them is much more noticeable among women. In France Mahaut d'Artois had a considerable library, ranging from Boethius to Marco Polo, and carried it on her travels, safely stowed in leather bags. However, we know more about the books of English women because of the larger number of available wills. Women not only possessed books, they passed them on to their daughters more often than their sons. The exception to this rule were the specially rich prayer books, often part of the family patrimony, which usually went to the principal heir. On her death in 1399 Eleanor, duchess of Gloucester, one of the two daughters of Humphrey de Bohun, earl of Hereford, left her son Humphrey a psalter 'well and richly illuminated with the clasps of gold enamelled with white swans and the arms of her father enamelled on the clasps, and other bars of gold on the tissues in the manner of mullets, which was left to her to be passed on from heir to heir'. This psalter, ornamented with Bohun heraldic symbols and rich covering, was more a testimony of distinguished ancestry than a simple prayerbook. The duchess had quite a library of her own, for she also gave other books to her son: a chronicle of France, a Latin treatise on the upbringing of princes, and a romance of the Knight of the Swan. One daughter got a *Golden Legend* (a collection of saints' lives), and another the psalter and primer (a child's first book including basic religious texts) which her mother had often used. The third daughter, a nun at the Minoresses in London, got the major share of books, as presumably she was the most literate and the whole convent could also benefit. These included a bible in French in two volumes, a book of decretals in French, a volume of the lives of the fathers, including Pope Gregory's *Pastorals*, two partial psalters in French, and even a book of fine tales.[28]

Among the highest rank of the English nobility French still seems to have been the most popular language. This was not as true further down the social ladder where English also appears. Lady Alice West in 1395 left all her books in Latin, English, and French to her daughter-in-law, except for the matins-book that had belonged to her husband which she left to her son. Some of the early fifteenth century wills even show the Lollard literary influence. In 1422 the will of Lady Perrin Clanvow, from the family of one of the most famous of the Lollard knights, strongly suggests her Lollard sympathies in its provisions about her funeral and burial. Among her books were a copy of *Pore Caitife*, a popular tract among the Lollards, and a psalter, which were left to two women serving among her executors. The occasional English woman even followed the example of Mahaut d'Artois and carried her books with her. When Alice, countess of Suffolk and Chaucer's grand-daughter, went back to her family home at Ewelme in the mid-fifteenth century she took with her one of Lydgate's works, a French book of romances, and a French book of *The City of Ladies*.[29]

And so we come back one last time to Christine de Pizan. Two of her works, *The City of Ladies* and *The Treasure of the City of Ladies*, have been frequently quoted because in them she expressed as a woman what she felt should be the rightful place of women within her society. Such testimony is particularly valuable since it stands alone – no other medieval woman speaks so unflinchingly for her sex at every social level. Nevertheless, Christine was not only a staunch supporter of women, she was one of the most prolific of fifteenth-century writers and the only medieval woman to earn her living by her pen and thus demands attention when describing women's contributions to medieval culture. Her first, rather tentative ballades appear in 1393, three years after her husband's death, and her first long work, the *Epistre au dieu d'amours* in 1399. It has been plausibly suggested that during the lean intervening years, she had served as a copyist. This would have allowed her to make some money and would also have put her in contact with such work-shops as the one which put the Boccaccio manuscripts in circulation c. 1400. In whatever way she gained their acquaintance, she knew many of the artists of her day, for her own later manuscripts were often lavishly illustrated – a necessity if she was to offer them to the queen or to the royal dukes, whose patronage and gifts of money were essential to her survival. In the first twelve years of the fifteenth century she produced some twelve major works, as well as a large number of ballades and short poems.

Her range was as extraordinary as her output, stretching as it did from conventional love poems to allegorical works (of which *L'Avision* was basically autobiographical) to didactic treatises and a spirited upholding of the woman's point of view in the quarrel over the attitude towards women of the *Roman de la Rose*. Her more factual works included a compilation and translation into French of a Latin military treatise combined with a contemporary work on military law, and above all, her biography of Charles V. That life was commissioned by Charles' brother, Duke Philip of Burgundy, and was an extraordinary gesture of confidence in her ability and the width of her knowledge. A woman's effectiveness in writing history depends to a great extent on her possible access to the sources needed, a particular difficulty for medieval women with the scarcity of books and their isolation from affairs of state. Christine was fortunate because her father's position at court had given her a privileged peephole into court life and the chance to observe King Charles. It is possible that she was allowed to use some of the very extensive royal library which Charles V had collected, and Duke Philip made available to her the relevant French chronicles. The *Livre des faits et bons meurs* is not a political history of the reign but an uncritical and vivid personal biography of a king at a time when the royal personality was still a major influence in shaping events. It stands comparison with Joinville's life of Louis IX, for Christine's work also provides a valuable human glimpse into the mystique of French royalty. Like Joinville, Christine deeply admired her subject and spoke from personal testimony, though as a subordinate, not a noble close to the king.

Christine's vigorous intervention in the quarrel over the *Roman de la Rose* brought her into touch with many of the leading writers and humanists of her day and won her the respect of Jean Gerson, the formidable chancellor of the university of Paris. She was not always popular among the men of her time, not surprisingly given her outspoken denunciation of the general denigration of women by men. That current of opposition has continued to have its supporters, for the author of a standard history of French literature at the beginning of this century dismissed Christine contemptuously as:

> a veritable bluestocking, the first of that unbearable line of women authors to whom no work on any subject is an effort and who, during the whole life that God lends them have to bustle about multiplying the proofs of their indefatigable facility, only equal to their universal mediocrity.[30]

Nevertheless, Christine had a considerable reputation among her contemporaries, not only in France but also in England. The earl of

56 Christine de Pizan at work at her desk, surrounded by Reason,
Rectitude and Justice who inspire her writings for women

Salisbury was impressed by her when he came to France on business for
Richard II and for a time had her only son in his household. Henry IV
knew of her poverty and even tried to entice her to his court, but with no
success. Her *Livre des faits d'armes* on military affairs, however, had a
surprising English connection. John Talbot, earl of Shrewsbury's
wedding present to Margaret of Anjou, whom he accompanied to
England for her marriage to Henry VI, was a splendid manuscript
containing a notable collection of romances and chivalric works but also
Christine's military treatise. Some years later, William Caxton translated it into English as one of his earliest printed works.[31]

It is not surprising that contemporary feminist scholars have shown
such a special interest in the career and works of this remarkable
fifteenth-century French woman, but Christine's real importance is as a
trail-blazer, not a rebel. She accepted the medieval framework, agreed
that woman was naturally subject to man, and praised the Virgin Mary

as the highest ideal to which a woman could aspire. However, like the forceful abbess Hildegard, three centuries before, Christine felt that such beliefs could be combined with a practical realisation of the complementary natures of men and women, a recognition of the valuable part women actually played, and the respect and sympathy which they deserved. Christine's last literary work was inspired by Joan of Arc's great victory over the English at Orleans in July 1429. By then elderly and living in retirement in a nunnery, Christine wrote with passion of Joan's virtue and ability but also with pride that it was a young woman who had recovered and made safe the kingdom of France, 'something that 5,000 *men* could not have done'.[32] How pleased she would have been with the praise of Matthieu Thomassin, who had attended Charles VII and later was the secretary of Louis XI! In a general eulogy of Joan of Arc as a gift to the kingdom of France Thomassin wrote that:

> a notable woman called Christine who has made many books in French (I have often seen them at Paris) made a *traitié* of the coming of the said Maid and of her deeds. . . . And I have desired to put Christine's *traitié* here rather than the others, in order to always honour the female sex.[32]

Such a statement seems a suitable ending to this account of what medieval women actually accomplished. The previous chapters have attempted to point out individual women and their activities at many levels of medieval life. Since it is indeed unwise to overlook the activities and concerns of half of the population, it is necessary to right the balance by a vigorous effort to uncover the less obvious traces which male historians have often unconsciously overlooked or considered unimportant because they only rarely dealt with great movements or major political events. Christine de Pizan is merely a final, very voluble reminder that medieval women might indeed be regarded as subordinate and inferior by medieval men, and might suffer from many restrictions, but they were neither invisible, inaudible, nor unimportant. Their contributions to the growth and development of their own society should not be overlooked or undervalued.

Abbreviations

ADH	*Annales de Démographie Historique*
BEC	*Bibliothèque de l'école des chartes*
BHM	*Bulletin of the History of Medicine*
BIHR	*Bulletin of the Institute of Historical Research*
BJRL	*Bulletin of the John Rylands Library*
CCM	*Cahiers de la Civilisation Médiévale*
CLibR	*Calendar of Liberate Rolls*, PRO publication
CPapL	*Calendar of Papal Letters*, PRO publication
CS	*Camden Series*
EETS	*Early English Text Society*
EHR	*English Historical Review*
MGH	*Monumenta Germaniae Historica*; SS, chronicles
PL	*Patrologia Latina*
PRO	Public Record Office
RHDFE	*Revue historique de droit français et étranger*
RHGF	*Recueil des historiens des Gaules et de la France*
RS	*Rolls Series*
SC	*Sources Chrétiennes*
SHF	Société pour l'histoire de France
TRHS	*Transactions of the Royal Historical Society*
VCH	*Victoria County History*
YAJ	*Yorkshire Archeological Journal*

Notes

Titlepage
C. Gilligan, *In a Different Voice* (Cambridge MA and London 1982), 6
R. H. Hilton, *The English Peasantry in the Later Middle Ages* (Oxford 1972), 95

INTRODUCTION
1 F. Heer, *The Medieval World* (London 1962), 265
2 *On the Properties of Things, John Trevisa's Translation of Bartholomaeus Anglicus,
   'De Proprietatibus Rerum'* (Oxford 1975), 307–9
3 E. Power, *Medieval Women*, ed. M. M. Postan (Cambridge 1975), 11
4 Gilbert Lunicensis, *De Statu Ecclesiae*, PL 157, 997, quoted by G. Duby, *The
   Three Orders* (Chicago and London 1980), 287
5 Hildegardis abbatissae, *Opera Omnia*, PL 197, 217–18

Chapter 1 THE PRECURSORS
1 Tacitus, *On Britain and Germany*, trans. H. Mattingly (London 1948), 116, 117,
   107
2 *Anglo-Saxon Chronicle*, rev. trans., ed. D. Whitelock (London 1961), 62–67:
   D. M. Stenton, *The English Woman in History* (London 1957), 4
3 A. Lehmann, *Le Rôle de la femme dans l'histoire de France au Moyen Age* (Paris
   1952), 260–64: C. Jourdain, 'Mémoire sur l'éducation des femmes au Moyen Age',
   Excursions historiques et philosophiques à travers le Moyen Age (Paris 1888, 1966),
   475
4 R. W. Southern, *The Making of the Middle Ages* (London 1967), 75
5 H. Waddell, *More Latin Lyrics* (London 1976), 123
6 S. F. Wemple, *Women in Frankish Society* (Philadelphia 1981), 183–85:
   Lehmann, *Rôle*, 163–80: H. Waddell, *The Wandering Scholars*, rev. 7th ed. (New
   York 1934), 23–27
7 Bede, *A History of the English Church and People*, trans. L. Sherley-Price, rev. ed.
   (London 1968), 245–50, 252
8 L. Eckenstein, *Women under Monasticism* (London 1896, 1963), 136–37: 'Life of
   Lioba', *The Anglo-Saxon Missionaries in Germany*, ed. C. H. Talbot (London
   1954) 205–26
9 M. Bateson, 'Origin and Early History of Double Monasteries', TRHS new ser. 13
   (1899), 175: Wemple, *Women*, 176
10 J. W. Thompson, *The Literacy of the Laity in the Middle Ages* (New York, reprint
   1960), 34–35
11 Dhuoda, *Manuel pour mon fils*, ed. P. Riché, SC 225 (Paris 1975), 352–53
12 P. Dronke, *Women Writers of the Middle Ages* (Cambridge 1984), 36
13 Ibid., 56–57
14 Some translated excerpts from this play, including the kitchen scene are included in

K. M. Wilson, 'The Saxon Canoness, Hrotsvit of Gandersheim', *Medieval Women Writers*, ed. K. M. Wilson (Athens GA 1984), 53–60
15 Dronke, *Women Writers*, 83
16 E. Power, *Medieval People*, 10th ed. (London 1963), 18–38: E. R. Coleman, *Journal of Interdisciplinary History* 2 (1971–72), 205–17

Chapter 2 THE MOULD

1 Christine de Pisan, *Treasure of the City of Ladies*, trans. S. Lawson (London 1985), 128–29: M. Girouard, *Life in the English Country House* (New Haven and London 1978), 27
2 D. Knowles and R. N. Hadcock, *Medieval Religious Houses: England and Wales*, new ed. (London 1971), 494
3 S. Medcalf, 'Inner and Outer', *The Later Middle Ages*, ed. S. Medcalf (London 1981), 109. Dronke, *Women Writers*, 180–83.
4 D. Herlihy, 'Life Expectancies for Women in Medieval Society', *The Role of Women in the Middle Ages*, ed. R. T. Morewedge (Albany 1975), 2–3, 11; C. T. Wood, 'The Doctor's Dilemma', *Speculum* 56 (1981), 723–24
5 V. Bullough and C. Campbell, 'Female Longevity and Diet in the Middle Ages', *Speculum* 55 (1980), 312–25: L. White jr., *Medieval Technology and Social Change* (Oxford 1962), 76
6 Herlihy, 'Life Expectancies', 11–13
7 Hildegardis, *Causae et Curae*, ed. P. Kaiser (Leipzig 1903), 78–79, 102–8, 121, 139
8 P. Dronke, *Poetic Individuality in the Middle Ages* (Oxford 1970), 149
9 F. Vercauteren, 'Les médécins dans les principautés de la Belgique et du nord de France du viiie au xiiie siècle', *Moyen Age* 57 (1951) 72–73, n. 36, quoting MGH SS 14, 282: P. P. A. Biller, 'Birth Control in the West in the Thirteenth and early Fourteenth Centuries', *Past and Present* 94 (1982), 21–24: J. T. Noonan, *Contraception* (Cambridge MA 1965), 227, 229
10 *Letters of Lanfranc, Archbishop of Canterbury*, ed. and trans. by H. Clover and M. Gibson (Oxford 1979), 161
11 M. M. Sheehan in his unpublished paper on 'The Wife of Bath and Her Four Sisters' has developed this point fully and I am grateful to him for making it available.
12 Wemple, *Women*, 100, quoting MGH SS 4, 163–64; *The Goodman of Paris*, trans. with notes by E. Power (London 1928), 210–14
13 Cesarius of Heisterbach, *The Dialogue on Miracles*, trans. H. von E. Scott and C. C. Swinton Bland (London 1929) I, 378
14 R. A. Helmholz, *Marriage Litigation in Medieval England* (Cambridge 1974), 92–93
15 R. C. Palmer, 'Contexts of Marriage in Medieval England', *Speculum* 59 (1984), 44–46
16 J. A. Brundage, 'The Crusader's Wife', *Studia Gratiana* 12 (1967), 427–41
17 E. C. McLaughlin, 'Equality of Souls, Inequality of Sexes', *Religion and Sexism*, ed. R. R. Ruether (New York 1974), 235–36
18 A. Manrique, *Annales Cistercienses* 3 (Lyons 1649), 525
19 Jouon des Longrais, 'Statut de la femme en Angleterre', *La Femme*, Recueils de la société Jean Bodin 12, pt. 2 (Brussels 1962), 140
20 Sharon Ady has kindly allowed me to quote from her paper, 'Women and Wills', read at the Berkshire Conference, May 1984
21 Orderic Vitalis, *Ecclesiastical History*, trans. and ed. by M. Chibnall (Oxford 1972) 3, 256–60; Prof. J. Shatzmiller kindly brought this text to my attention, the

translation was made by one of his students from A. M. Hoberman, *The Crusades in Germany and France* (Jerusalem 1945) 165–67

22 *Letters of Peter the Venerable*, ed. G. Constable (Cambridge MA 1967) 1, Letter 53, 153–73: W. G. Hoskins, *Two Thousand Years in Exeter* (London 1969), 38

23 *Towneley Plays*, EETS n.s. 71 (1897), play 3, ll.388–96

24 Sharon Ady, 'Women and Wills', and further discussion

25 A. Lecoy de la Marche, *Anecdotes historiques, légendes et apologues tiré de recueil inédit d'Etienne de Bourbon* (Paris 1877), 217, 39

26 B. Jarrett, *Social Theories of the Middle Ages 1200–1500* (Westminster MD 1942), 84, quoting Holcot, *In Proverbia Salamonis*

27 Summaries of Robert of Blois and Philip of Novara can be found in A. A. Hentsch, *De la littérature didactique du Moyen Age s'addressant specialement aux femmes* (Cahors 1903, 1975). They also appear in C. V. Langlois, *La Vie en France d'après les moralistes du temps*, 2 (Paris 1925, 1970), 176–204, 205–40: Vincent de Beauvais, *De Eruditione Filiorum Nobilium*, ed. A. Steiner (Cambridge MA 1938), 172–219

28 Langlois, *Vie en France* 4, 42–46

29 *The Book of the Knight of La Tour Landry*, ed. G. S. Taylor (London n.d.), xxii

30 Ibid., 171, 197–98, 279–80, 257–59, xxii–xxiii

31 E. Power, 'The Ménagier's Wife', *Medieval People*, 96–119: *Goodman of Paris*, 113–37

32 'How the Good Wijf taughte Hir Doughter', *Babees Book*, ed. F. J. Furnivall, EETS OS 32 (1868, 1969), 48

33 Christine de Pizan, *The Book of the City of Ladies*, trans. E. J. Richards (New York 1982: *The Treasure of the City of Ladies*, trans. and intro. by S. Lawson (London 1985). These recent translations have made Christine's works available to the general public, but full critical editions of both are needed.

34 Pisan, *Treasure*, 59–76

35 Ibid., 130–33

Chapter 3 QUEENS

1 Jacobus de Cessolis, *The Game of Chess*, trans. and printed by Wm Caxton c. 1483, facsimile ed. (London 1946), 4b

2 Eadmer, *History of Recent Events*, trans. G. Bosanquet (London 1964), 126–31

3 William of Malmesbury, *De gestis regum Anglorum*, RS 90 (1889) 2, 493–94: 'Vita S. Margareta', in Symeon of Durham, *Opera et Collectanea*, Surtees Society 51 (1868), 234–35

4 E. J. Kealey, *Medieval Medicus* (Baltimore MD 1981), 18–20: R. W. Southern, *Saint Anselm and His Biographers* (Cambridge 1963), 191–93

5 Malmesbury, *De gestis* 2, 494–95

6 Waddell, *Wandering Scholars*, 216

7 *Grandes chroniques de France*, ed. J. Viard (Paris 1932) 7, 38

8 RHGF 24, pt. 1, nos. 18–20, 117, 126, 130

9 Matthew Paris, *Chronics Majora*, RS 57 (1876) 3, 166–69: *Grandes Chroniques* 7, 60–61

10 M. Bloch, *Mélanges Historiques* (Paris 1963) 1, 462–90

11 Paris, *Chron. Maj.* 5, 254

12 Comte Riant, 'Déposition de Charles d'Anjou pour la canonisation de Saint Louis', *Notices et Documents publiées pour la Société de l'histoire de France à l'occasion du cinquantième anniversaire* (Paris 1884), 175

13 Joinville, *The Life of St. Louis*, trans. R. Hague, text ed. N. Wailly (London 1955), 606–7

14 A. Bailly, *Saint Louis* (Paris 1949), 55

15 Guillaume de Nangis, 'Vie du Saint Louis', RHGF 20, 317

16 *The Political Songs of England*, ed. and trans. T. Wright, CS 6 (1839), 67: Paris, *Chron. Maj.* 5, 475–82

17 Aldebrandin de Sienne, *Le Régime du Corps*, ed. L. Landouzy and R. Pépin (Paris 1911, 1978), 68–70, 71–78, 87–89

18 Joinville, *Life*, 397–400, 370

19 Ibid., 645–47

20 E. Boutaric, 'Marguerite de Provence', *Revue des questions historiques* 3(1867), 422–23

21 M. A. E. Green, *Lives of the Princesses of England* (London 1849) 2, app. XI, 457–58: Boutaric, 'Marguerite', 457

22 Paris, *Chron. Maj.* 3, 477

23 E. Boutaric, *Saint Louies et Alphonse de Poitiers* (Paris 1870), 108–10: Boutaric, 'Marguerite', 434–39

24 H. M. Colvin, *The King's Works: 2, The Middle Ages* (London 1963), 950–52, 730–31

25 M. D. Legge, *Anglo-Norman Literature and Its Background* (Cambridge 1963), 233–35

26 M. Prestwich, *The Three Edwards* (London 1980), 25

27 M. Champollion-Figeac, *Lettres des Rois, Reines et autres personages des Cours de France et Angleterre* (Paris 1839) 1, 154

28 J. C. Parsons, *The Court and Household of Eleanor of Castilein 1290* (Toronto 1979), 10–14: Legge, *Anglo-Norman Literature*, 225–26

29 J. Froissart, *Chroniques*, ed. K. de Lettenhove (Brussels 1868) 5, 214–16: C. Given-Wilson, 'The Merger of Edward III's and Queen Philippa's Households, 1360–9', BIHR 51 (1978), 184

30 Colvin, *King's Works* 2, 167–68: J. Harvey, *Mediaeval Gardens* (Oregon 1981) 87: R. H. Robbins, 'Medical Manuscripts in Middle English', *Speculum 45 (1970), 401*

31 C. R. Sherman, 'Taking a Second Look; Observations on the Iconography of a French Queen, Jeanne de Bourbon', *Feminism and Art History*, ed. N. Broude and M. D. Garrard (New York 1982), 101–17

32 Christine de Pisan, *Livre des fais et bonnes meurs de Charles V*, ed. S. Solente, SHF (Paris 1936) 1, 53–57 and *Treasure*, 45–81

33 Shakespeare, *Henry VI*, Pt. 3, Act I scene 4, ll, 111–12

34 Christine de Pisan, Letter to Queen Isabeau, in *Anglo-Norman Letters and Petitions*, ed. M. D. Legge (Oxford 1941), 144–49

35 P. M. Kendall, *The Yorkist Age* (New York 1970), 423

Chapter 4 NOBLE LADIES

1 *Register of Letters of Br. John Peckham, archbishop of Canterbury* 1, RS 77, 250–53

2 *Letters of Queen Margaret of Anjou*, ed. C. S. Monro, CS o.s. 86, 97–98

3 *Testamenta Vetusta*, ed. N. H. Nicolas (London 1826), 205: S. L. Thrupp, *The Merchant Class of Medieval London* (Ann Arbor 1962), 266

4 T. F. Tout, *Chapters in the Administrative History of Medieval England* 2 (Manchester 1937), 182–83

5 R. Grosseteste, 'Les Reules Seynt Roberd', *Walter of Henley's Husbandry*, trans. E. Lamond (London 1890), 122–50: M. T. Clanchy, *From Memory to Written Record* (London 1979), 151–54: Pisan, *Treasure*, 129

6 *Aucassin and Nicolette*, trans. E. Mason (London 1910), 27

7 *Self and Society in Medieval France*, ed. J. F. Benton (New York 1970), 38–39

8 *Chanson du Chevalier du cygne et de Godefroid de Bouillon*, quoted G. G. Coulton,

Life in the Middle Ages 3 (Cambridge 1967), 30–31: G. Webb and A. Walker, *St. Bernard of Clairvaux* (London 1960), 13–14, 18–19

9 Vitalis, *Ecclesiastical History* 5, 325

10 *Les Oeuvres poétiques de Baudri de Bourgueil*, ed. P. Abrahams (Paris 1926), 196–231, 232–53

11 Vitalis, *Ecclesiastical History* 6, 44–45 and n. 2

12 *Histoire Générale de Languedoc*, ed. C. Devic et J. Vaissete (Toulouse 1879) 6, 151–53, and see further 7, 437, 440

13 *Rotuli Hundredorum, temp. Henry III et Edw. I* (London 1812) 1, 309, quoted R. Graham, *English Ecclesiastical Studies* (London 1929), 365

14 Paris, *Chron. Maj.* 5, 437, 440

15 Aquinas, *Selected Political Writings*, ed. A. P. d'Entrèves (Oxford 1948), 84–95
    L. E. Boyle, O. P., 'Thomas of Aquinas and the Duchess of Brabant', unpublished paper given at Pontifical Institute of Medieval Studies, Toronto. I am much indebted to Fr. Boyle for allowing me to see his copy describing Marguerite of Flanders as the proper addressee

16 *Manners and Household Expenses of England in the Thirteenth and Fifteenth Centuries*, ed. H. T. Tanner, intro. by B. Botfield (Roxburghe Club 1841), 15–16, 31, 33

17 VCH Hampshire 4, 645

18 N. Denholm-Young, *Seigniorial Administration in England* (Oxford 1937), 77 and 'The Yorkshire Estates of Isabella de Fortibus', YAJ 31 (1934)

19 N. Denholm-Young, 'Edward I and the Sale of the Isle of Wight', EHR 44 (1929), 435–36

20 Godefroy-Menilgaise, *Mémoires de la société des antiquaires de France* 28 (1865) gives the various documents of the trial. See also P. Lehugeur, *Histoire de Philippe le Long, roi de France (1316–1322)*, (Paris 1877, 1975), 168–74

21 J. M. Richard, *Mahaut comtesse d'Artois et de Bourgogne* (Paris 1887), 39–40

22 Ibid, 94–95

23 Dehaisnes, *Documents et extraits concernant l'histoire de l'art dans la Flandre, l'Artois et le Hainaut avant le XVᵉ siècle* (Lille 1886), 183, 207, 272, 276, 236

24 C. A. Musgrave, Household Administration in the Fourteenth Century with special reference to the Household of Elizabeth de Burgh, unpublished MA thesis, University of London 1923

25 H. Rashdall, *The Universities of Europe in the Middle Ages*, new ed. rev. by F. M. Powicke and A. B. Emden (Oxford 1936) 3, 302–4

26 J. Nichols, *Collection of the Wills of the Kings and Queens of England* (London 1780), 22–43

27 H. Jenkinson, 'Mary de Sancto Paulo, foundress of Pembroke College, Cambridge', *Archaeologia* 66 (1915), 411–46

28 CPapL 3, 285–86, 433

29 R. R. Sharpe, *Calendar of Wills proved and enrolled in the Court of Hustings London 1258–1688* (London 1889–90) 2, 194–95 and printed in full in Jenkinson, op. cit., 432–35

30 *Household Book of Dame Alice de Bryene 1412–1413*, ed. V. B. Redstone, Suffolk Institute of Archaeology and Natural History (Ipswich 1931)

31 E. Rickert, 'A Leaf from a Fourteenth-Century Letter Book', *Modern Philology* 25 (1927), 253–54

32 *Household Book*, 123

33 Ibid., 25–28

34 M. T. Riley, *Memorials of London and London Life 1276–1419* (London 1868), 430–32

Chapter 5 NUNS AND BEGUINES
1 *Letters of Abelard and Héloïse*, trans. B. Radice (London 1974), 217–18
2 Dronke, *Women Writers*, 144
3 G. Constable, 'Aelred of Rievaulx and the nun of Watton', *Medieval Women*, ed. D. Baker (Studies in Church History: Subsidia I 1978), 206–9
4 *The Register of Eudes of Rouen*, trans. by S. M. Brown, ed. J. F. O'Sullivan (New York, London 1964), 110, 293: *Register . . . Peckham* 1, 82–83
5 Langlois, *Vie en France* 2, 341–42
6 Dronke, *Women Writers*, 175: Hildegardis, *Causae*, 104
7 *Letters . . . Abelard*, 160–78
8 P. Dronke, *Abelard and Héloïse in Medieval Testimonies* (Glasgow 1976), 23, 51: E. McLeod, *Héloïse* (London 1971), 226–27
9 *Letters . . . Abelard*, 199–201
10 VCH Wiltshire 3, 244–51
11 *Issues of the Exchequer*, ed. F. Devon (Record Commission 1836), 144
12 Legge, *Anglo-Norman Literature*, 300
13 *Life of Christina of Markyate*, ed. and trans. C. H. Talbot (Oxford 1959), 40–55, 73–93
14 A. Manrique, *Annales Cistercienses* (Lyon 1649) 3, 200
15 R. W. Southern, *Western Society and the Church in the Middle Ages* (London 1970), 314 quoting E. L. Hugo, *Annales Praemonstratenses* 2, 147
16 W. Dugdale, *Monasticon Anglicanum* (London 1830) 6, pt. II, 502: E. Power, *Medieval English Nunneries* (Cambridge 1922), 121
17 VCH Hampshire 2, 132–33
18 *Register . . . Peckham* 2, 650–55: *Visitations of Religious Houses in the diocese of Lincoln*, ed. A. Hamilton Thompson (Canterbury and York Society 1915) 1, 67
19 E. M. Hallam, 'Philip the Fair and the Cult of St. Louis', *Religion and National Identity*, ed. S. Mews, Studies in Church History 18 (1982), 205–6: A. W. Lewis, *Royal Succession in Capetian France* (Cambridge MA 1981), 140–42
20 Christine de Pisan, *Oeuvres poétiques*, ed. M. Roy (Paris 1891, 1965) 2, 155–222
21 Nichols, *Collection . . . Wills*, 31: VCH London 1, 518: CPapL 4, 37–38
22 *Butler's Lives of the Saints*, ed. H. Thurston and D. Attwater (London 1956) 2, 623–26, trans. from *Acta Sanctorum*, June 5
23 Hefele-Leclerq, *Histoire des Conciles* (Paris 1873) 9, 431
24 For Mechtild, see infra, 133; for Marguerite, infra, 209
25 E. W. McDonnell, *The Beguines and Beghards in Medieval Culture* (New Brunswick N.J. 1954), 148–49, quoting J. Bethune, *Cartulaire du béguinage de Sainte-Elisabeth de Gand* (Bruges 1893), 74
26 J. L. Connolly, *John Gerson, Reformer and Mystic* (Louvain 1928), 23–27
27 Langlois, *Vie en France* 2, 343–44: *Not in God's Image*, ed. J. O'Faolain and L. Martines (New York 1973), 157

Chapter 6 RECLUSES AND MYSTICS
1 Cesarius, *Dialogues* 1, 402, 381
2 *Butler's Lives* 1, 76: D. Weinstein and R. M. Bell, *Saints and Society* (Chicago 1982), 88–89
3 CLibR Henry III, 1240–45, 435
4 J. Stow, *The Survey of London*, rev. ed. (London 1959), 333
5 C. H. Talbot, 'The "De Institutis Inclusorum" of Ailred of Rievaulx', *Analecta Sacri Ordinis Cisterciensis* 7 (1951), 177–216: Aelred de Rievaulx, *La Vie de Recluse*, intro. and trans. by C. Dumont, SC 76 (Paris 1961): *The Ancrene Riwle*, trans. M. B. Salu (Notre Dame, Ind 1956)

6 Aelred, *Vie*, 44–53
7 Ibid., 60–79
8 E. J. Dobson, *The Origins of Ancrene Wisse* (Oxford 1976)
9 *Ancrene Riwle*, 185
10 Cesarius, *Dialogues* 1, 428
11 R. M. Clay, *The Hermits and Anchorites of England* (London 1914), 203–63
12 F. M. Powicke, 'Loretta, countess of Leicester', *Historical Essays in Honour of James Tait* (Manchester 1933), 247–71: Dobson. *Origins*, 304–11
13 Thomas of Eccleston, *De adventu fratrum* in *Monumenta Franciscana* (RS 4) 1, 16
14 L. W. Vernon-Harcourt, *His Grace the Steward* (London 1907), 125–26
15 Clay, *Hermits*, 74–75: Calendar of Fine Rolls 1319–27, 99
16 Musgrave, Household Administration, 7–8, 37–38
17 *Visitations*, ed. Thompson, 1, 113–15
18 *A Book of Showings to the Anchoress, Julian of Norwich*, ed. E. Colledge and J. Walsh (Toronto 1978) 1, 43–47
19 *Concise Oxford Dictionary of the Christian Church*, ed. E. A. Livingstone (Oxford 1977), 350
20 Hildegardis abbatissa, *Opera Omnia* PL 197
21 C. Singer, *From Magic to Science* (New York 1958), 215–16
22 Hildegardis, *Causae*, 47
23 Hildegardis, *Opera*, 216–18
24 *The Revelations of Mechtild de Magdeburg*, trans. L. Menzies (London 1953), 98, 164–69, 169–70, 188
25 The Latin edition is to be found in *Revelationes Gertrudianae ac Mechtildianae*, ed. by the monks of Solesmes (Paris 1877) 2, 1–422: the English version, *The Booke of Gostlye Grace of Mechtild of Hackeborn*, ed. T. A. Halligan (Toronto 1979)
26 Gertrude of Helfta, *Le Héraut* SC 139 (Paris 1968)
27 C. W. Bynum, *Jesus as Mother* (Berkeley 1982), 170–262
28 Ibid., 262
29 Clay, *Hermits*, 232–37
30 Julian of Norwich, *Revelations of Divine Love*, trans. by C. Wolters (London 1966)
31 *Les Révélations célestes et divines de Sainte Brigitte de Suède*, trans. J. Ferraige (Paris 1859) 3, 461
32 J. G. Dickinson, *The Congress of Arras* (Oxford 1955), 146
33 *Révélations célestes* 3, 381–82
34 E. Colledge, '*Epistola solitarii ad reges*: Alphonse of Pecha', *Medieval Studies* 18 (1956), 19–49: *Révélations célestes* 2, 401–7
35 Connolly, *John Gerson*, 240
36 C. A. J. Armstrong, 'The Piety of Cicely, Duchess of York', *England, France and Burgundy in the Fifteenth Century* (London 1983), 149
37 *The Book of Margery Kempe*, trans. W. Butler Bowdon (London 1936), 215–16, 82
38 Ste-Marie Perrin, *Ste. Colette and Her Reform*, trans. C. Maguire, ed. G. O'Neill (London 1923), 313
39 The complete *Book of Margery Kempe*, ed. by S. B. Meech with notes by S. B. Meech and H. E. Allen, is EETS o.s. 212 (1940). The Butler Bowdon translation previously cited is more accessible to the non-expert and references are to that unless otherwise noted
40 *Self and Society in Medieval France*, ed. J. F. Benton (New York 1970)
41 *Book of Margery Kempe*, 47
42 C. W. Atkinson, *Mystic and Pilgrim* (Ithaca 1983); D. Knowles, *The English Mystical Tradition* (London 1961), 138–50: E. Colledge, 'Margery Kempe',

Pre-Reformation English Spirituality, ed. J. Walsh (London n.d.), 210–23 and *Showings* 1, introduction 25–38

43 *Book of Margery Kempe*, 59

Chapter 7   TOWNSWOMEN AND PEASANTS

1 Pisan, *Treasure*, 145–49
2 Ibid., 153–54
3 *Menagier*, 310
4 Pisan, *Treasure*, 167–68
5 'How the Good Wijf', 36–47
6 Pisan, *Treasure*, 168–71
7 Riley, *Memorials*, 68–69
8 R. B. Cook, 'Some Early Civic Wills of York', *Associated Architectural Societies Reports and Papers* 33, pt. 1 (1915), 167–76. Juetta as executrix, 173
9 Ibid., 161–62
10 *Fifty Earliest English Wills*, ed. F. J. Furnivall, EETs o.s. 78 (1882), 103
11 G. A. Williams, *Medieval London* (London 1963), 58–59
12 S. L. Thrupp, *The Merchant Class of Medieval London* (Ann Arbor 1962), 106–7
13 *Le Livre des Métiers d'Etienne Boileau*, ed. R. Lespinasse et F. Bonnardot, Histoire Générale de Paris (Paris 1879)
14 A. G. I. Christie, *English Medieval Embroidery* (Oxford 1938), 36
15 P. Verlet, 'Gothic Tapestry', *Great Tapestries*, ed. J. Jobé (Lausanne 1965), 16: A. W. Carr, 'Women as Artists in the Middle Ages', *Feminist Art Journal* Spring 1976, 9
16 Riley, *Memorials*, 375–76
17 H. Geraud, *Paris sous Philippe les Bel*, Paris 1837: *Livre de la taille de Paris 1313*, ed. K. Michaelsson, Acta Universitas Gotoburgensis 57 (Goteborg 1951), xvii: J. Favier, *Les Contribuables parisiens â la fin de la guerre de Cent Ans* (Geneva 1970), 11–12
18 E. Ekwall, *Two Early London Subsidy Rolls*, Skrifter Utgivna ov Kungl. Humanistiska vetenskapssamfundet Lund 48 (Lund 1957), 104–5, 309, 216
19 *Taille . . . 1313*, 228–34, 219
20 Ibid., 60, 93; 159, 129; xviii–xix; 17
21 *Early Gild Records of Toulouse*, ed. with intro. M. A. Mulholland (New York 1941); K. Rogerson, Women in business in Late Medieval Montpellier, lecture at Toronto Medieval Conference March 1985
22 Sharpe, *Calendar of Wills* 2, 198–99; 1, 450; 1, 445
23 Riley, *Memorials*, 123–25: 446–47
24 Ibid., 162–65; 319; 643
25 Ibid., 385–86; 433–34; 662
26 Pisan, *Treasure*, 176–77
27 'Hosebonderie', *Walter of Henley's Husbandry*, ed. E. Lamond (London 1890), 82–83
28 Hilton, *English Peasantry*, 106
29 Ibid., 98
30 Z. Razi, *Life, Marriage and Death in a Medieval Parish* (Cambridge 1980), 82–83
31 J. M. Bennett, 'Medieval Peasant Marriage', *Pathways to Medieval Peasants*, ed. J. A. Raftis, Papers on Medieval Studies 2 (Toronto 1981), 193–208
32 J. M. Bennett, Gender, Family and Community: a Comparative Study of the English Peasantry 1287–1344, unpubl. Ph.D. thesis, Pontifical Institute of Medieval Studies (Toronto 1981), 98
33 T. McLean, *Medieval English Gardens* (New York 1980), 219

34　Hilton, *English Peasantry*, 103–4: Cesarius, *Dialogues* 2, 271–72

35　B. A. Hanawalt, 'Childbearing among the Lower Classes of Late Medieval England', *Journal of Interdisciplinary History* 8 (1977), 8–19

36　Cesarius, *Dialogues* 2, 198–99

37　This information comes from as yet unpublished work by Ann De Windt on Ramsey women involved in trades, and I am most grateful for her generosity in sharing it with me at an early stage.

38　Bennett, Gender, 320

39　G. Duby, *Rural Economy and Country Life in the Medieval West* (Columbia SC 1976), 485–86

40　J. G. Greatrex, Church, Society and Politics in a Fourteenth Century Rural Setting, paper read to the Ecclesiastical History Society at York, July 1974. My thanks to Dr. Greatrex for allowing me to use her portrait of a peasant widow

41　Bennett, Gender, 207–8: Razi, *Life*, 87

42　Hilton, *English Peasantry*, 109

43　M. T. Lorcin, 'Retraite des veuves et filles au couvent', ADH 1975, 193

44　Ibid., 190–96

Chapter 8　WOMEN AS HEALERS

1　Vitalis, *Ecclesiastical History* 4, 28–30

2　*Aucassin and Nicolette*, trans. E. Mason (London 1928), 27: W. von Eschenbach, *Parzival*, trans. H. M. Mustard and C. E. Passage (New York 1961) 304–7: *Le Livre de Seyntz Medicines*, ed. E. J. Arnould, Anglo-Norman Text Society 2 (Oxford 1940), 144–45 and passim: *Paston Letters*, ed. J. Gairdner (Edinburgh 1910) 3, no. 898

3　Hildegardis, *Vita* PL 197, 153; *Letters of Abelard and Héloïse*, 215: *Dictionnaire Biographique des médecins en France au Moyen Age*, ed. E. Wickersheimer, (reprint Geneva 1979), 532

4　P. Dubois, *The Recovery of the Holy Land*, trans. with intro. and notes W. I. Brandt (New York 1956), 118–20, 138–39

5　*Chartularium universitatis Parisiensis*, ed. H. Denifle and E. Chatelain (Paris 1889–97) 1, 488–90; *University Records and Life in the Middle Ages*, ed. L. Thorndike (New York 1975), 83–84: *Chartularium* 3, 16–17; *University Records*, 235–36

6　Riley, *Memorials*, 519–20; Robbins, 'Medical Manuscripts', *Speculum* 45 (1970), 394

7　*Dictionnaire*, Wickersheimer, 273, 522: D. Jacquart, *Le Milieu médical en France du XIIe au XIVe siècle* (Geneva 1981), 478

8　*Dictionnaire*, Wickersheimer, 294–95; M. L. Hughes, *Women Healers in Medieval Life and Literature* (reprint 1968), 88–89, quoting Louis' grant to Hersend

9　C. H. Talbot and E. A. Hammond, *Medical Practitioners in Medieval England*, (London 1965), 200: M. C. Barnet, 'The Barber Surgeons of York'. *Medical History* 12 (1968), 27: Talbot and Hammond, *Medical Practitioners*, 10

10　Talbot and Hammond, *Medical Practitioners*, 209

11　P. Kibre, 'The Faculty of Medicine at Paris', BHM 27 (1953), 7: *Dictionnaire*, Wickersheimer, 100: Lehmann, *Rôle*, 472

12　*Chartularium* 2, 255–67; Kibre, 'Faculty', 8–12 (although Yvo, servant of the Paris court, was not a woman)

13　*Dictionnaire*, Wickersheimer, 537, 549, 732 and 730: Lehmann, *Rôle*, 472–73

14　*Dictionnaire*, Wickersheimer, 543; *Chartularium* 4, 198–99; *University Records* 289–90: *Dictionnaire*, Wickersheimer, 267

15 Ekwall, *Early . . . Rolls*, 241, 266: Talbot and Hammond, *Medical Practitioners*, 28, 100

16 E. F. Tuttle, 'The *Trotula* and old Dame Trot', BHM 50 (1976), 62–65: C. H. Talbot, *Medicine in Medieval England* (London 1967), 80–82

17 B. Rowland, *Medieval Woman's Guide to Health* (Kent Ohio 1981), 59

18 Jacquart, *Milieu medical*, 48–49

19 *Supplément*, ed. E. Wickersheimer and D. Jacquart, Hautes Etudes médiévales et modernes 35 (Geneva 1979), 33, 191

20 Talbot and Hammond, *Medical Practitioners*, 209–10

21 *Supplément*, 12, 222

22 T. R. Forbes, *The Midwife and the Witch* (New Haven 1966), 133–38; *Supplément*, 222

23 E. J. Kealey, *Medieval Medicus* (Baltimore MD 1981), 83

24 J. Vitry, *Historia Occidentalis*, ed. J. F. Hinnebusch (Fribourg 1972), 146–51, 276–84: J. H. Mundy, 'Charity and Social Work in Toulouse, 1100–1250', *Traditio* 22 (1966), 211–30, 235–37

25 D. L. Mackay, *Les Hôpitaux et la Charité à Paris au XIIIe siècle* (Paris 1923), 28–29, 71

26 Kealey, *Medieval Medicus*, 90

27 *Statuts d'Hôtels-Dieu et de Léproseries*, ed. L. Le Grand (Paris 1901), 78

28 Richard, *Mahaut comtesse d'Artois*, 89, n. 2; app. VIII, 399–401

29 L. Lallemand, *Histoire de la Charité*; III, *Le Moyen Age* (Paris 1907), 146–48: *Statuts*, 13, 115, 124, 162

30 H. Bordier et L. Briele, *Les Archives Hospitalières de Paris* (Paris 1877), 146–49

31 Lallemand, *Histoire* 3,87: R. Coyecque, *L'Hôtel-Dieu de Paris au Moyen Age* (Paris 1889–91) 1, 160–61

32 *Statuts*, 120, 129, xii–xvii

33 L. Le Grand, *Les Maisons-Dieu et léproseries du diocèse de Paris au milieu du XIVe siècle, d'après le registre de visites du délégué de l'evêque (1351–69)*, Mémoires de la société de l'histoire de Paris et de l'Ile-de-France 24 (Paris 1897), 61–64

34 Coyecque, *Hôtel-Dieu* 1, 92 n. 3

35 *Collection de documents pour servir à l'histoire des hôpitaux de Paris*, ed. M. Briele: 3 *Collection des comptes de l'Hôtel-Dieu de Paris* (Paris 1883), 45

36 Coyecque, *Hôtel-Dieu* 1, 80 n. 2

37 Ibid., 31–34

38 Coyecque, *Hôtel-Dieu* 2, Doc. 533, 80–81

39 Knowles and Hadcock, *Medieval Religious Houses*, 38, 407

40 VCH London 1, 520–25; Kealey, *Medieval Medicus*, 98–101

41 Lallemand, *Histoire* 3, 240–67, 271–99

42 A. Higounet-Nadal, 'Hygiène, salubrité, pollutions au Moyen Age', ADH 1975, 88–89

43 A. Bourgeois, *Lépreux et maladreries du Pas-de-Calais (Xe-XVIIIe siècles)* (Arras 1972), 17–19, 51–52

44 D. Angers, La bourgeoisie de Falaise et ses lépreux à la fin du Moyen Age, unpublished paper which Prof. Angers has kindly allowed me to use.

Chapter 9 WOMEN ON THE FRINGE

1 Thomas of Chobham, *Summa confessorum*, ed. F. Broomfield (Louvain 1968), 346–53; quotation, 352

2 R. Gutsch, 'A Twelfth Century Preacher-Fulk of Neuilly', *The Crusades and other Historical Essays presented to Dana C. Munro*, ed. L. J. Paetow (New York 1928, 1968), 191

3 Thomas of Chobham, *Summa*, 349

4 Le Grand, *Maisons-Dieu*, 252–58

5 Pisan, *Treasure*, 172–74

6 A. Terroine, 'Le roi des ribauds de l'hôtel du Roi et les prostituées parisiennes', RHDFE 56 (1978), 255–64

7 J. Rossiaud, 'Prostitution, jeunesse, et société dans les villes du sud-est au XVᵉ siècle', *Annales* 31 (1976), 292, 290: L. Le Pileur, *La Prostitution du XIIIᵉ au XVIIᵉ siècle* (Paris 1908), 8

8 J. B. Post, 'A fifteenth-century customary of the Southwark stews', *Journal of the society of Archivists* 5: 6 (1976), 422–28

9 Le Pileur, *Prostitution*, 3, 6–7: S. M. Newton, *Fashion in the Age of the Black Prince* (London 1980), 76

10 A. Porteau-Bitker, 'Criminalité et delinquance feminines dans le droit pénal des XIIIᵉ et XIVᵉ siècles', RHDFE 58 (1980), 27, n. 134 Riley, *Memorials*, 267, 458–59: Le Pileur, *Prostitution*, 11: J. Evans, *Dress in Medieval France* (Oxford 1952), 55

11 Post, 'Fifteenth-century custumary', 422–28

12 E. Le Roy Ladurie, *Montaillou* (New York 1978), 153–68

13 Le Pileur, *Prostitution*, 4, 6

14 Rossiaud, 'Prostitution', 293–301: J. Bellamy, *Crime and Public Order in England in the Later Middle Ages* (London 1973), 58–59

15 Porteau-Bitker, 'Criminalité', 38

16 Ibid., 47, n. 204.

17 Riley, *Memorials*, 484–86

18 B. Hanawalt, 'The Female Felon in Fourteenth-Century England', *Viator* 5 (1974), 267–68 and *Women in Medieval Society*, 135–37

19 C. Elder, Gaol Delivery in the Southwestern Counties, 1416–1430, unpubl. MA thesis, Carleton University 1983, 109–10

20 Porteau-Bitker, 'Criminalité', 49: supra, 154

21 Lehmann, *Rôle*, 246–47

22 Riley, *Memorials*, 368

23 Porteau-Bitker, 'Criminalité', 51–52

24 Ibid., 296–98, 196

25 Porteau-Bitker, 'Criminalité', 33: Elder, Gaol Delivery, 83–84

26 Porteau-Bitker, 'Criminalité', 49: Elder, Gaol Delivery, 136

27 B. Hanawalt Westman, 'The Peasant Family and Crime in Fourteenth Century England', *Journal of British Studies* 13 (1974), 11

28 K. E. Garay, 'Women and Crime in Later Medieval England', *Florilegium* 1 (1979), 93

29 J. R. H. Moorman, *Church Life in England in the Thirteenth Century* (Cambridge 1955), 228

30 M. D. Lambert, *Medieval Heresy* (London 1977), 177–78: Dronke, *Women Writers*, 217–28

31 William of Puylaurens, *Historia Albigensium* RHGF 19, 200d: R. Abels and E. Harrison, 'The Participation of Women in Languedocian Catharism', *Medieval Studies* 41 (1979), 227–28

32 Abels and Harrison, 'Participation', 241

33 *Chronicon Henrici Knighton* (RS 92) 2, 152: Hoccleve, *Minor Poems*, EETS ES 61 (rev. reprint 1970), 1, 13–ll, 145–52 of To Sir John Oldcastle

34 M. Aston, 'Lollardy and Literacy', *History* 62 (1977), 355

35 *Heresy Trials in the Diocese of Norwich 1428–31*, ed. N. P. Tanner, CS Fourth Ser, 20 (1977)

36 Ibid., 66, 68, 200, 43
37 Ibid., 42, 46; 47–48
38 Ibid., 141–42
39 M. Aston, 'Lollard Women Priests?', *Journal of Ecclesiastical History* 31 (1980), 444–51
40 Knighton, *Chronicon* 2, 316–17
41 A good recent summary and guide to the material is M. Warner, *Joan of Arc: The Image of Female Heroism*, London 1981
42 J. B. Russell, *Witchcraft in the Middle Ages* (Ithaca and London 1972), 182–84; 214
43 A. R. Myers, 'The Captivity of a Royal Witch', BJRL 24 (1940), intro. 263–77; text, 277–84
44 R. A. Griffiths, 'The Trial of Eleanor Cobham', BJRL 51, 381–99
45 Supra, 86

Chapter 10 WOMEN AND MEDIEVAL CULTURE

  1 Dronke, *Women Writers*, 84–92
  2 A Feather on the Breath of God, Hyperion Records A66039: text of *Ordo Virtutum* in P. Dronke, *Poetic Individuality in the Middle Ages* (Oxford 1970), 180–92; performance by Society of Old Music, Kalamazoo, Michigan, May 1984
  3 Herrad of Hohenbourg, *Hortus Deliciarum*, ed. R. Green, M. Evans, C. Bischoff, M. Curschmann, Studies of the Warburg Institute 36 (London 1979) 2 v
  4 Ibid., 2, plate 154 and text 1, 227: 2, plate 124 and text 1, 201
  5 Legge, *Anglo-Norman Literature*, 60–72: J. C. Russell, *Dictionary of Writers of Thirteenth Century England*, special supplement BIHR 3 (London 1936, 1967), 23
  6 *Gesta Abbatum* (RS 128d) 1, 127: C. J. Holdsworth, 'Christina of Markyate', *Medieval Women*, ed. D. Baker, 189–95
  7 McDonnell, *The Beguines*, 405
  8 Herrad, *Hortus* 2, 398, no. 1810
  9 RHGF 22, 592b; CLibR 1240–45, 278
 10 Y. Rokseth, 'Les femmes musiciennes de xiie au xive siècle', *Romania* 61 (1935), 473–74
 11 Paris, *Chron. Maj*, 4, 147: C. Bullock-Davies, *Menestrellorum Multitudo* (Cardiff 1978), 137–38, 55–60
 12 'Vita S. Margareta', Surtees Society 51, 239: Langlois, *Vie en France* 2, 27: Bourgueil, *Oeuvres poètiques*, 253–55
 13 Paris, *Chron. Maj*, 4, 546–47
 14 *Gesta Abbatum* 1, 93: T. S. R. Boase, *English Art 1100–1216* (Oxford 1953), 202–3
 15 R. K. Lancaster, 'Artists, Suppliers and Clerks: the Human Factor in the Art Patronage of King Henry III', *Journal of the Warburg and Courtauld Institute* 35 (1972), 83–85; Christie, *Eng. Med. Embroidery*, 33
 16 Christie, op. cit., 36; Riley, *Memorials*, 52
 17 G. Fagniez, *Etudes sur l'industrie et la classe industrielle au Paris 13e–14e siècles* (Paris 1884), app. 47, 376–77
 18 F. Baron, 'Enlumineurs, peintres et sculpteurs parisiens des xiiie et xive siècles d'après les rôles de la taille', *Bulletin archéologique des travaux historiques et scientifiques* n.s. 4 (1968), 37–115
 19 Ibid., nos. 19, 168, 135 and 8, 29 and 137, 74
 20 D. Miner, *Anastaise and Her Sisters* (Baltimore MD 1974), 11–12 and Walters Art Gallery, Baltimore, W 26, f. 64: D. Jackson, *The Story of Writing* (New York 1981), 76
 21 Miner, *Anastaise*, 18–19
 22 Pizan, *City of Ladies*, 85

23 V. W. Egbert, *The Medieval Artist at Work* (Princeton 1967), 82–83
24 Miner, *Anastaise*, 23
25 M. Bogin, *The Woman Troubadours* (New York 1976), 82–91; Dronke, *Women Writers*, 103–6
26 Denis Pyramus, *La vie seint Edmund le Rei*, quoted G. Olson, *Literature as Recreation in the Later Middle Ages* (Ithaca 1982), 150
27 E. J. Mickel jr., *Marie de France* (New York 1974), 23
28 *Testamenta Vetusta*, ed. N. H. Nicolas (London 1826), 147–49
29 *Fifty Earliest Eng. Wills*, 5, 49–51: D. Gardiner, *English Girlhood at School* (London 1929), 113
30 G. Lanson, *Histoire de littérature Française*, 22nd ed. (Paris 1912) 1, 167
31 Christine de Pisan, *Book of Fayttes of Armes and of Chyvalrye*, ed. A. T. P. Byles, EETS 189 (1932), xvi–xviii
32 A. J. Kennedy and K. Varty, 'Christine de Pisan's "Ditié de Jehanne d'Arc"', pt. 2, *Nottingham Medieval Studies* 19 (1975), verse 34, 70
33 R. Thomassy, *Essai sur les écrits politiques de Christine de Pisan* (Paris 1838) xlvii–xlviii, quoting the Registre Delphinat

Further Reading

As this study of medieval women is meant primarily for the general reader, it would seem inappropriate and ponderous to list the wide variety of sources from which the inevitably fragmentary information has been gathered. Those directly quoted can be found in the Notes. Two earlier bibliographies: C. Erickson and K. Casey, 'Women in the Middle Ages: A Working Bibliography', *Medieval Studies* 37 (1975), 340–59, and M. M. Sheehan, *Family and Marriage in Medieval Europe*, Vancouver 1976, are comprehensive to the date of their compilation. The list, therefore, merely suggests the most important general studies and collections of essays which could aid further research and points out the most useful books and essays dealing more specifically with the content of each chapter. Because there has been so much new work in certain fields it has attempted to draw attention to the most recent useful works. Many of the books cited have very extensive bibliographies which can assist those with particular interests.

General

Bennett, H. S., *Six Medieval Men and Women*, Cambridge 1955

Casey, K., 'The Cheshire Cat: Reconstructing the Experience of Medieval Women', *Liberating Women's History*, ed. B. A. Carroll, Urbana IL 1976, 224–49

Dronke, P., *Women Writers of the Middle Ages*, Cambridge 1984

Ferrante, J., *Woman as Image in Medieval Literature: from the Twelfth Century to Dante*, New York 1975

Harksen, S., *Women in the Middle Ages*, New York 1976

Herlihy, D., *Women in Medieval Society*, Houston 1971

Kemp-Welch, A., *Of Six Medieval women*, 1913, Williamstown MA 1979

Lehmann, A., *Le Rôle de la femme dans l'histoire de France du Moyen Age*, Paris 1952

Pernoud, R., *La femme au temps des cathédrales*, Paris 1980

Power, E., *Medieval People*, London 1924 and many editions: *Medieval Women*, ed. M. M. Postan, Cambridge 1975: 'The Position of Women', *The Legacy of the Middle Ages*, ed. G. C. Crump and E. F. Jacob, Oxford 1926, 401–33

Shahar, S., *The Fourth Estate: A History of Women in the Middle Ages*, London 1983

Stenton, D. M., *The English Woman in History*, London 1957

Collections of Essays

Becoming Visible: Women in European History, ed. R. Bridenthal and C. Koonz, Boston 1977

Beyond Their Sex, ed. P. H. Labalme, New York 1980

Feminism and Art History: Questioning the Litany, ed. N. Broude and M. D. Garrard, New York 1982

Fossier, R. et al., 'La femme dans les sociétés occidentales', *CCM* 20 (1977), 95 ff

Leyerle, J. et al., 'Marriage in the Middle Ages', *Viator* 4 (1973), 413 ff

Literature and Western Civilisation: The Medieval World, ed. D. Daiches and A. Thorlby, London 1973

The Role of Women in the Middle Ages, ed. R. Morewedge, Albany 1975
Roles and Images of Women in the Middle Ages and Renaissance, ed. D. Radcliffe-Umstead, Pittsburgh 1975
Women in Medieval Society, ed. S. M. Stuard, Philadelphia 1976

Chapter I
Facinger, M. F., 'A Study in Medieval Queenship: Capetian France 987–1237', *Studies in Medieval and Renaissance History* 5 (1968), 3–47
Riché, P., *Education and Culture in the Barbarian World*, Columbia SC 1976
Stafford, P., *Queens, Concubines and Dowagers: The King's Wife in the Early Middle Ages*, Athens GA 1983
Wemple, S. F., *Women in Frankish Society: Marriage and the Cloister 500–900*, Philadelphia 1981

Chapter II
d'Alverny, M-T., 'Comment les théologiens et les philosophes voient la femme', CCM 20 (1977), 105–29
Bornstein, D., *The Lady in the Tower: Medieval Courtesy Books for Women*, Hamden CT 1983
Bullough, V. L., *The Subordinate Sex: A History of Attitudes towards Women*, Urbana IL 1973
Duby, G., *The Knight, the Lady and the Priest*, New York 1983
Goody, J., 'Inheritance, Property and Women: some comparative comments', *Family and Inheritance: Rural Society in Western Europe 1200–1800*, ed. J. Goody, J. Thirsk, E. P. Thompson, Cambridge 1976, 10–36
Herlihy, D., 'Land, Family and Women in Continental Europe 701–1200', *Traditio* 18 (1962), 89–120, *Women in Medieval Society*, ed. Stuard, 13–45
Jourdain, C., 'Mémoire sur l'education des femmes au Moyen Age', *Excursions historiques et philosophiques à travers le Moyen Age*, Paris 1888, Frankfurt 1966, 465–99
La Femme, Recueils de la Société Jean Bodin pour l'histoire comparative des institutions 12, pt. 2, Brussels 1962
Lucas, A. M., *Women in the Middle Ages: Religion, Marriage and Letters*, New York 1983
McLaughlin, E. C., 'Equality of Souls, Inequality of Sexes: Women in Medieval Theology', *Religion and Sexism*, ed. R. Ruether, New York 1974, 213–65
McLaughlin, M. M., 'Survivors and Surrogates: Children and Parents from the Ninth to the Thirteenth Century', *History of Childhood*, ed. L. de Mause, New York 1974, 101–81
Sheehan, M. M., 'Formation and Stability of Marriage in Fourteenth Century England', *Medieval Studies* 33 (1971), 228–63
Warner, M., *Alone of All Her Sex: The Myth and Cult of the Virgin Mary*, New York 1976
The Welsh Law of Women: Studies presented to Prof. Daniel A. Binchey, ed. D. Jenkyns and M. E. Owen, Cardiff 1980

Chapter III
Bagley, J. J., *Margaret of Anjou, Queen of England*, London 1948
Combridge, K., 'Ladies, Queens and Decorum', *Reading Medieval Studies* 1 (1975), 70–83
Crawford, A., 'The King's Burden?: the Consequences of Royal Marriage in Fifteenth-

century England', in *Patronage, the Crown and the Provinces in Later Medieval England*, ed. R. A. Griffiths, Gloucester, 1981 has become available to me too late for use but is valuable for its period.

Dupuy, M., *Françaises, Reines d'Angleterre*, Paris 1968

Eleanor of Aquitaine: Patron and Politician, ed. W. W. Kebler, Austin 1976

The Household Book of Queen Isabella of England, ed. F. D. Blackley, Edmonton 1971

Johnstone, H., 'Isabella, the She-Wolf of France', *History* 21 (1936), 208–15

Parsons, J. C., *The Court and Household of Eleanor of Castile in 1290*, Studies and Texts 37, Toronto 1977

Pernoud, R., *Blanche of Castile*, London 1975
                Eleanor of Aquitaine, London 1967

Petit, K., 'Le Mariage de Philippa de Hainaut', *Moyen Age* 87 (1981), 373–95

Chapter IV

Altschul, M., *A Baronial Family in Medieval England: The Clares, 1217–1314*, Baltimore 1965

Bennett, H. S., *The Pastons and Their England* 2nd ed., 1932, 1979

Bezzola, R., *Les Origines et la formation de la littérature courtoise en Occident 500–1200*, 3 v

Du Boulay, F. R. H., *An Age of Ambition: English Society in the Late Middle Ages*, London 1970

Mathew, G., *The Court of Richard II*, London 1968

McFarlane, K. B., *The Nobility of Later Medieval England*, Oxford 1973

Chapter V

Bolton, B., *'Mulieres Sanctae', Sanctity and Secularity*, ed. D. Baker, Studies in Church History 10, Oxford 1973 and *Women in Medieval Society*, ed. Stuard

Eckenstein, L., *Women under Monasticism*, London 1896, 1963

Gilson, E., *Héloïse et Abelard*, Paris 1938, 1953

McDonnell, E. W., *The Beguines and Beghards in Medieval Culture,* New Brunswick, NJ 1954

McLaughlin, M. M., 'Peter Abelard and the Dignity of Women: Twelfth Century "Feminism" in Theory and Practice', *Pierre Abelard-Pierre le Vénérable*, Colloques Internationaux du Centre National de la Recherche Scientifique Juillet 1972, Paris 1975, 289–333

McLeod, E., *Héloïse*, London 1971

Mens, A., 'Les béguines et les béghards dans le cadre de la culture médiévale', *Moyen Age* 64 (1958), 205–15

Pernoud, R., *Héloïse et Abelard*, Paris 1970

Phillips, D., *Beguines in Medieval Strasbourg*, Ann Arbor MI 1941

Power, E., *Medieval English Nunneries*, Cambridge 1922

Roisin, S., 'L'efflorescence Cistercienne et le courant féminin de piété au xiiie siècle', *Revue d'histoire ecclesiastique* 39 (1943), 342–75

Schmitt, J-C., *Mort d'une hérésie: l'Eglise et les clercs face aux béguines et aux béghards de Rhin supérieur du XIVe au XVe siècle*, Paris 1978

Singer, C., 'The Scientific Views and Visions of Saint Hildegard (1098–1180)', *Studies in the History and Method of Science*, ed. C. Singer, London 1917, 1955

Thorndike, L., 'Hildegard of Bingen', *A History of Magic and Experimental Science* 2, New York 1967

Weinstein, D. and R. M. Bell, *Saints and Society*, Chicago and London 1982

Chapter VI

Ancelet-Hustache, J., *Mechtild de Magdebourg (1207–1281)*, Paris 1982

Atkinson, C. W., *Mystic and Pilgrim: The Book and the World of Margery Kempe*, Ithaca and London 1983

Bynum, C. W., *Jesus as Mother: Studies in the Spirituality of the High Middle Ages*, Berkeley and London 1982

Clay, R. M., *The Hermits and Anchorites of England*, London 1914

Collis, L., *The Apprentice Saint*, London 1964; American title, *Memoirs of a Medieval Woman*, New York 1964 (Margery Kempe)

Flavigny, C., *Sainte Brigitte de Suède,* Paris 1910

Georgianna, L., *The Solitary Self: Individuality in the Ancrene Wisse*, Cambridge MA 1981

Jorgenson, J., *Saint Bridget of Sweden*, 2 v., London 1954

Jones, R. M., *The Flowering of Mysticism*, New York 1939, 1971

Underhill, E., *The Mystics of the Church*, reprint New York 1971

Chapter VII

Abram, A., 'Women Traders in Medieval London', *Economic Journal* (1895), 276–85

Bennett, H. S., *Life on the English Manor*, Cambridge 1956

Bloch, M., *French Rural History*, Berkeley 1973

Dixon, E., 'Craftswomen in the *Livre des Métiers*', *Economic Journal* 5 (1895), 209–28

Duby, G., *Rural Economy and Country Life in the Medieval West*, London 1968

Franklin, A., *Les corporations ouvrières de Paris 12ᵉ–18ᵉ siècles après les documents*, Paris 1877

Gies, J. and F., *Life in a Medieval City*, New York 1973

Goody, J., *Production and Reproduction*, Cambridge 1976

Hilton, R. H., *The English Peasantry in the Later Middle Ages*, Oxford 1975

Homans, G. C., *English Villagers of the Thirteenth Century*, Cambridge MA 1941

Raftis, A. J., *Tenure and Mobility*, Toronto 1964

Smith, J. Toulmin, *English Gilds*, EETS OS 40, 1870

Thrupp, S. L., *The Merchant Class of Medieval London (1300–1500)*, Ann Arbor MI 1964

Chapter VIII

Bienvenu, J-M., 'Pauvreté, misères et charité en Anjou aux XIᵉ et XIIᵉ siècles', *Moyen Age* 72 (1966), 389–424; 73 (1967), 5–34, 189–216

Engeberg, G. M., 'Saint Hildegard, Twelfth Century Physician', BHM 8 (1940), 770–84

Hughes, M. J., *Women Healers in Medieval Life and Literature*, Freeport NY reprint 1968

Jacquart, D., *Le Milieu Medical en France du XIIᵉ au XVᵉ siècle*

Kealey, E. J., *Medieval Medicus*, Baltimore 1981

Lallemand, L., *Histoire de la charité: 3 Le Moyen Age*, Paris 1906

Mundy, J. H., 'Charity and Social Work in Toulouse 1100–1250', *Traditio* 22 (1966), 203–87

Chapter IX

Bellamy, J., *Crime and Public Order in England in the Late Middle Ages*, London 1972

Bullough, V. L., 'The Prostitute in the Middle ages', *Studies in Medieval Culture* 10 (1977) 9–17

Lambert, M. D., *Medieval Heresy*, London 1977

McFarlane, K. L., *John Wycliffe and the Rise of English Non-Conformity*, London 1952

Nelli, R., *La vie quotidienne des Cathars de Languedoc au XIIIe siècle*, Paris 1969

Porteau-Bitker, A., 'Criminalité et delinquance feminine dans le droit penal des XIIIe et XIVe siècles', RHDFE 58 (1980), 13–56

Russell, J. B., *Witchcraft in the Middle Ages,* Ithaca and London 1972

Strayer, J. R., *The Albigensian Crusade,* New York 1971

Chapter X

Christine de Pizan: A Bibliography of Writings by Her and about Her, ed. E. Yenal, Metuchen NJ 1982

Kendrick, A. F., *English Needlework*, 2nd ed. rev by P. Wardle, London 1967

Legge, M. D., *Anglo-Norman Literature and Its Background*, Oxford 1963

Lejeune, R., 'La femme dans les littératures française et occitane du XIe au XIIIe siècle', CCM 20 (1977), 201–17

McLeod, E., *The Order of the Rose: The Life and Ideas of Christine de Pizan*, London 1976

Mickel, E. J., *Marie de France*, New York 1974

Petersen, K. and J. J. Wilson, *Women Artists: Recognition and Reappraisal from the Early Middle Ages to the Twentieth Century*, New York 1976

Schuette, M. and S. Muller-Christiansen, *A Pictorial History of Embroidery,* New York 1963

Willard, C. C., *Christine de Pizan: Her Life and Works, New York 1984*

List of Illustrations

Index